WHAT CRITICS ARE SAYING DR. ELLIOT ENGEL, WHOSE POPULAR LECTURES INSPIRED

A Dab of Dickens
&
A Touch of Twain

"Professor Elliot Engel is quite possibly the most insightful, personable, and entertaining academic lecturer to come out of academia in the last fifty years. His witty, engaging speaking style imparts hard, factual information while leaving his audiences virtually spellbound."

—*Wisconsin Bookwatch*

"Good storytellers are rare these days; Paul Harvey, Charles Kuralt, and Andy Rooney are just a few that come to mind. Add to this illustrious list Elliot Engel, a most remarkable professor."

—*Video Librarian*

"Dr. Engel revives the genius of my great-grandfather—and every other author he touches!"

—Cedric Charles Dickens,
Charles Dickens' great-grandson

"Professor Elliot Engel is a scholar and performer whose infectious enthusiasm and radiant wit create an imaginative and delightful presentation."

—*Video File* magazine

A Dab of Dickens

& A Touch of Twain

Literary Lives from Shakespeare's Old England to Frost's New England

ELLIOT ENGEL, PH.D.

POCKET BOOKS

New York London Toronto Sydney Singapore

An *Original* Publication of POCKET BOOKS

 POCKET BOOKS, a division of Simon & Schuster, Inc.
1230 Avenue of the Americas, New York, NY 10020

Copyright © 2002 by Elliot Engel

ISBN: 0-7434-4897-9

First Pocket Books trade paperback printing October 2002

10 9 8 7 6 5 4 3 2 1

POCKET and colophon are registered trademarks of Simon & Schuster, Inc.

For information regarding special discounts for bulk purchases, please contact Simon & Schuster Special Sales at 1-800-456-6798 or business@simonandschuster.com

Book design by Jaime Putorti

Cover design by Min Choi
Front cover illustration by Kent Barton

Printed in the U.S.A.

For:

Andrew Chappelow (age 4)
Benjamin Chappelow (age 4)
Thomas Chappelow (age 6)

Future Readers

Present Listeners

From E, whose recent Past you've made so rich

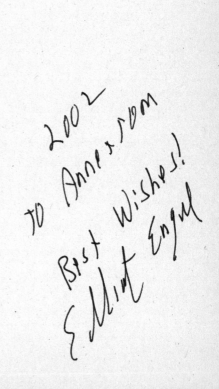
2002
to Ann & Tom
Best Wishes!
E Mint Engel

Acknowledgments

Although we're all taught how important it is to settle our debts, I have incurred two enormous liabilities in writing this book that can never be adequately discharged, but they can be gratefully acknowledged.

The first is to Christina Boys, my editor at Simon and Schuster, who not only approached me with the idea for this book but who gave generous counsel that sharpened the focus of innumerable paragraphs in the following pages.

The second is to Quinn Hawkesworth, who helped me transform the loose verbiage of my lectures into the tight vocabulary of the essay form. Her performance of this difficult role, like Mrs. Crummles' performance of the original *Blood Drinker*, was "too tremendous."

Contents

Contents

Introduction

I assume you're reading these words because my title interested you enough to purchase this book, or someone has
been kind enough to give it to you, or you're standing there
in the bookstore debating whether to buy it. And though we
all know that we're not supposed to judge a book by its
cover, how can you help but form a judgment of the contents based on the title that appears there?

Believe me, you have no idea how difficult it was to think
up a title for this book of literary essays on familiar authors
usually studied in school. My editor and I must have conceived, tossed around, and discarded fifty dreadful titles
before settling on the current one.

As I hope the title indicates, what unites all my essays are
facts, anecdotes, and insights about the lives of famous
authors whom you either read or at least heard about in the
classroom. That is why we were tempted to call the book
Literary Lives You Never Learned in English Class. But that
title was discarded early on because we certainly did not
want to offend English teachers by intimating that they had
not done a thorough job of teaching these famous writers.

Personally, I had nothing but superb English teachers in
high school and college. All of them seemed to me either

born in a cradle of chalk dust or directly descended from Mr. Chips. Far be it from me to denigrate such soft-spoken, hard-working, underpaid, and overextended professionals. They are the reason I became an English professor.

But let's face it, all sorts of tantalizing tidbits were left out of our English teachers' lectures due to the impossibility of their task. How were they ever supposed to teach that semester course "American Literature from Cotton Mather through Last Night" or that other one "British Literature from Beowulf through Virginia Woolf"? They simply had no time to do the kind of research on each author that would have yielded the assortment of gems that I have hoarded through years of study and teaching and that I now unearth for you in the following pages.

With hundreds of authors to choose from in British and American literature, you may wonder why I decided upon the nineteen you'll find in the table of contents. I suppose more than any other criterion, I selected authors based on whether their lives enormously influenced the works that now make them famous. As you'll certainly be able to tell, I am a proud member of the school of *biographical* literary criticism and have always been truant from the Freudian, Marxist, deconstructionist, poststructuralist, and other literary schools that seem to concentrate on illuminating the supposed genius of the critic while all too often ignoring and distorting the real genius of the famous writer.

Because biography plays such a central role in my essays, you'll notice that I include only two authors—Chaucer and Shakespeare—who lived before 1750. Since we know so little about the lives of medieval and Renaissance writers, a biographical approach to them is bound to yield rather skimpy and dubious results. On the other hand, more than half of my chapters are devoted to writers born during the brief period from 1800 to 1850. Is this because authors of this era are especially fascinating? No. Is this because as a professor I specialize in authors born in the first half of the nineteenth century? You bet.

You'll notice that the chapters are arranged chronologically in order of the authors' deaths rather than births. That is because the influence of a writer on contemporary literature often increases in direct proportion to how long he or she lived. For example, Thomas Hardy was born fourteen years *before* Oscar Wilde, but because he lived more than forty years longer than Wilde, he was very influential on both modern poetry and the twentieth-century novel. Poor Wilde, who died at forty-six, seems a much more dated author than Hardy, who lived to be eighty-eight.

As a critic who is devoted to studying authors' lives as the basis for fully understanding their works, I suppose I should reveal just a little bit about my own literary background. No research was required for the following biographical morsels.

Before my love for the individual authors in this volume came my love and respect for the written word. I distinctly remember how my initial glee for reading came into being. I was about eight years old. Every summer my father promised me one trip to Riverside Amusement Park in Indianapolis, where I grew up. It was the highlight of my entire year. As soon as we entered the park that summer, I spotted a young man selling helium balloons. I begged for one and Dad agreed. Dad warned me to hold tightly to the string or else the balloon would float away.

With the peculiar logic of an eight-year-old, I decided I'd let go of the string for just a second so that I could enjoy the thrill of catching it right before it was too late. Robert Browning said that a man's reach should exceed his grasp—but not so with little boys. That balloon quickly exceeded not only my reach and my grasp but my father's as well.

Up and up it flew, leaving behind one heartbroken little boy. Dad did not lecture me, nor did he buy me a replacement. Quite soon, the excitement of the rides made me feel better. But I did not forget about that balloon.

At breakfast the next morning, I asked sadly, "Where do you think my balloon is now?"

"Well, Elliot," I can still hear my father say, "since the wind was blowing from the west, your balloon must now be over Ohio."

"Where's Ohio?" Dad walked over to a bookshelf in our den, pulled down the O volume of the *World Book Encyclopedia*, and showed me the colored map of Ohio. I'll never forget the pale green color of the state speckled with all the large and small black dots that located the various Ohio cities. The memory, in fact, revives every time I eat mint chocolate-chip ice cream.

Dad then read to me all about Ohio, my balloon's temporary home. I was intrigued. The next morning, of course, I asked about the location again and was told the balloon was over Pennsylvania. But where's Pennsylvania? This time Dad took down the proper volume, but it was *I* who started—slowly—to read about my balloon's latest home. By the time that balloon was over New Jersey, I had fallen in love with maps, geography, the encyclopedia, and—most especially—words. I was blessed with a wise father who could turn a minor disaster at an amusement park into the inspiration for an amusement that will last my entire life.

It is one thing to love reading but quite another to become an English professor who writes books on literary lives. Actually, through my senior year of college I assumed I would become a lawyer. As an undergraduate I had indeed been an English major but simply because it was an approved pre-law major. Then a superb Chaucer course followed by a "superber" Dickens seminar convinced me that I could only be happy in a career of teaching English.

But convincing my family that my love of literary lives was the basis for a career proved a bit tricky.

I am descended from a long line of owners of dry-goods stores. As one of my relatives aptly phrased it: "Our family has been in dry goods ever since the first good was dried." Somehow, deciding on a career in English literature seemed exotic and rather bizarre. "But, Elliot," my aunt Anna reminded me, "you know you can't open up an English store."

My experience working at my father's hosiery store during summer vacations in high school and college had already convinced me that I would not regret choosing a different career path, even though my father was a most lenient employer. My summer hours at work were basically from when I felt like coming in (nine-thirty always seemed congenial) until either I grew bored or Dad ran out of energy thinking up busywork for me.

But I do believe that my love of literature was shaped during those few hours a day that I spent at my father's business. My grandmother, who had come to America from Russia when she was in her teens and who had helped run a successful dry-goods business without the benefit of an MBA, had always said, "You stand behind a counter, you learn life." The flow of humanity that came through the doors of Midwestern Hosiery Company was my own version of the Canterbury pilgrims, each with a unique tale to tell me. And I listened—and fell in love with the stories of lives.

Although I've chosen a career that is seemingly quite different from sales, I've discovered that in reality my teacher's apple has not fallen far from my family tree. A few years ago, I was sharing my upbringing with some students I was teaching in a seminar on the novels of Dickens. I had just mentioned to the class that my teaching career had broken a family tradition of dry-goods sales. A witty student in the back of the room raised her hand to disagree.

"Wouldn't you say," she began, "that you've devoted your career to selling your students on the virtues of Charles Dickens?"

I admitted that this was true.

"Well," she added, "Some of the Dickens novels we're studying are about as dry as anything I've ever read. It looks to me like you've become the ultimate dry-goods salesman."

So consider this book just another indication that my English store continues to operate.

Oh, one warning before you proceed. The following essays were originally conceived as lectures. That is why you will find no footnotes. Should you crave them, please go to the library and check out any of the thousands of books written by my brethren English professors. Due to the strictness of scholarly publications, professors must footnote or endnote their articles and books with mind-numbing thoroughness. But the following chapters were delivered orally to my students to educate, entertain, and inspire. Thus, a statement here or there may stretch the truth just a little. But as the great Emperor of Exaggeration, Mark Twain, once opined: "It is both apt and fitting to stretch the truth, for if it is indeed The Truth, it can always stand the strain of being stretched."

I hope I've convinced you to move on to chapter 1, in which you just might fall victim to the thrill of the quill that my nineteen literary legends have given to me and to countless other readers. Enthusiasm is contagious. Charles Dickens, as enthusiastic a writer as ever put quill to paper, often bemoaned that the very word *enthusiasm* with its complex Greek derivation did not sound nearly exciting enough to represent such a thrilling, fervent emotion. So he invented a new and much more onomatopoeic term for it: *enthoozymoozy.* May you catch a severe case of literary enthoozymoozy within these chapters and may you be confined in bed or on a comfy couch or chair with a raging reading fever that can only be broken by those two dreadful, medicinal words: The End.

Elliot Engel

January 3, 2002
Raleigh, North Carolina

Geoffrey Chaucer

(1343–1400)

© Michael Nicholson/CORBIS

Although I want this essay to feature one of the earliest and best humorists in the English language, Geoffrey Chaucer, I want to begin by quickly looking at humor in general during the Middle Ages. Now, if you form an image of the Middle Ages in your mind, you might assume this will be a brief interlude before we arrive at Chaucer. You might think the medieval period had little humor—and you would probably be right. *Beowulf* has rarely been studied for its humor, although I did have a professor who pointed out that the villain of *Beowulf*—the monster Grendel—would sneak out of its lair after midnight and devour a few soldiers from Denmark. He then reminded us that this beastly act has led to an early morning eating tradition that is still with us: having a couple of danish for breakfast.

We begin the Middle Ages in the year 500. Why? You might assume it is because we begin with the fall of Rome in 476. Not the British—they date the Middle Ages starting in 500 because they say that was the year King Arthur died. Now, that assumption requires a leap of faith, since no one has ever been able to prove that King Arthur lived in the first place. Research has been going on for hundreds of years trying to prove Arthur's existence. As far as we know, there was likely no King Arthur, but if there was, he did die about 500.

We need, then, to examine what came right before the Middle Ages, in regard to humor. We tend to ignore that the age before the Middle Ages, the first period of English litera- ture, was the Roman age. Rome conquered England in 55 B.C. and remained there until A.D. 476. They were there for five hunded years, yet few of us ever consider them. Is it because they were so early and so barbarian? Hardly. During the Roman period in England most men and women who were not peasants not only had baths in their houses, but hot run- ning water for those baths. After Rome fell in 476 the next time the English had hot baths in their houses was 1885!

The Romans were an extremely cultivated people, and their literature influenced the humor of the Middle Ages. Of all Roman comedy, only the names of two playwrights come down to us: Plautus and Terence. And I want to tell you the difference between these two and delineate their contribu- tion to the development of humor, because their talents would affect the rest of British and American literature.

Both lived about 200 B.C., but Plautus was one generation older than Terence. Plautus was a jovial fellow; he had a devil-may-care attitude and a huge tolerance for all sorts of people. Everything he wrote was jolly; everything he wrote was for the purpose of escape. His plays had horrible plots— really, no plots at all. In a play's prologue he would tell the audience everything that was going to happen; invariably the action involved a set of twins that no one recognized as twins, except for the audience, because it had been told ahead of time. The laughs arose from actors pretending they weren't aware which twin they were addressing—but the clever, forewarned audience did. If you want a taste of the spirit of Plautus, a good modern representation of his kind of comedy is *A Funny Thing Happened on the Way to the Forum.*

It is Terence, however, who influenced the course of British humor, and humor in general. He was the opposite of Plautus. Plautus was a hail-fellow-well-met, Santa Claus type. Terence was an African slave brought up in a noble Roman household. He was extremely talented, which led his master to free him and educate him. So although Plautus, being white and a Roman, had the advantages of noble birth and education, it was Terence, the African slave, who wrote superior comedy.

Terence did not write for the general public, but for a small group of friends who gathered under the banner "Never be vulgar." His plays are about sophisticated young men on the town, a cosmopolitan nobility; because of his upbringing he understood the nobility and their taste. His plays are always clever and amusing, never knee-slapping. Above all he was brilliant at plotting, providing abundant suspense and surprise in one episode after another. He led his characters along from one adventure to the next—there seems to be no rhyme nor reason to these adventures, but at the end every-thing pulls together and makes sense. Terence invented what came to be called the picaresque novel. A novel such as *Tom Jones* probably couldn't have been written had not Henry Fielding known Terence's plays. One critic noted that a for-mula applies both to the plays of Terence and the picaresque novel of Fielding. The formula is simply ODTAA, which stands for One Damn Thing After Another (which pretty much describes our lives, come to think of it). Terence is so enjoyable because our own lives are usually one damn thing after another, but at least in Terence the events are all tied up neatly at the end, and everyone is happy.

The primary reasons Terence's works have relevance today and Plautus' do not are (1) Terence's plays led to the picaresque novel and (2) his plays had morals attached to them. During the Middle Ages when monks were translating Roman literature from the Latin, Plautus was forbidden to them because of his "pagan" immorality—but Terence they could translate and claim as a Christian because his plays contained valuable moral lessons.

It is interesting that Christianity evolved in a period of extremely low moral values; the Christian movement replaced Rome as the primary influence on Western civilization. It is not coincidental that a rock-bed principle of Christianity is strict morality, formed in response to a decadent era. The church's disapproval of immorality focused upon the drama of the time. The church closed the theaters as early as A.D. 500, and once the theaters were gone, the actors had to earn a meager living as wandering minstrels.

When the Anglo-Saxons invaded England at about this same time, these Teutonic tribes were so serious that even harmless secular amusements were viewed as antireligious and were banned. Literary historians say, "With the Anglo-Saxons comes the *lugubriossification* of England." They would, wouldn't they? What in the world does that long word mean? It's obviously a $50 term for a 5¢ thought and simply means "a somberness." How many of us have heard poor speakers and felt that a *lugubriossity* was setting over the hall. It is an appropriate word, *lugubriossification*, because the word *ossify* means "to change into bone"—a hardening to something lumpy and sad.

These traveling minstrels who used to be actors became tired of having to earn a meal by singing the praises of nobles, and they eventually struck back with what we call satire. They would criticize the nobles and the clergy; they would especially satirize the hypocrisy and the cupidity of the Church and its strictures. These minstrels invented the term *merry monks* to illustrate that monks were not always at their books, that they too had a life most people didn't know about. Trouvères of northern France (as opposed to the troubadours of southern France) were educated minstrels who went around the country singing of chivalrous deeds; they would set up a rigid code of social manners and then poke fun at it in their songs. (In their own way the trouvères lead directly to Jane Austen, because her period was one of chivalry where men and women were governed by strict rules of conduct. Her novels always look at society's conduct and show how it falls short of the mark.) Both trouvères and troubadours created works known by Chaucer through his travels in France.

Finally we arrive at the first comedic artist of English literature, Geoffrey Chaucer. I cannot give you copious detail about his life because he lived too long ago. But because he was from an aristocratic family, we do have an unusual amount of information on his life—had he been a commoner like Shakespeare, living as early as he did, we would have virtually no information about him.

First of all his name, Chaucer: it is from the French *chaussure*, which means "shoe." His family had likely made footwear or were shoemakers and perhaps his paternal grandparents were French. Chaucer's father, however, was an aristocrat, a man of property. His name was John Chaucer and he served as deputy to the king's butler, a high position. We don't know when Chaucer was born, but we think it was around 1343. Chaucer became a page of the Countess of Olster, who was the wife of Lionel, a son of King Edward III.

The first mention of Chaucer in writing is in 1357, when he would have been about fourteen. Because he came from such a fine family, the countess reported that she bought this teenager a short cloak, a pair of shoes, and red-and-black parti-colored breeches. He was a page in the royal house-hold, a coveted position. As a page he only had three tasks, none of them to be coveted: Chaucer (1) made the beds; (2) carried the candles; (3) ran the errands. The work itself was not what made the position so special, but because for a young man of the fourteenth century it provided an oppor-tunity to continue his education with the noble children of the family. It was also a way to learn how polite society acted, and to become known to persons who could further one's education and advancement later on.

Chaucer, as did all young men, went into the army at about age sixteen. When he was twenty, he was taken pris-oner in France during the Hundred Years' War, and Edward III himself paid part of the ransom to have him returned to England. Chaucer then married a woman named Phillipa, who came from as good a background as Chaucer's, and both of them were taken into the service of John of Gaunt. John of Gaunt was not only the son of Edward III the king, he was the uncle of Richard II, who would be the next king.

Once Richard II came to the throne, Chaucer, because of his education and intellect, was viewed as a diplomat, and he was sent to France and Italy to gather diplomatic informa-tion. At the time he was in Italy, Petrarch and Boccaccio had recently died, but their works were everywhere. In Italy, Chaucer soaked up the marvelous stories of the time, stories that would eventually come out of the mouths of the pilgrims going to Canterbury. In France he learned French stories. He was fluent in both French and Italian. As a diplomat he was able to absorb stories firsthand that he would never have had access to otherwise, because the printing press had not yet been invented.

In 1386, John of Gaunt fell out of power and Chaucer was left without royal employment. He had time now to sit and write, and so he began *The Canterbury Tales*. Had not John of Gaunt fallen out of power, Chaucer would have had in his head all the tales he'd heard abroad, but we believe he wouldn't have had the time to sit down and write them. Beginning in 1386, Chaucer worked on *The Canterbury Tales* up until the day of his death in 1400.

Three years after he fell from grace John of Gaunt returned to power, and Chaucer was given the lucrative privilege of supervisor of the repairs of walls and ditches between Greenwich and Woolwich. He never actually went to Greenwich or Woolwich; he simply took in the money for being in charge and hired subcontractors; in other words he had no responsibility to be anywhere except in his study writing. The king rewarded him for success in this position with a scarlet robe trimmed with fur and the annual gift of a tun of wine (the equivalent of 252 gallons of wine a year). No wonder there is so much levity in *The Canterbury Tales*! This cheerful good luck of Chaucer's—receiving the well-paying jobs, being in the right place, never having to work— they're all reflected in the *The Canterbury Tales* and in their delightful levity of spirit.

In 1399, Chaucer's last year, Henry IV deposed Richard II—a terribly weak king. Fortunately Chaucer was too ingrained in English society for any king to kick him out. He took a house in the garden of Westminster Abbey. He would only live eight more months—fifty-seven was a ripe old age in that era—but in a touch of whimsy, he took a fifty-three-year lease on that little house.

Chaucer died on October 25, 1400. Because his house was at Westminster Abbey, when asked where he wished to be buried, he said, "Could there be a corner for me in the Abbey?" He was buried, alone, in an unused corner. But because of his exalted reputation, his grave led the corner to be christened Poets' Corner, where Dryden and Dickens and so many literary giants would be buried.

Chaucer had a remarkably wonderful life, a life whose richness is reflected in his many works. We will concentrate, of course, on his masterpiece, *The Canterbury Tales*. Let me emphasize that Chaucer is the only prominent author we have who lived in a pre–printing-press era. Chaucer died almost fifty years before the printing press was developed. There *were* other authors, William Langland is one—but almost all are unfamiliar to us. And of course there is the anonymous *Beowulf*. *The Canterbury Tales* is the only early work we have that was not meant to be read by large numbers of readers. When Chaucer wrote *The Canterbury Tales*, he was thinking of the oral tradition of literature, and he read *The Canterbury Tales*, for amusement, to the court.

Poetry written to be read is different from poetry written to be heard, so the first point I wish to make regarding *The Canterbury Tales* is to emphasize why Chaucer wrote the work the way he did. If you are writing poetry that is only going to be heard, you had better make your points strongly the first time, because there is no going back—no one in the audience will raise a hand and say, "I need to hear line one oh eight again." Therefore, none of the allusions in *The Canterbury Tales*—mythological, biblical, geographical—have footnotes, because he read it to people who could comprehend what he was talking about.

The other point related to oral poetry is the tone of the work: *The Canterbury Tales* was in the voice of the author. Tone is the author's relationship to the material he's writing, and to the audience listening to it. Like a tone of voice, a poem's tone can be ironic, sentimental, light, serious, satirical. Chaucer knew anyone listening to *The Canterbury Tales* would hear the tone he wished to get across; he knew he could do it for the audience through his reading.

We do not know how Chaucer spoke his words or how he might have used gestures or facial expressions or pauses. Is that lack of knowledge a negative? No, it is a positive. It makes Chaucer mysterious in some way; we have to imagine what tone he was trying to convey. Though Chaucer didn't realize it, he was making his work far more ambiguous by never realizing that he wouldn't be there to guide us as we were reading his tales.

Let's examine the setting of this work of literature. You know the setting must be important because it is mentioned in the title: *The Canterbury Tales*. (Ironically, of course, the setting is never actually Canterbury because the characters never get there.) What we have as *The Canterbury Tales* is not what Chaucer intended to write. If you read the "General Prologue," you know that the work was intended to feature each pilgrim telling two tales en route to Canterbury, and two tales coming back. There were thirty pilgrims; thirty pilgrims times four tales would have been one hundred twenty different tales. Chaucer barely finished thirty. The work, therefore, is considerably incomplete; it is only a quarter of what he wanted to write. (And all my students who suffer with *The Canterbury Tales* are thankful that the man died when he did.)

The setting is a pilgrimage, a stroke of Chaucer's genius, because only on a pilgrimage could you have characters from every walk of life brought together. Only on pilgrimages were all levels of English society on common ground—with two exceptions. The only two classes that would never have been on a pilgrimage were the highest class, royalty, and the lowest class, the peasantry. But those two classes only made up a small percentage of the English public; most of the English public could be represented on a pilgrimage. The three most fundamental classes of society were represented on religious pilgrimages: people of prayer, people of war, people of labor. Of course Chaucer's couldn't be a bona fide pilgrimage because he only gives us one of each type: there is an educator, but only one; a man of war, but only one. Not only were the classes brought together, but they could also socialize freely because the occasion was religious. And the religious purpose freed the pilgrims to tell stories because otherwise travel was spent looking behind every bush for highway robbers. But even robbers knew that if they stole from someone on a religious pilgrimage or killed that person, their souls went straight to hell. The pilgrims, thus free of worrying about brigands, could entertain one another.

It has also been pointed out that on a religious pilgrimage most pilgrims wore a voluminous cape with a hood. If a bandit did indeed try to seize a pilgrim, the cape was so flowing that the victim could easily slip out of it and run away. We have a word today that goes back to Chaucer's pilgrimage: *escape*. *Escape* comes from *ex*, "out of," and *capus*, "cape"—go out of your cape. Thus, personal safety allowed lighthearted social mingling free rein; the holiday spirit of a pilgrimage promoted festivity. It was literally a holiday—a holy day—going to Canterbury.

The Canterbury Tales is known most of all for the opening lines:

> Whan that Aprille, with his shoures soote,
> The droghte of March hath perced to the roote
> And bathed every veyne in swich licour,
> Of which vertu engendred is the flour;
> Whan Zephirus eek with his swete breeth
> Inspired hath in every holt and heeth
> The tendre croppes, and the yonge sonne
> Hath in the Ram his halfe cours yronne,
> And smale foweles maken melodye,
> That slepen al the nyght with open eye—
> So priketh hem Nature in hir corages—
> Thanne longen folk to goon on pilgrimages.

It is beautiful language, and not much like our modern English. It seems almost Scandinavian, perhaps, in its singsong lilt. Now let's translate the verse:

> When that April with his showers sweet,
> The drought of March has pierced to the root
> And bathed every vein in such sweet liquid,
> That eventually there comes forth the flower.

This is a lovely description of springtime in England, but why would Chaucer, writing about a religious trip to Canterbury, open with rather trite lines about how the showers of April make the ground that was very dry in March produce the flowers that we think of in May? I think those opening lines are some of the most brilliant and inspired in English literature. What Chaucer is trying to say in this poem is that these pilgrims set out for Canterbury because in the spring they feel a need for renewal; it is time for a new life—what we much later have been calling "born again" —revived spiritually.

And why did the pilgrims always go to Thomas of Becket's shrine in Canterbury in April? April was the month for thanksgiving. And what did one give thanks for? If you've ever been to England in the winter, you know—you were literally thanking God for having made it through another wretched English winter. In the fourteenth century a third of those that died each year did so from something contracted in winter.

The journey signified spiritual rebirth, so of course Chaucer was inspired to begin his work with one of the loveliest metaphors in English poetry about the physical rebirth of nature. But let us look at those opening lines again, because they are not so much about rebirth as they are about creation—creating something anew—just as the pilgrims desired to re-create their spiritual vows. What you need to know to fully appreciate the four opening lines is that, in Chaucer's day, everyone was familiar with astrology, knew it backwards and forwards. They knew April was the most masculine month of the year because astrologically it is the sign of Aries the Ram—the most masculine sign in the zodiac. March, on the other hand, was the most feminine sign of the zodiac, because in March you have Pisces the Fish, a water sign—the most feminine. So April was regarded symbolically as a man; March was regarded as a woman. Now go back to those opening lines again, and try not to blush as you reread them this time: "When April with his shower pierces March and spreads within her such sweet liquid that eventually comes forth the flower." You see? You do not have to belong to the "dirty old man school" of literary criticism to see it. It's there. It's right there. When I tell students that the opening four lines of Chaucer are some of the most sexually explicit lines ever written, they come up to me and say, "I must have the wrong edition—let me see yours." It is there whether you admit it or not. Chaucer's people certainly knew it was there. They knew everything about it that we think today—except that it was dirty. In the Middle Ages, sex was not dirty, it was a fact of nature. Chaucer illustrates the renewal of life through the sexual act in nature, just like the pilgrims going down to Canterbury to be renewed—physically re-created in the same way.

To me, the most remarkable part of *The Canterbury Tales* is the "General Prologue." Critics have said that it is unique in all literature. Nothing else is comparable to Chaucer's "General Prologue" because it comprises concise portraits of an entire nation. Everyone is on that pilgrimage: the high and the low, the old and the young, males and females, laypeople and clerical people, learned people and ignorant people, rogues and the righteous, people who make their living by land, people who make their living by sea, town people and country people. Every one of them is represented. And each pilgrim is relatively normal; there are no extremes.

ELLIOT ENGEL

They're fascinating characters, but they are true to life. The critic George Edelen said that Chaucer's *Canterbury Tales* is full of "the perennial progeny of men and women." Yes, they are sharply individual, but they are universal—we still see the same people today.

John Dryden wrote about Chaucer's "General Prologue," "Here is God's plenty." And certainly it is. I want to give you, in translation, what I consider some of the greatest characterizations in all literature, from the "General Prologue." I will begin with a less familiar character, the Cook. His is one of the shortest descriptions of the "General Prologue," only nine lines:

> A cook there was perchance among them, too
> With marrow-bones to boil a chicken stew,
> Add tarts with spices that would never fail
> He knew for sure a draft of London ale.
> And he could roast and scald and boil and fry,
> And make thick soups and bake a wondrous pie.
> But what a dreadful thing it seemed to me
> That on his shin a scabrous sore had he.
> A creamy chicken he cooked with the best.

Now this reads like an innocent enough description, but because it is Chaucer, we know there is more besides. It opens as we would expect: Chaucer praises this cook for what we would call today "signature dishes": his "chickens with marrow-bones," the ales he can distinguish, his ability to "roast and scald and boil and fry." And then Chaucer, just as an aside, as if it's something he just happened to notice, says, "But what a dreadful thing it seemed to me that on his shin a scabrous sore had he." Now a scabrous sore would be an ulcer, and the only reason you would have one back then was because you had a disease that gave you ulcers in unmentionable places; it was the badge of syphilis to have an ulcer. It was called an "ulcer" because it was runny, and if you had an ulcer on your shin, you likely had them on your arm as well. Think about what he does for a living: broiling, baking, and frying. He is a cook, but he's not a chef, is he? He is a low-class fellow who cooked, probably for the military, and with his ulcers and his syphilis is standing over these boiling cauldrons making goodness knows how many people sick to death by his work. But Chaucer doesn't end with this medical tidbit, just drops it in. He ends instead with "A creamy chicken he cooked with the best." This chicken dish has the texture of a pudding, something rather liquid, a dish supposedly high class. Chaucer closes his cook's portrait with the distasteful idea of him standing over a hot stove making a blanc-mange and dripping heaven knows what in it. In nine little lines we have a brutal satire upon the sort of people who called themselves cooks, yet it's delivered in the tone of "Isn't he a charming man, aren't we lucky to have him?"

The portrait, however, that I consider Chaucer's most brilliant is that of the nun—the Prioress:

> There also was a Nun, a Prioress
> That in her smiling simple was and coy.
> Her greatest oath was only "By Saint Loy"
> And she was known as Madame Eglantine
> Full well she sang the offices divine,
> Intoning through her nose the proper way.

And French she spoke with ease, but, truth to say,
'Twas of the school of Stratford-at-the-Bow
For French of Paris-folk she did not know.
Well taught she was at table how to eat;
She from her lips let fall no scrap of meat,
Nor dipped her fingers deeply in the sauce.
She carried well each morsel without loss
So that no drop should fall upon her breast.
To study courteous manners pleased her best.
Her upper lip she always wiped so clean
That in her cup no slightest trace was seen
Of grease, when she had drunk her draft of wine;
She reached her hand for food with manners fine.
And surely she was apt for jest and sport,
For she was pleasant, amiable of port,
The way of court she sought to imitate,
And she was ever stately and sedate,
Full worthy to be held in reverence.
And now to tell of her beneficence.
She was so kind and gently piteous
That she would weep if she should see a mouse
Caught in a trap, if it were dead or bled.
Some little dogs she had, the which she fed
With roasted flesh or milk or wheaten bread;
And sore she'd weep if one of them were dead
Or if one struck it with a yardstick smart;
She was all gentleness and tender heart.
A pleated wimple round her head was draped;
Her eyes were gray as glass, her nose well-shaped;
Her mouth was small and also soft and red;
And certainly she had a fair forehead—

It was almost a hand in breadth, I swear,
For truly she was neither short nor spare.
Her cloak was neatly made, as I could see.
About her arm was wound a rosary
Of coral beads, the larger beads of green,
And thereon hung a brooch of golden sheen
On which there first was a writ a crowned A
And after, Amor Vincit Omnia.

On the surface this description leaves you with the impression you couldn't have a more pleasant nun on a religious pilgrimage. But let us go back to it and notice what Chaucer has done:

There also was a Nun, a Prioress
That in her smiling simple was and coy.

The first thing he mentions about the nun is her coy smile—an odd beginning. And then:

Her greatest oath was only "By Saint Loy"

You think, what an odd thing, to praise a nun for not swearing very often.

And she was known as Madame Eglantine

Eglantine is honeysuckle, and you think what a pleasant name, Madame Honeysuckle, how sweet. And then you think about being in a warm room with honeysuckle, and you understand that honeysuckle is after a while oppressively sweet and cloying. But we wish to be told what exactly she does as a nun, and Chaucer tells us:

> Full well she sang the offices divine,
> Intoning through her nose the proper way.
> And French she spoke with ease . . .

No mention of the religious nature of what she's singing, only that she knew how to sing it so it sounded most impressive. The longest part of the description you would assume would describe her religious order or perhaps the reason she became a nun, or acts of charity she has performed for the poor. No. One-third of the description is about her table manners:

> Well taught she was at table how to eat;
> She from her lips let fall no scrap of meat,
> Nor dipped her fingers deeply in the sauce.
> She carried well each morsel without loss
> So that no drop should fall upon her breast.

Then we read that when she drank, you noticed there wasn't any grease around the cup's edge (a wonderful description because it tells you what it was like to eat and drink back then). But by this point, when the description is half over, you begin to wonder, "Why would Chaucer spend so much time elaborating upon how she sang French through her nose and how beautiful her table manners were?" And then you realize, that's all we know about her because obviously she has not shown one iota of a religious nature to anyone.

And what about her charitable instincts? Chaucer wrote:

That she would weep if she should see a mouse
Caught in a trap, if it were dead or bled.

This is impressive until you recollect that twenty-five years before this was written the bubonic plague had swept through London, killing one out of three people. Here is a nun who cries at a mousetrap's victim, yet says nothing about the thousands of human beings who died in agony from the plague. And then:

Some little dogs she had, the which she fed
With roasted flesh or milk or wheaten bread;

This pilgrimage came during a terrible famine, yet we see the nun hoarding delicacies for her dogs.

The most damning evidence against the Prioress is the last part of her description:

Her eyes were gray as glass, her nose well-shaped;
Her mouth was small and also soft and red;
And certainly she had a fair forehead—

This is a description all the other pilgrims could have related to, because in every work of romantic poetry this was how the heroine was described—red lips, beautiful forehead. And you wonder, "Why would a nun be described in the same way as a romantic heroine?" Clearly this is a woman who took up the nunnery not because she cared a thing for religious impulses, but because she had some romantic notion about going out and helping others, when in fact her heart was closed to everything except her self-absorbed world.

And then we are given the ending:

> About her arm was wound a rosary
> Of coral beads, the larger beads of green,
> And thereon hung a brooch of golden sheen

And on that brooch was the inscription "Amor Vincit Omnia"— "Love conquers all." Not an unusual motto for a nun, but on most nuns you would assume "Love conquers all" refers to God's love. Chaucer, however, has described her so completely as a romantic heroine that we realize the phrase refers to physical love—the last thing that should be on a proper nun's mind.

What is brilliant about this description is not Chaucer's satire against the clergy. What was so challenging for Chaucer was to offer a damning portrait of a nun with every line seeming to be praise of her. It is hard enough to create satire that is obvious; to make it praise that is not praise at all is wonderful.

Those are only two of the thirty descriptions in the "General Prologue"—unique in all literature not only because they give such devastatingly clever insights into the foibles of the folk of Chaucer's day, but also because Chaucer set himself the impossible task of putting it all in the mouth of a narrator who supposedly sees nothing but benign aspects of all the pilgrims. And because Chaucer has such a keen genius for observing human nature, his characters seem as fresh and recognizable to us now as they did to the audiences of his time.

William Shakespeare

(1564–1616)

When you turn to William Shakespeare you almost have to begin by giving *the* most impressive statistic about this man, which, of course, is this: from the time he died in 1616 right down to our time, he has always been considered the greatest writer in the history of the English language. That fact alone would be impressive, but it becomes even more so when you realize that William Shakespeare is regarded as not only the greatest writer in our language, but as the greatest writer of all time in *any* language.

It is our extreme good fortune that we were born into a culture that speaks and writes the language that was written and spoken by Shakespeare. Of course if you say that to high school students and then give them a text of William Shakespeare's to read, they insist that there must be some mistake. Students see immediately that Shakespeare's language is not, of course, the language they speak every day. And yet given that in English we have had three distinct periods—Old English, Middle English, and Modern English—some may find it surprising that Shakespeare does not belong to the Old English or Middle English period, but actually belongs to our own period—he is the first great writer in the Modern English language. Obviously over four hundred years our language has changed significantly, but Shakespeare remains a writer in the modern period, the one in which we live.

Shakespeare's contribution to world literature has been in the field of drama. He did write poetry, but the works that secure his immortality are the thirty-seven plays we believe he wrote. Because he wrote plays, he is different from all the other authors we examine in this book (with the exception of Oscar Wilde). Almost all other great writers in the English language became famous either because they wrote poetry or they wrote fiction. Shakespeare stands virtually alone as a genius who wrote plays, and because he wrote plays, we have to treat him a bit differently. With other writers—Frost for example, who wrote poetry, or Dickens, who wrote novels—if you want to know how worthy that author is, you simply take the book, you read the poem or the fiction, and you decide on its merit. But Shakespeare never wanted anyone simply to read his plays. He would think it absolutely ridiculous that today if we want students to understand the greatness of Shakespeare, we assign them one of his plays. All too often students sit in a classroom with the text before them, examining Shakespeare in the form of words (often difficult words) on a page.

I also assume that he would be highly amused at all the doubt as to whether he actually wrote those brilliant plays attributed to him. I know I am. I have never had one person ask, "Do you think Charles Dickens really wrote *Great Expectations* or might it have been William Makepeace Thackeray?" What is it about Shakespeare that has given rise to so much questioning of the authorship of the plays?

It is true that he wrote long ago and therefore many of

the confirming biographical facts have been lost. But think of Chaucer—he wrote two hundred years before Shakespeare and nobody to my knowledge ever questioned the authorship of *The Canterbury Tales*. No, those who are convinced that Shakespeare could not be the writer of those immortal plays tend to have a rather snobbish objection to his authorship.

You will notice that these doubting Thomases always put forward as the real playwright a man of much higher birth than the commoner Shakespeare. Their candidates are generally noblemen who traveled widely, mingled with the best minds of the age, and led exciting lives overflowing with incidents and anecdotes. They point out that the few facts we do have concerning the life of one William Shakespeare are peculiarly dull. He never seemed to go anywhere of interest.

Well, of course Shakespeare's life was dull. He spent it writing, directing, and occasionally performing in thirty-seven brilliant plays. I tend to eliminate all noblemen as possible authors for these plays; they simply were too busy living it up to sit down and do much thinking, let alone all that magnificent writing.

Ah, the Shakespeare doubters continue, but we know that Shakespeare dropped out of school at about age fourteen—and the school he left was in the backwater town of Stratford. How could an eighth-grade dropout of a common country schoolhouse go on to write *any* play, let alone *Hamlet* or *King Lear*?

How indeed? This argument stumped us Shakespeare advocates until scholars recently began investigating the state of education in sixteenth-century England. This was the Renaissance period of English history, and the stress on education was so remarkable then that a brilliant young student—even in Stratford—could have absorbed enough classical learning by eighth grade that he could have left school with the equivalent knowledge of one of today's Ph.D. candidates in English history plus a master's candidate in Greek and Roman mythology.

Occasionally, I admit, our defenses for Shakespeare's authorship reach the height of divine absurdity. My favorite is the critic who used numerology to prove that Shakespeare was not only capable of writing all the plays but was also an unacknowledged author of the King James translation of the Bible. The Bible was indeed translated in England at the height of Shakespeare's writing power—the year 1611, when he was forty-six. This critic reminds us that Shakespeare loved all sorts of word and number games as demonstrated by the constant game-playing in all the plays. Thus, he is convinced Shakespeare left a clue to his authorship of the Bible translation by placing it in a biblical section corresponding to his current age, forty-six. The only such section would be Psalm 46. The critic read the psalm carefully but found no hidden clue.

But then he was inspired by a new—and even dumber— idea. Counting down exactly forty-six words from the opening of the psalm, he came to the word *shake;* counting up exactly forty-six words from the end, he came to the word *spear.* If this convinces you of Shakespeare's authorship of the King James version of the Bible, you should receive free membership in a new literary touring club—Gullible's Travels.

I mention all this because with so much unknown and

unknowable concerning Shakespeare's personal background, I think we are on safer ground to rebuild the wondrous experience of attending a dramatic performance of his works rather than investigating the man himself.

To fully experience a play is to go to a playhouse today and see the play performed—the curtain goes up and Shakespeare's words wash over you in glorious richness and vitality. He wanted you to experience the words by listening to them, not by reading them. It is this combination of *hearing* and *seeing* a work of art that makes drama so exciting. What I would like to do for you is to take you back about four hundred years to Elizabethan England, London in particular. I want to leave you with an impression of what it was like to attend the Globe playhouse when Shakespeare was its most prominent playwright.

You would have walked into the Globe just as you walk into a movie theater today; the doors were in the back, the stage was up front. Admission for a seat to a Shakespeare play in the 1590s cost exactly four pennies; even back then, though four pennies certainly had more weight than they do today, that was inexpensive for three and a half hours of live entertainment.

You did not give the four pennies to the usher; instead, the usher held out a small, locked metal box, the moneybox. You put your four pennies in that box so the usher couldn't run off with your money. This system had a problem, however: the moneyboxes were tiny, but pennies were enormous, larger than silver dollars are today. After only a few people had put in their four pennies, the little box became so full you couldn't jam in another penny. The usher then had to get someone to watch the back gate so people wouldn't sneak in. Then he would run as fast as he could backstage, to a little office with a lock on it. He would unlock the office door, throw in the full moneybox, grab an empty box, and run back. But after only a few more people had come in, that empty box would be filled, so he had to run behind the stage all over again.

You may wonder why the theater management simply did not supply a larger metal box to hold all of the pennies. They *had* thought of that, but discarded the idea. Shakespeare's playhouse was south of the river Thames in a highly unsavory neighborhood. The only people who daily frequented that area were prostitutes, robbers, and murderers. Any of these folk, had they seen a huge metal moneybox, would have stolen it without hesitation. The theater managers craftily assumed that no robber in his right mind would risk trying to steal a few pennies in a tiny box. Of course you may have guessed by now what that office backstage where the moneyboxes were locked up was called . . . the box office; that is why, four hundred years later, you still cannot go to a public form of entertainment—a movie, a rock concert, a play—without first visiting the "box office."

Once you paid your four pennies to see a play, you did not immediately take a seat. As you came down the aisles, on either side of you against the walls were large refreshment stands. Shakespeare's age was the first to move the refreshments from outside the playhouse to inside the playhouse. Theater managers cleverly figured out that if you could only buy refreshments once you paid for your ticket and were inside the playhouse, you were trapped. They could charge any exorbitant amount of money they chose on those refreshments, and you would have to pay it because there was no competition. If you went outside for refreshments, you would have to pay to get another ticket to get back inside. And that is why, four hundred years later, when you go to a movie, you will pay $3.75 for a box of buttered popcorn. That box of buttered popcorn that costs you $3.75 costs the owner of the movie theater 11¢ a box. That 11¢ includes the cost of the popcorn and the employee's salary. This is the highest markup in retail American business, and we never give it a second thought. Theater policy in Shakespeare's age taught us to overcharge the audience on the refreshments to generate profits.

Inside the playhouse, three refreshments were usually for sale. If you wanted dessert, they sold you an orange; oranges were cheap, they were sweet, and when you ate an orange, you really did not make enough noise to distract the actors onstage. If you wanted an entire meal, then they sold you a meat pie. We have no idea what the ingredients were for these pies, but we do know, because of diaries, that you would not encounter a live cat or dog within a five-square-mile area of the theater. One other item was for sale, which sold more than the first two combined. If you did not want an orange nor a meat pie, you could purchase a tomato. Now it seems odd that you could buy a tomato at a Shakespeare play, because in the sixteenth and early seventeenth centuries when Shakespeare was writing, no one in England ate tomatoes. The English believed the tomato to be deadly poisonous. Yet tomatoes sold like the proverbial hotcakes at Shakespeare's theater. You bought the tomato, you took it to your seat, and you waited. If after the first fifteen minutes of the performance you concluded that this was a waste of time and the most excruciatingly boring experience you had ever had to endure, you now had a convenient method of letting the actors know that this was not your idea of entertainment. You simply waited for the actor you deemed the worst offender to step to the edge of the stage and deliver his soliloquy. You then picked up your tomato, aimed it, and let it fly. Not surprisingly, this practice distracted many actors. Don't forget, they thought they were poisoned missiles. An actor, if enough tomatoes were being tossed at him, would lose concentration. If you have ever been on a stage and lost your concentration, you know what follows—you forget your lines. In Shakespeare's day, prompters would cue actors who forgot their lines, but a prompter was told not to help an actor who forgot his lines because so many tomatoes were being hurled at him. Therefore there was no helpful cue, the play would stop, and the audience was told to go home.

Unfortunately for Elizabethan playwrights, if a play was stopped because countless tomatoes were being hurled, the audience received a complete refund. In Shakespeare's day, you did not have to pay for a play that was below standard. Obviously, had Shakespeare not been a gifted playwright, he would have starved. Granted, Shakespeare was paid through a complex system of patronage, theater ownership, and author fees, but all of these payments depended on the quality of the plays themselves. As far as we can tell, not one tomato was ever tossed at a Shakespeare production, because William Shakespeare had the ability to keep an audience spellbound from the opening lines until the last word of the last act.

Although Queen Elizabeth I and her courtiers were

treated to command performances of all Shakespeare's plays, he could not afford to write solely for the queen and the court. To earn a living he had to write for the general public, and because the general public was largely uneducated, he had to write at a lesser level. Scholars tell us that 40 percent of the audiences at a Shakespeare play were people who possessed no more than the equivalent of a fifth-grade education today. Yet these folk loved Shakespeare and attended his plays in huge numbers. The poor and uneducated could only save about one penny for entertainment. It cost four pennies to get a seat at a Shakespeare play, so what did these people do if they only had a penny? Shakespeare was a good businessman. Why should he turn away almost half the population of London just because they did not have four pennies for a seat? If all a person had was a penny, he was told to put the penny in the moneybox. The usher, however, did not seat him; instead, he was taken all the way down to the front of the stage to join the rest of the "groundlings," as the standees were called. In Shakespeare's time, the stage was rather low, so if you stood close to the stage, you could still see the play's action. You were in fact so close that you could reach out and touch the actors as they came downstage.

This proximity to the groundlings could prove uncomfortable or even dangerous for the actors. In a diary from that time one actor tells us that if he saw too many groundlings standing up against the stage before the play started, he would not go out to perform because he was afraid he would get hurt. Why? Did he think they were going to throw tomatoes from such a close angle that he would be injured? No; the groundlings could not afford to buy tomatoes. But when the play would begin, the groundlings, an unsophisticated lot, would become so excited and so caught up in the action that their mouths would hang open; they would be gaping up at the actors, slack-jawed, watching the play unfold. This rapt attention was not what bothered the actors, but when the play became exciting and suspenseful, as in the early fight scenes in *Romeo and Juliet*, the groundlings would start to salivate. That saliva would drip down their chins and eventually fall onto the edge of the stage, where it made this little rivulet at the actors' feet. In his diary the actor wrote, "I feared when it was time for me to give my soliloquy and step to the edge of the stage, I was in grave danger of slipping in the drool left by the groundlings."

This particular performing hazard led to a superstition still firmly held by actors today. In Shakespeare's day actors believed that if someone said "good luck" to them before they went onstage, it was sure to bring bad luck. Rather than "good luck," the well-wisher would say, "Perform so the groundlings become so enthralled that they slobber on the stage; may you slip in it and break your leg." Even today one still says to a performer, "Break a leg." (Of course this is not to be taken literally. Tonya Harding may be the only person who took the expression as advice.)

The groundlings made their influence felt in the shaping of Shakespeare's plays. What is the first thing you see in *Macbeth?*—three hideous witches incanting over a bubbling cauldron. The play does not begin with a discussion of succession to the throne, it begins with what was sure to enthrall the groundlings: a hellish prophecy. When the curtain goes up on *Julius Caesar*, what is the first thing we see?

Not Caesar. We see a conspirator who says, in effect, I cannot wait until we stab Caesar and his blood flows all over the forum. The groundlings relished this especially, because they knew that before every performance of *Julius Caesar* a pig was slaughtered offstage, and its bladder carefully removed, because the bladder had the most concentrated deep red blood. Still warm, the bladder would be tied underneath the toga of the actor playing Julius Caesar. When Brutus stabbed Caesar, he made certain to burst the pig bladder with the stage knife, and all that rich, red pig blood would gush right down the costume onto the stage. And since in Shakespeare's day all stages were tilted downward (that is why we still have the terms *downstage* and *upstage*), all that blood would flow down to the edge of the stage, where it mingled with what had already been left there thanks to the droolers. Diaries of the day tell us that during productions of *Julius Caesar*, the groundlings would take the fingers of their right hand, dip them in the mixture of drool and pig's blood, and wave back at the actors to let them know they were enjoying this production.

Of all of Shakespeare's thirty-seven plays, the one the groundlings turned out in the largest numbers for is still, today, his most popular play: *Romeo and Juliet*. Why would such an uneducated crowd regard *Romeo and Juliet* as Shakespeare's best play? If you think about it, how much intelligence is really needed to become involved in this story? Early in act 1 you see a handsome teenage boy, in tights no less, named Romeo. A few lines later you see coming out from the other side of the stage what appears to be a lovely teenage girl, Juliet. (As you probably know, females were not used onstage in Shakespeare's day.) Someone on that stage, Romeo or Juliet, is going to strike your fancy, and you're going to pay attention through sex drive alone. Scholars tell us that the opening scene of every one of Shakespeare's plays always promises the audience one of three things: supernatural creatures, violence, or youthful sex. Shakespeare knew that if he did not titillate the groundlings early, he would lose their favor.

One play Shakespeare wrote is so difficult it is almost never taught in high school, only in college: *King Lear.* Yet even *King Lear* was written for the groundlings. To understand *King Lear,* all you need is to see the play with an eight-year-old. When the curtain goes up on act 1, turn to the eight-year-old and say, "Look! There's old King Lear and there are his three beautiful daughters. I hear two of those daughters are rotten beyond belief, but one of them is good and kind and loving." Then ask the eight-year-old, "I wonder, which of those daughters is the good one?" And any eight-year-old will look up at you as if you are an idiot and say, "The youngest daughter is the good one." Sure enough, at the end of act 1 we learn that the two eldest daughters are rotten beyond belief, and the youngest is good.

How would an eight-year-old child know the plot of Shakespeare's most difficult play? Shakespeare knew most of those groundlings sitting up front were illiterate. He also knew his audience had been raised on oral fairy tales and the folk tales of England. So in every major play Shakespeare wrote, he made the central plot a fairy-tale motif. That eight-year-old you took with you to *King Lear* knows fairy tales. He knows that in any fairy tale, if you see three children, you can be certain that the two eldest children will be rotten and the youngest good. It's that way in *Cinderella,* it's that way in every fairy tale that has three children; the elder two are either wicked or stupid (or both) and the youngest is wise and good. Shakespeare was telling people who couldn't read, this play is going to follow a motif that you know from the good old-fashioned fairy tale.

If this is true, if Shakespeare in his time was so simple and accessible, why do most high school students of today studying Shakespeare need a creative teacher, or Cliff's Notes, to understand his plays? One answer, of course, is the language; after four hundred years it has changed. But language is not the sole reason. The real reason Shakespeare seems so hard today is not Shakespeare's fault, and it's not the students' fault—it is actually my fault. I am an English professor, and it is English professors who are guilty. When Shakespeare was alive, he wrote comedies, tragedies, histories, long poems, short poems, and sonnets. Of those genres, the critics have always cited his tragedies as the most difficult. Yet what do we teach high school students today? As freshmen they read *Romeo and Juliet*—tragedy. As sophomores they read *Julius Caesar*—tragedy. Juniors read American literature, but seniors usually read *Macbeth*, yet another tragedy. Should they go on to college, as freshman they are often taught *Othello*, of course a tragedy. Should they survive to sophomore year, that's when we give them *King Lear*. All we ever seem to shove down students' throats today are Shakespeare's tragedies. They are his most difficult form, so of course they seem difficult to students.

The tragedies are actually difficult for anyone. Let me give you a philosophical key to help you unlock the mystery of almost any tragedy by Shakespeare you read. First of all, how do you know a play is a tragedy? Remember what they taught you in high school? You know it is a tragedy if at the beginning of the play the character is at a high level of society, but by the end of the play the character has fallen to a low level of society. Look at *Romeo and Juliet*. Where are Romeo and Juliet at the beginning of the play—are they at a high level of society? Yes, they are from two of the noblest families in Italy. Where are they at the end of the play? They are dead. You cannot fall further in society, obviously, than death. In all Shakespeare's tragedies characters begin at a high social level; at the end they are almost always dead. So, is a Shakespearean tragedy any play where at the beginning the character is at a high level of society but takes a long fall during the play?

The answer is, absolutely not; that is not the foolproof answer. If all it took to qualify for tragedy was someone on high taking a long fall, according to that definition our greatest tragic hero would, of course, be none other than Humpty-Dumpty. "Humpty-Dumpty sat on a wall, Humpty-Dumpty had a great fall." "Humpty-Dumpty" was not originally a nursery rhyme. Originally "Humpty-Dumpty" was written to teach uneducated people the basic principle of great tragedy. There is more about Shakespearean tragedy in the opening line of "Humpty-Dumpty" than in almost any other source.

"Humpty-Dumpty sat on a wall" does not sound complex, but it is. What does it mean? Suppose you are walking around in your neighborhood some late afternoon. You come to a wall. You look at the wall and there's a little boy sitting on the wall, playing with a yo-yo. Harmless enough. You walk a little longer, you come to another wall, there's a good-looking man and woman sitting on the wall, holding hands, gazing at the sunset. That doesn't excite you either. You keep walking and come to a third wall, a really high one, and you look up and sitting up there you see Humpty-Dumpty! You take one look at Humpty-Dumpty precariously perched on the wall, and you are immediately concerned. Why? Humpty-Dumpty is an egg.

And this observation leads us to Shakespearean tragedy. Because if you walk by a high wall and you see Humpty-Dumpty the egg up there, you know what you're going to think: "If I were an egg, I might be at the grocery or I might be in an omelette, but I think the last place on earth I would choose to sit would be upon a high wall." Which brings up the question "Well, Humpty-Dumpty, if you are an egg, what are you doing sitting on a high wall at the beginning of your poem?" The answer to that question is an insight into every Shakespearean tragedy. Basically Humpty-Dumpty is saying, "Tragedy, come scramble me. If I didn't want to be scrambled, why, as an egg, would I be on a wall?"

How does this relate to Shakespeare's tragedies? In every one of Shakespeare's tragedies the main character, just like Humpty-Dumpty, puts himself in the worst possible place, and therefore the only way he has to go is down. Look at *Romeo and Juliet* again. Early in the play Romeo learns that he may marry anyone on earth except Juliet; a little later Juliet learns she may marry anyone on earth except Romeo. So what do these two teenagers decide to do? Get married. The marriage is doomed, they know it is doomed, but they marry nevertheless—and pay a mortal price. Look at *Macbeth*. In act 1 of *Macbeth*, Macbeth takes his political counsel from a witch. Should any intelligent person listen to a witch for political advice? Macbeth does and is fated to fall. All Shakespearean tragedy is united by characters who ignore common sense, who enact something foolish and are bound, then, to fall.

Of everything I have told you about Shakespeare, I believe I have saved the best for last. Every playwright must invent dialogue for his characters. But Shakespeare is the only writer who, when he had to devise words for his characters to say, invented phrases so perfect and clever in their expression that, when the characters delivered them onstage to the other characters, the people in the audience recognized these phrases as works of genius and they stole these gems of speech on the spot. They went home, used them in front of their children. Those children used them—on and on, until right down to our time, out of our mouths will come phrases borrowed from the works of William Shakespeare.

Perhaps you were not aware you borrowed his words because you never knew they were Shakespeare's creations. But you will now, because I can think of no better way to end this look at Shakespeare than by quoting him for you. Every phrase that follows was first invented by the genius of William Shakespeare: If you've ever been *footloose and fancy free*. If you've ever thanked someone from the *bottom of your heart*. If you've ever been *left high and dry*. If you ever took a test that you thought was *a piece of cake*. If you've ever *refused to budge an inch*. If you've ever been *tongue-tied, a tower of strength, hoodwinked,* or *in a pickle*. If you've ever *knitted your brow, made a virtue of necessity, insisted on fair play, slept not one wink, stood on ceremony, laughed yourself into stitches,* or had *short shrift, cold comfort,* or *too much of a good thing*. If you've ever *cleared out bag and baggage* because you thought it was *high time* and that is *the long and short of it*. If you've ever believed *the game is up*, even if it involves *your own flesh and blood*. If you ever *lie low, till the crack of dawn, through thick and thin*, because you suspect *foul play*. If you've ever had your *teeth set on edge, with one fell swoop, without rhyme or reason*. And finally, if you now *bid me good riddance* and *send me packing*. If you wish I were *as dead as a doornail*. If you think I am *an eyesore, a laughingstock, a stony-hearted villain, bloody-minded*, or *a blithering idiot*, well then, *by Jove, O Lord, tut tut, for goodness' sake*, and (my personal favorite) *what the dickens!* It is *all one to me*, even if *it's Greek to you*, for you are quoting Shakespeare.

Jane Austen

(1775–1817)

I've always been amazed that, with all the detailed examination of Jane Austen in literary circles, I never hear remarked upon what I find the most remarkable aspect of her writing career: Jane Austen is the first great female author in our language. I am not saying that there were no other good women authors before she wrote, but Austen is indeed the first great female author. The few female authors before her have nowhere near the status that Jane Austen has acquired; she is a classic. We have to wonder then why there were great male authors from long before Chaucer, and yet we had to wait until almost 1800 before a great female author makes her appearance. Is the answer simply this: men by their very gender have always had an advantage in becoming great authors? This we know is not possibly true; if you have ever looked at any SAT scores, intelligence tests, or any other kinds of tests of native capabilities, you will discover that in general males score higher on science and math; females score higher on verbal and written skills. There are of course thousands of exceptions—many men are better at English than at math, many women are better at engineering than English. In general, however, females have always been more likely to become writers and authors by their inherent skills than men have; yet there is virtually no female author of any great reputation before Jane Austen.

The primary reason women have not become authors is simply that men had absolute power in all things, and they certainly controlled the types of literature that were written. Men made certain that the very areas they considered literary were the very areas in which most women were ignorant. For example, the first great age of writing in most societies is the epic age. What is an epic about? An epic can encompass almost any aspect of human life, but the one constant in all epics is war, and of course the one area that women never had any firsthand experience in, until recently, is war. Since epics must cover war and women knew nothing about war, no epics were written by women as far as we know. The age that replaced the epic age, in England at any rate, is the Renaissance. One of the most popular types of poetry written in this period is love poetry, especially love sonnets. Now, with the introduction of the subject of love you would assume many women would try their hands at this genre. Yet how many great women authors wrote love poetry in the Renaissance? As far as we know, not one. Why? Of course love sonnets focus upon love, but since men controlled literature, they decreed that in love sonnets one had to praise one's mistress. Let's face it: unless a woman was singularly adventuresome during the Renaissance, she didn't have a mistress, and without a mistress she obviously couldn't write in praise of one.

Next comes the Restoration and the early eighteenth century. What three topics were considered (by men) to be obligatory? Politics, religion, and society—which topics excluded most areas with which women were familiar. In fact, a woman could not be an author until recently. The original term for "writer" was not *author*. *Author* is what we've called such a person for quite some time, but it is really a shortened form. The word was not originally *author*, but *authority*. Women therefore could not be authors because they couldn't be authorities on anything except domestic issues, and until the novel genre really came about, domestic issues were of no importance to literature in general.

In fact, the whole act of writing was regarded as male. You can read in hundreds of sources from early days that when men discussed their writing, they talked about "fathering" a work of literature; you never heard of "giving birth" to a work of literature. Men went so far as to say that the very tool one used for writing, the pen, was a particularly male object and should not be used by females. If you look at a pen you notice that it is long and thin and pointed—I don't want to go into too much detail here, all of us are familiar with Freudian symbolism—but indeed you can see why men started to say that the pen was the ultimate phallic symbol and therefore women should have nothing to do with it. Indeed, why is a pen called a *pen*? *Pen* comes from the Latin word *penis*, which actually meant "tail," like a dog's tail. The very word we use for the writing tool is indisputably male.

You see, then, the entrenched tradition Jane Austen had to overcome. When Charles Dickens picked up his pen to write a novel, if he worried whether he could actually earn a living by writing, he could take security in a centuries-old tradition of men, a brotherhood, that stretched all the way back to Chaucer and beyond. Whom could Jane Austen look back to? Virtually no one—no female, no sister, had gone before to earn a living as an author.

Before we turn directly to Jane Austen's life, let us think about the fact that a writer has words and words alone as tools to build a work of art. If you're a painter, you have pigments; if you're a sculptor, you have clay; but if you're a writer, you just have words. And those words, in the English language, have tended to put women in their place; words by their nature are occasionally very antifemale, and Austen had to overcome this bias as well.

For example, if you have a little girl who acts more like a little boy than a little girl, we call her a tomboy. No girl has ever really minded being called a tomboy; it has no really negative connotation. However, if a little boy is acting like a little girl, we have a word for him too: *sissy*. Think of the difference in connotation between *sissy* and *tomboy: tomboy* has no negative connotation, *sissy* has no positive connotation. No little boy has ever wanted to be called a sissy, because men have always felt that the male is the superior sex and the female inferior. So when men regarded a little girl, considered inferior, behaving like a little boy, who was superior, they thought, now here's a spunky little girl. She's trying to act like a more important person; let's encourage her and call her a tomboy. But if they saw a little boy, the superior sex, trying to act like the inferior sex, well, they had to discourage him. They had to think up a negative name for the errant boy, and so they came up with *sissy*. *Sissy* is simply short for "sister," which tells you pretty much what men think about the concept of sisterhood. The opposite, though, brotherhood, is used as one of the founding symbols of America.

Notice the difference between male and female things and the connotations they have in our words. Now let's say that little girl grows up and as a woman she's still not acting like a woman, she's acting like a man. If we look in the dictionary, what's the worst thing in the dictionary to describe a woman who acts like a man? Well, the worst thing we could call her that is not slang is *masculine*, and although no woman wants to be called masculine, it does have a rather positive connotation. You call a woman masculine and you at least mean she knows what she wants, she has a strong personality, she gets ahead, nothing stops her, so it's not a terribly negative term. But let's say that little boy grows up to be a man, and rather than acting like a man, he's acting like a woman. Do we have a word in the dictionary to call a man who acts like a woman? We do, we call him *effeminate*. That is the exact word we call him. And what does *effeminate* mean? It means acting like a woman and being disgusting. Now isn't it odd that there is no word in the dictionary that means acting like a man and being disgusting? We have no word on the other side of *effeminate*. We have to call a woman like that *masculine*, and yet we have the word that means acting like a woman and being disgusting. How come we don't have a word for acting like a man and being disgusting? Well, because men controlled the power and the power of words. They weren't going to invent a word that meant acting like a man and being disgusting because, since they were men, they figured, well, if you're acting like a man, it can't be all that disgusting no matter what sex you are.

Let us look at one final example of the very nature of the words that Jane Austen and other female authors had to surmount before we turn to her directly. You have all learned from earliest days in school that in English we have prefixes, added to the beginnings of words, and suffixes, added to the ends of words. The most common suffix is *er*. If you end a verb in *er*, it always connotes a strong or violent action. That's why we call someone who labors a laborer, we call someone who murders a murderer, and we call someone who strangles a strangler—all strong actions. Now consider the much more sophisticated, accomplished suffix *ist*. If a noun ends in *ist*, it means having a particular talent or skill. We call a person skilled at working with teeth a dentist, we call a person who seeks perfection a perfectionist, and we call people who take up anthropology, anthropologists. It means having a particular talent or skill. Now given that *er* means taking a strong action and *ist* means having a talent or skill, we all know what we should call someone who rapes. We should call him a raper, meaning taking a strong action. However, because men controlled the language when a name was needed for this despicable man, they decided to call him a rapist, meaning possessing a particular talent or skill. It is one of the only examples in our language of a word that ends in *ist* that does not mean having a skill.

Now, having shown you how many obstacles Jane Austen faced as a female author, let me inspire you with how her unique genius would not be denied. Jane Austen's life does not seem the kind of life that would lead to such a revolutionary title as First Great Author in the English Language Who Was Not a Man. Her life can rather quickly be told. She was born in 1775 in the bucolic village of Stephenton, in the county of Hampshire, about an hour and a half west of London by car today, gorgeous rural country then as it is now. She was born into a secure world where every person knew his place. Her father was a rector in the Anglican

Church, so although he wasn't wealthy, his, and his family's, status was high. Because her father was a rector, we would place her in the upper middle class; because she lived in a rural setting, her class was the country gentry. In her novels *Pride and Prejudice, Emma, Sense and Sensibility*, she never writes about any other class at any length but the country gentry, which she knew so well. There were eight children in her family but only one other girl, a sister named Cassandra, with whom Austen was very close.

As a little girl Jane was shy and quiet around people her age and well behaved within her family. Her father and mother were bright, her brothers and sister extraordinarily bright; two of her brothers would go on to hold the two highest positions in the British navy. She lived amid a remarkable family that loved to be entertained by such exercises of the mind as conversation and reading aloud to one another. Jane took up writing at a young age to contribute to the family entertainment. At first she thought she would be a poet and write the first ever epic about a young woman. Any two lines from this early work would do to give you the flavor of her as a budding poet:

> She then left to go to dinner,
> after which she wasn't thinner.

Clearly poetry was not her calling, but Austen did not go directly to writing a novel. She had tried the epic form at fifteen; at sixteen she decided to write nonfiction prose, history in particular, and she decided to focus upon the history of England from the beginning of time. The result is a wonderful brief history of England; its chief glory was the title: "The

History of England by a Partial, Prejudiced and Ignorant Historian." (How many of us have read histories by ignorant historians? Austen is the only one forthright enough to publicly declare her ignorance.) I can't resist giving you just one typical selection, the segment she wrote about the reign of Henry VIII: "It would be an affront to my readers were I to suppose that they were not as well acquainted with the particulars of King Henry VIII's reign as I am, myself. Therefore, since it will be saving them the task of reading again what they have read before, and myself the task of writing what I do not perfectly recollect, I will give only the slightest sketch of this king's reign in the following two sentences." She does so and moves on. By the age of nineteen she decided to try writing a novel, and we are forever grateful she did.

She wrote her first novel at age twenty. She at first called it *Eleanor and Maryanne*, but eventually retitled it *Sense and Sensibility*. It was not, however, the sole focus of her writing. In her spare time she was writing another novel, which she decided to call *First Impressions*. That title didn't suit her, so she changed it to *Pride and Prejudice*. Both *Pride and Prejudice* and *Sense and Sensibility* were finished by the time she was twenty-two years old. If any other author had died at twenty-two—Chaucer, Shakespeare, Dickens, Byron— what would we have to read from them? Nothing. In her twenty-third year she wrote a work she called *Susan*, which became *Northanger Abbey*. By age twenty-three she has these three manuscripts—three of the six novels she wrote. Of course none of them were published; women didn't publish novels in that era, not only at her young age, but at any age. Her novels were written to entertain her brilliant family, and indeed they must have.

In 1800, when she was twenty-four, an event occurred that in terms of intensity was probably the climax of her emotional life. Her father announced one day at breakfast that taxes were so high and rectors paid so little—some things don't change in two hundred years—they could no longer afford to live as they desired in Stephenton, and he planned to move the entire family to the fashionable, thriving city of Bath. The minute Jane Austen heard her father announce his plan, she fainted dead away. Now why would she take it so terribly hard, this relocation to Bath? Because she knew the country-gentry set of this small town of Stephenton, she felt comfortable with it, she had her niche in society. She felt her father was wrenching her away from everything she knew and loved to go to a strange, anonymous city; it was a drastic transition for her.

The family did move to Bath, and almost immediately the future seemed to become more promising for Jane, because she received a proposal of marriage, from Harris Wither. We do not know much about Harris Wither, but fortunately a cousin of his wrote about him in a letter, trying to describe Wither to a friend: "He is a stutterer, he is huge, he is awkward, terribly flabby and above all unbelievably rude. These are his better qualities." Obviously, for Jane Austen he was no prize. In addition to his miserable personality, he was only twenty-one; she was twenty-seven. Do we have any glimpse of what she thought about him? As far as we can tell, the only emotion probably evoked from Jane Austen by Harris Wither was pity. It would seem to be a terrible match; it was not terrible at all, it was a most desirable match. Personality at the beginning of the nineteenth century, in Jane Austen's class, counted for naught. The two things that mattered were the two things Wither had in abundance, land and money. Desirable as the match was, Jane Austen certainly did not have to say yes; she could have respectfully declined. But although the two had only known each other for a few days, when he proposed early one evening, she accepted.

When Jane Austen went to sleep that night, it was clearly the worst night of her life, because when she awoke the next morning, she did the unthinkable. She retracted her acceptance and told him no. British society dictated that one could either say yes or no, but one never said yes and then the next morning retract to say no. It must have been horribly difficult for Jane Austen to have to refuse Wither so immediately after accepting. Why change her mind? Her refusal had nothing to do, we feel, with any fears she may have felt that he would be a miserable companion. More to the point, she loved her family so much and found such delight and stimulation with them, that she was not going to give up such ideal society for Harris Wither.

Less than two years later, in 1805, Jane Austen's father died, a doubly traumatic event. She was of course close to her father, but if you have ever read her novels, you can imagine what would become of Jane, her mother, and her sister. Often when a father died, the women of the family got nothing; they became dependent either upon the sons or often upon a distant male cousin, who took control of the women's fates. So Jane, her mother, and Cassandra for the next four years were homeless. Of course they had a place to live—and it was not a shabby place—but it was not their own. They had to go from brother's house to brother's house or, in Mrs. Austen's case, from son's house to son's house, depending on the mercy of their own kith and kin for a place to live. It clearly was unsatisfactory for all concerned.

I have now described the next ten years in Jane Austen's life, yet I have not told you one word about what she was writing, for good reason—she wasn't writing anything. This woman who produced three great novels by the time she was twenty-three wrote almost nothing for the next ten years. She had been so traumatized by the burdens of those ten years—the Bath experience, the proposal and her retraction, her father's death, and the resulting homelessness—that she was too emotionally unstable to write one decent word. In 1809 life blessedly changed. Jane's brother Edward had become exceptionally close to a childless couple, distant relatives. They were a wealthy landowning family, and when they died, they left the estate to him. Not only did the estate have a lovely manor house where Edward and his family would live, but also another charming house, called Chawton, just down the road. Edward made a gift of Chawton to his mother and his two sisters. Now Jane could move into her own home, and immediately she began to write, and to write quickly. The very year they moved in she completed her fourth novel, *Mansfield Park*, and during that year her first novel, *Sense and Sensibility*, was published.

The title page of this first published work of Austen's did not announce *"Sense and Sensibility*, by Jane Austen."* Instead it read, *"Sense and Sensibility*, by a lady."* But the very next year, because *Sense and Sensibility* did respectably, *Pride and Prejudice* was published. Probably one of the proudest moments of Jane Austen's life came when she was sent the title page of this novel, because the title page read, *"Pride and Prejudice*, by the author of *Sense and Sensibility*."*

While these novels were being published, Austen was starting her next one, *Emma*, which many consider her masterpiece. It was finished in 1814, as *Mansfield Park* was being published. The next year she began *Persuasion* and published *Emma*. *Northanger Abbey* would not be published until after her death. Once Austen had found a stable home, she again began writing finely crafted novels at a remarkable rate. Yet even in the security of Chawton, writing was complicated. When Jane was at home with no one but her mother and sister, if anyone came into the room where she was writing, she would instantly put the manuscript away. Even in front of her family it would have been improper for it to seem she was writing anything of substance. Of course her family knew what a talented writer she was, and all of them were proud of her. But this was a great age of manners and decorum, so the appearances—even in the home—had to be kept up. When the Austen women moved into Chawton the door to their parlor had a squeak, which Jane refused to let anyone fix. If she was working on a novel and she heard the squeak of the door, she would know someone was coming in and thus she couldn't be caught, red-handed, being an author. She could quickly hide her writing in the desk and get out her knitting. And because she constantly had to put away her writing, she couldn't write on anything that looked like a manuscript: her work had to be written on scraps of paper so she could quickly throw them in a drawer. She would occasionally have to put the scraps in chronological order and simply feel the weight of them in her palm to realize how far she had gone and how far she probably had to go.

Despite these impediments she still wrote one glorious

novel after another. Unfortunately this prolific time was brief. When she had just finished *Persuasion*, at age thirty-nine, she developed what is today called Addison's disease, still a serious malfunction of the adrenal gland. She began her last novel, which she could not complete, called *Sanditon;* ironically, its setting is a health spa. Two months before her death she moved to the city of Winchester, seeking medical help. There was no help, and she died July 18, 1817, only forty-one years old.

At Winchester Cathedral, where she is buried, there is a lovely monument to Jane Austen. The inscription says all sorts of wonderful things about her, but not one word indicates she ever wrote anything. She is described as a fine Christian woman and daughter; there is no mention that she crafted some of the most enduring works in the English language.

Now then, what can we say about Jane Austen as a writer, other than that she is the first great *female* writer in English? Is there any literary technique she mastered better than anyone else—even Shakespeare? Yes. That technique is irony of a particular type: comic irony. Critics consider her the foremost comic ironist in the English language.

If you say, in certain situations, "It's ironic," you pretty much know what you're talking about, but irony is hard to define. Irony is the audience being *given* by the author what is other than, or opposite of, what was *expected*. For example, if I said to you, "The police station is unsafe," that is ironic. Why? Because you expect the police station to be safe.

The above example, however, is not great irony; if I wanted to turn the statement into great irony, it would not be difficult. Simple irony is "The police station is unsafe."

But great irony is "The police station was robbed." Why? Because irony is when you get *other* than what you expect; great irony is when you get the *opposite* of what you expect. Throughout Austen's novels she gives you comic irony unequaled by any other author. In fact, the most famous sentence she ever wrote is regarded as probably the most clever, ironic statement in any English novel. It is the opening sentence of *Pride and Prejudice:* "It is a truth universally acknowledged that a single man in possession of a good fortune must be in want of a wife."

So, first, Jane Austen is the greatest comic ironist in the novel genre. What sounds more impressive but is not is the observation that she could write what we call "the perfect novel" better than any other author. What do I mean by "the perfect novel"? Jane Austen is one of those rare novelists in whom there is no progression of genius. She's perfect at the beginning and she's perfect at the end. What she cleverly did was focus upon the smallest segment of society, a milieu she knew extremely well: small, rural town, country gentry, and—above all—eligible young ladies in search of husbands. Plots revolve around meeting the wrong men, meeting the right men, and eventually, marrying and living happily ever after. It seems a narrow world, and it is, but because it is so narrow that it can probe deeply. In other words, though Austen's novels offer a narrow view of life, that view is perfect, there are no flaws. There is nothing she ever tackles that she does not do brilliantly.

And now we come to my third point, which lovers of Jane Austen will probably dismiss outright. No matter how beloved and respected an author is, that author will always have a weakness. Austen's weakness is this: she was unparalleled at irony, she wrote perfect novels, but *because* she was so very ironic, she seems to us quite detached from her characters, and she gives the impression of coldness. She judges her characters harshly. We applaud this now because we live in an age where no judgments are made in our society. We are a most socially uncivilized age, and we love Jane Austen today because her age *was* so judgmental and knew how to behave properly. But we also have to admit that her attention to the social mores of her era, her cool judgment of others, leaves us feeling that she was perhaps too intellectual, too distant, with too little heart.

Let me illustrate this point. Austen and her sister, Cassandra, rarely left home, but on one occasion Cassandra left on a distant journey and the sisters wrote letters back and forth. When Cassandra was about to leave, their neighbor, Mrs. Hall, was about to give birth to a child. Naturally when Cassandra was away, she wrote Jane and asked, "Has Mrs. Hall had her baby yet?" Jane replied, "Mrs. Hall was brought to bed yesterday, but delivered a dead child weeks before it was due, owing, the Doctor said, to a fright. I suppose she happened to look unawares at her husband." Amusing, perhaps—yet Jane Austen cannot refrain from making a joke about a tragedy so close to home.

My final observation is this: there are two literary societies, very different and very popular, in England and America. These societies are devoted to two great authors: Charles Dickens and Jane Austen. I am certainly heavily involved in the Dickens societies, or as we so aptly call them, Dickens Fellowships. Do you know what we call people who belong to the Dickens Fellowships, people who love Dickens? We are called Dickensians. And that word

Dickensian is a perfect word if you love Dickens, because *Dickensian* is a kind, gentle word, rather like the soft sentimentality of Dickens himself.

There are Jane Austen Societies as well, people who love Austen. You might think that if Dickens lovers were called Dickensians, Austen lovers would be called Austenians. But if you are in a Jane Austen Society, you are called a Janeite. And that is the perfect word for a lover of Jane Austen. As opposed to *Dickensian*, *Janeite* has a bite to it, an intellectual snap. So the difference between the sound of *Dickensian* and *Janeite* fairly well sums up the divergent gifts of these two great authors.

Edgar Allan Poe

(1809–1849)

Everyone wants to know, "Was Poe's life really as horrible as I have heard?" Actually, it was far worse: Edgar Allan Poe had what could be considered the most bizarre, grotesque, horrific, and pathetic life of any literary figure we ever studied in school. And when Poe picked up his pen to write a short story or a poem, he distilled his horrible life into everything he wrote. Nothing he wrote was strictly autobiographical, but everything he wrote ultimately had to do with his personal history.

The first important detail of Poe's life concerns the one person who shaped his imagination more than anyone else. That person was his mother. Poe's mother was not like yours or mine. Anyone who ever met his mother always had the same thing to say about her: "Edgar Allan Poe's mother has to be one of the most beautiful women who ever lived." She was, in fact, so exquisite that when she was only eight years old, her parents schemed a way to profit from her looks. Poe's mother was born in England, but when she was only eight, her parents left England and came to America. They thought that because Elizabeth was so beautiful, clever, and "foreign," she could be cast in starring roles in plays written for American audiences. Sure enough, by the age of ten

Elizabeth was a prominent child star. When she was only thirteen, her parents married her off to the comedian who was the opening act of their theatrical company. He died within the first year of their marriage; at the age of fourteen Elizabeth was a widow, wearing black onstage. The theater company now had no opening act, so little advertisements were placed in journals throughout the country, advertising for men to audition. Many tried out; one man got the job, David Poe. He was not a comedian but a dancer, such a good dancer that even though the company had been looking for a comedian, when they saw this man perform, they hired him on the spot. David Poe was young, thin, pale, and handsome; Elizabeth was gorgeous. The two took one look at each other, fell in love, and married. It was a doomed marriage, but it did produce this one child, Edgar Poe.

Three weeks after the baby was born his father lost all interest in his newborn son, his wife, and his marriage. He perfected a new act—a disappearing act—and he was gone. He was found, eventually, in a cheap Chicago hotel room, dead of alcoholism.

Elizabeth had to return to the stage three weeks after young Poe was born because without a husband she needed to earn money. Elizabeth was sixteen, lovely, and possessed of a wonderful British accent, so you may intuit what role she was given—Juliet in Shakespeare's famous tragedy *Romeo and Juliet*. She performed Juliet eight times a week, every night but Sunday, and on Wednesday and Saturday afternoons. She was onstage most of the time and she had her little Edgar; what could she do with him while she was performing? The only thing she could think to do was to reserve the middle seat of the front row of whatever playhouse she was performing in, and there she would leave him during the play.

So when Poe was one, two, and three years old, he sat in the front row of the theater, watching his mother perform *Romeo and Juliet* eight times a week. Was this exposure wise? You may remember that the last scene in *Romeo and Juliet* takes place in a crypt, an underground burial vault. The newly wed Juliet comes to the crypt early for a secret rendezvous with her husband, Romeo. She drinks a magic potion that causes her to fall asleep on a tomb amid the bones of her ancestors. Romeo enters the crypt, sees his beautiful wife sleeping, but believes she is dead. Wild with grief, he takes poison and falls dead at her feet. Juliet then wakes and finds Romeo dead. Distraught, she seizes the dagger from Romeo's belt, plunges it through her heart, dies, and the final curtain comes down.

Well, there was little Edgar sitting in the front row, watching his mother take a knife, eight times a week, put it right in the middle of her heart and die. Then the stage manager would come out from behind the curtain, take little Edgar by the hand, and escort him backstage, where he watched his mother take the knife out her heart, get up, and take him out to dinner.

Was this a healthy environment for the young Poe? Hardly. Did it affect the future writing of Edgar Allan Poe? Most certainly. Scholars can tell you that in the stories and poems of Edgar Allan Poe, innumerable beautiful, dead young women refuse to stay dead. They seem dead in the beginning, they come back to life in the middle, and someone stabs them in the final paragraph. Poe was always confusing life and death within his women characters because, when he was age one, two, and three, he saw his mother die and come back to life over and over.

Unfortunately Edgar discovered the reality of death when he was three and a half. He and his mother moved to Richmond, Virginia, where she was to star in *Romeo and Juliet*. Elizabeth never performed again because once they arrived in Richmond, she fell ill with the most deadly disease of that era—consumption. It is called consumption because the disease attacks the lungs and consumes, or eats away, the lung lining. The infection made the lungs so weak that the blood the heart was supposed to pump to the rest of the body would accumulate in the lungs. The test for consumption was simple: you took a handkerchief and you coughed into it. When you took that handkerchief away from your mouth, if even one bright red drop of arterial blood was on your handkerchief, it meant you had consumption and were fated to die a lingering, painful death. The cause of death was actually drowning—eventually so much blood would fill your lungs that you literally drowned.

So many women got consumption in the early 1800s that, if you walked into an antique store today and asked to see a woman's handkerchief from the early nineteenth century, you would know immediately if the one they showed you was authentic. If it was truly a woman's handkerchief from Poe's day, it would not be pure white. At the bottom border the handkerchief manufacturer would have embroidered one of three things: a row of cherries, a row of strawberries, or, the one used most often, a tiny row of roses. All three motifs were, of course, bright red. If a consumptive woman was out in public and coughed into her handkerchief, the cherries, strawberries, or roses would disguise any spots of blood.

The playhouse where Elizabeth was to have performed Juliet set up a little cot backstage that became her deathbed. The wealthy women of Richmond would come to the theater during the day bringing nourishing meals in the hopes of reviving the lovely, dying creature. But their efforts came to naught. Elizabeth died, and it was poor Edgar's ill fortune that he was looking at his mother's face the moment she drew her last breath.

Poe later said something so mesmerizing happened to his mother right after she died that he never forgot it, and he spent the rest of his life writing about it. The ravages of consumption had eventually destroyed his mother's preternatural loveliness. But once she was dead and finally at peace, he claimed that her face became so beautiful again that she looked far better in death than she had ever looked in life. And because he saw his mother transformed from such haggard devastation at the very moment of her death, to ethereal beauty after she was dead, four images fused in his brain that day, and he never forgot them. The images that would haunt him to the end were youth, beauty, women, and death. Poe became fixated on his dead mother's face that day, an obsession that would cause him enormous pain the rest of his life.

Now, at age three, Poe was an orphan. He would likely have starved but for one of those wealthy Richmond ladies, Frances Allan, who had visited the actress before her death. When she heard that Elizabeth had died, she went home and told her wealthy husband, John Allan, that they should adopt Edgar and give him a home since they could not have their own children. Allan rejected the idea because Edgar Poe was the son of an actress. At that time almost the lowest job a woman could have to make money was as an actress. Prostitutes were at the bottom of the social scale; actresses were only one rung higher. John Allan refused to taint his fine Virginia bloodline by bringing this child into it. Frances Allan gave up on the possibility of adoption, but won permission to absorb the boy into the household, to feed him and rear him. And so Edgar Poe, who should now have become Edgar Allan had he had a compassionate stepfather who had legally adopted him, moved in with the family. Because he wasn't legally adopted, he used Allan in the middle of his name and called himself, for the rest of his life, Edgar Allan Poe.

John Allan did not send Edgar to school in Richmond. He enrolled him in a school in England, in what John Allan thought was an exclusive, private church school. Poe tells us later, this school *was* church and *was* private, but it was hardly fancy. According to Poe, the headmaster was so cheap he would not buy books and texts for the students. Instead, because the school was in a church and right outside the church was the churchyard where all the dead parishioners were buried, the headmaster forced the teachers to use the cemetery in their lesson plans. When students had to learn subtraction, they were given a piece of chalk and a slate and were then sent out to the cemetery. Choosing a tombstone, each pupil had to write down the year the dead person was born, then subtract that date from the year the person died, because the arithmetic problems always concerned how old Mr. X was when he dropped dead—the only way to solve the problem was to use the cemetery. But the oddest schooling concerned physical education. Each child was given a little wooden shovel on the first day of autumn semester. If anyone subsequently died in the parish, the gravedigger was instructed to stop at the school and commandeer the older children, who were expected to help dig the grave for aerobic activity. Poe said the only benefit he received from his schooling was that it gave him the settings for many future stories. He begged his stepfather to bring him back to Richmond.

And so beginning at age twelve, Poe attended school in Richmond. None of the students liked Poe because they didn't know him; he had grown up in England. It took Poe three years to make one good friend. When he was a sophomore in high school, his best friend was a young man named Richard. One day Richard said to Poe, "I want you to come home with me after school today because I want to show you my squirrels, my rabbit, and my mother."

We don't know what Poe thought about the squirrels and the rabbit, but we certainly know what Poe thought about the mother. Not only was she rather young and very beautiful, but unfortunately for Poe, her petite, dark beauty was uncannily similar to that of his beloved, lost mother. Poe was obsessed by his own mother's face, and this woman, Richard's mother, looked enough like Poe's dead mother to be a sister. Poe fell hopelessly in love.

Two weeks later Richard's mother went to a doctor because she had been having terrible headaches; the doctor informed her she had a brain tumor so advanced it would kill her within five weeks. When Poe learned that this woman he loved was dying, he made a nightly pilgrimage to her bedside, to hold her hand, and he was there the night she died in frightful agony from the brain tumor. For the next year after Richard's mother had died, Poe could be found every night in the cemetery where she was buried, walking round and round her tombstone as if in a trance. One bizarre critic of Poe's suggested that this did not prove Poe was devoted to Richard's mother. It only proved Poe was confused and thought he was back at that school in England trying to get extra credit.

So here was the second woman that Poe loved who had died before his eyes, but one woman remained who was a source of goodness in Poe's life, Frances Allan, his stepmother. No one could have been a more kind, giving, loving mother than Frances Allan. Unfortunately, as wonderful as Mrs. Allan was as a mother, that is how oppressive John Allan was as a stepfather. Allan despised Edgar Allan Poe and wanted him out of the way, but he could never act against Poe because Mrs. Allan was there to protect the youth. Allen's hatred was due to his intense jealousy of Poe since Frances delighted far more in Edgar's company than in her own husband's, and Allen never tried to overcome his snobbishness regarding Poe's low birth. Poe was sheltered, until he was sent to college at the University of Virginia shortly after Thomas Jefferson opened it, in 1826. Poe came home one spring break, walked into the house, and there was Mrs. Allan in the parlor. She looked at him and said, "I have consumption, I am dying."

After her death, no one stood between Edgar Allan Poe and the stepfather who despised him. As soon as Frances was buried, John Allan threw all of Poe's possessions onto the front lawn of the house (subtlety was not his strong suit) and told him, "I want you out of my house and out of my life today. If you ever come back onto my property, you will be arrested on the spot."

Poe was twenty years old, no mother, no father, and not one person in the world who cared whether he lived or died. He was so poor he had to rent a room that had no fireplace. He tells us that before he could write in that frigid little room, he would have to hold his fingers over a candle to get rid of the frostbite. But at this point, at the nadir of Poe's life, he struck upon the one thing that would guarantee his fame. Alone in his room he decided to write something so beautiful, so moving, that the world would fall in love with him and reward him.

His nature, however, worked against this fantasy. Because his mind was so warped and influenced by his miserable childhood and all the deaths, the only thing he seemed able to write were stories and poems about dead people who return from the grave. At the age of twenty Edgar Allan Poe invented "the tale of terror" when he began writing his first stories.

Am I telling you Poe was the first person to write a scary story? Of course not—scary stories actually go back to the cavemen. But Poe *is* the first to write a scary story from the psychological point of view of the killer or the mad person himself. He crafted the theme of terror into a form both artistic and respectable. For better or worse there could be no Stephen King today without Edgar Allan Poe.

He created something else, far more important than "respectable terror"—he invented the modern short story. Poe developed the principle that every sentence of a story must contribute to a single effect. In the case of Poe, the effect is horror. If you read any short story today, all of them meet Poe's criterion.

How much money did Poe receive for inventing the tale

of terror and the short story? Nothing—no one wanted to read such twisted tales. Poe would probably have starved, except yet another woman took hold of his life, Mariah Klemm. Her brother was David Poe, Edgar's dissolute father, the dancer. She had spent two years looking for Poe, to make amends for her brother's desertion. She had heard from a cousin that her nephew was a struggling writer and therefore felt great pity for his wretched condition. She wished to adopt Poe as her son and give him a comfortable haven in which to write.

This was what Poe had thought he always wanted, a family who could nurture and love him. But like everything else in Poe's life, it turned into disaster. He moved in with his aunt and discovered that she already had five children. Her husband had died and she was the family's sole support. Poe looked over his new brothers and sisters, who were actually, of course, his first cousins, and his heart was immediately snared by the youngest, a lovely creature named Virginia. She was young and beautiful in the exact way his dead mother, Elizabeth, had been—a fatal resemblance.

Within a few months Poe approached his aunt and expressed his yearning to marry Virginia. Mariah refused— not because Virginia was Edgar's first cousin, but because Virginia was ten years old. Mariah told Edgar he would have to wait until Virginia was thirteen; at that time she would allow the marriage. Mariah was as demented as Edgar; it obviously ran through the entire family.

Three years passed. And when Poe was twenty-six and his cousin Virginia was thirteen, they married. Before the marriage Poe was writing stories of the macabre; no one bought them and he was starving. Once married, he continued writ-

ing such stories, which still went unsold—the only differe
was that now his wife was starving too. We don't know w
would have happened to them without the man who n
entered the scene, who turned Edgar Allan Poe's life cc
pletely around and made him famous as we know him toc
His name? Charles Dickens, the great English novelist.

What does Dickens have to do with Poe? When Poe v
starving in Richmond in 1842, Charles Dickens was 1
most famous young novelist of his time. So famous was
that American readers paid him handsomely to tc
America on the first international superstar tour. And a s
he was—oglers pulled at his clothes, women fainted in t
streets, hordes begged for his autograph. One of the cit
Dickens visited was Richmond, where Poe was struggling
hard. When Poe heard that the great Charles Dickens w
coming to Richmond, he sent such a clever letter to Char
Dickens inviting him to lunch at a downtown Richmo:
hotel that Dickens not only accepted, he came alone.

They sat down to lunch. Poe looked at Dickens, realiz
that Dickens had been crying, and of course asked the re
son. And Dickens related the story: "I was hoping yc
wouldn't notice, Mr. Poe, but since you asked, I'll give you :
honest answer. I had a personal tragedy in my family befor
left England to come to America, and I was thinking abo
it. I have a wife and three children, and we had a pet by tl
name of Grip. We loved our pet Grip almost as much as v
love each other. Before I came away, I took my family on
weekend holiday. We did what we always did with Grip: v
locked him in our stable. We left plenty of food and wat
and thought he would be fine during our absence. But w
did not realize there was a large can of paint in the stabl

and its lid had fallen off. Unfortunately the paint was of a color that looked just like water. Poor Grip became confused and drank up all the paint by mistake [paint that was heavily laced with lead and of course deadly poison]. Imagine our shock, Mr. Poe, when we unlocked the stable door upon our return, and there was poor Grip, flat on his back, stiff as a board, legs sticking straight up, stone-cold dead."

Of course the moment Edgar Allan Poe heard the phrase "stone-cold dead," he perked up; this was his kind of conversation! Poe asked, "What was poor little Grip? A cat or a dog?" And Dickens replied, "Oh, no, Mr. Poe, we have no normal pets in my family. Actually Grip was a big, lovable black raven." And Poe thought, raven.

He had never really thought about a raven before; we know this from his diary. He went home that night and opened up a drawer. Within was a poem he had already written, about a beautiful dead young woman named Lenore. Poe had sent the poem to publishers—no one had wanted it. But on this evening, because he was inspired by the grotesque story Dickens had told him, he decided to change the poem. He kept as the centerpiece the dead young woman, but he erased the title "To Lenore" and changed it to "The Raven." He put the ominous black bird in every stanza and gave it one mysterious utterance: "Nevermore." And he sent the poem out again. This time, as "The Raven," it was accepted and immediately caught the public's fancy. Everyone wanted a copy of "The Raven." Even in Poe's day it was a mystery why this poem was so wildly popular. It became, indeed, the most popular poem ever published.

Poe was asked why he thought "The Raven" had so captured the public imagination. First, he said, perhaps it was because he had wanted to write the first adult fairy tale. And people said, well, if you were going to write the first adult fairy tale, why didn't you open it with the four famous words of most fairy tales, "Once upon a time"? And Poe said, "But I did open it that way. In my mind *all* time is midnight dreary."

The other reason Poe gave for the popularity of "The Raven" had to do with rhythm. He said he had tried to capture, in the beat or cadence of each line, the way a stately raven would actually walk. Whether that was actually a consideration we don't know. But we certainly do remember the unusual and haunting beat of "The Raven":

> Once upon a midnight dreary,
> while I pondered, weak and weary,
> Over many a quaint and curious volume
> of forgotten lore—
> While I nodded, nearly napping,
> suddenly there came a tapping,
> As of someone gently rapping,
> rapping at my chamber door.

How much money did Poe make on "The Raven"? He made nothing because he was ignorant of copyright laws. He decided to bring out "The Raven" in a newspaper first so he could hurry it into print, not realizing that if one published a poem in a newspaper there was no copyright protection. Any second-rate poet could copy out "The Raven" and immediately bring out a book called *My Greatest Poems* including "The Raven Illustrated." It took Poe so long to bring out his own edition, because he needed to find sponsors, that by the time it came out no one would buy it because they'd bought someone else's.

It was a costly mistake. One day, not long after "The Raven" was published, Poe went home to his young wife, who told him she had consumption and was dying. Poe had so little money while Virginia lay ill that he could not afford to buy a blanket for her bed, where she lay in chills. They did, however, have a pet, a longhaired cat named Katarina. Poe would pick up the cat and place it on Virginia's chest for her to hug as the only warmth in their tiny apartment.

Virginia died, and Poe was consumed by grief. There was, however, a token silver lining to his misery. He wrote what is perhaps his most brilliant poem to his dead wife, Virginia. He took it to a publisher who refused it because of its title: "To Virginia." Readers wouldn't know if the poem was written to Poe's home state or to his dead wife. Poe changed the name to "Annabel Lee."

"Annabel Lee" was instantly successful, and Poe's career finally seemed to be established. Even the short stories— "The Gold Bug" in particular—were now finding great favor with the reading public. And then the one success he had always prayed for seemed about to happen. A wealthy man in New York City named Davis McCarthy made Poe an offer: "You are the greatest living author. I own the finest poetry magazine in America. If you will move to New York, not only will I hire you to edit my magazine, I'll pay you twice as much as any editor is currently getting." Finally Poe had acquired the respect of the literary world. All he needed to do to start his new life was to move to New York. He tried; he never arrived.

En route from Richmond to New York, travelers had to

change trains in Baltimore, Maryland. Poe got off the train in Baltimore thinking he would walk down the track, get on the train to New York, and begin his new and glorious life.

Poe arrived in Baltimore on election day for mayor. If a political candidate wanted more votes back then, he simply found people to vote over and over for him under false names at different polling places. No one in Baltimore would risk doing this for a candidate, because if anyone was caught changing his name to vote illegally more than once, the penalty was ten years in the federal penitentiary. The candidates got around this by sending henchmen down to the train stations, hoping someone gullible would get off a train.

Poe disembarked. A man approached him and said, "This is Baltimore, the friendly city. We'd like to buy you a drink." Poe replied, "You can't buy me a drink, I'm an alcoholic." You have to admire Poe: he had sworn off alcohol for good and had been on the wagon six months. He should have said no more. But just to be friendly he said, "You know, when I used to drink, if I only had one shot of liquor, I'd get so drunk I'd do anything. And then I wouldn't even know I'd done it." "Oh, really?" said the candidate's man. "We didn't want to get you alcohol. It's hot—we thought you might like a lemonade. Do you have time?"

The political flacks took Poe across the street to the railroad tavern where they bought him something called Baltimore lemonade: 5 percent lemons, 95 percent vodka. Poe had seven shots of this deceptive drink, all poison to his system. The men steered the nearly insensible Poe to the polling place, where he cast his vote—and was then cast aside to make his way back to the train station. An eyewitness tells us Poe took only three steps down that Baltimore street before he collapsed in the gutter in a deep alcoholic coma. A horse ambulance happened by, and they saw Poe. They threw him in the wagon and dumped him at the front gate of the charity ward of a hospital. Poe survived three days. On the third day he opened his eyes wide, raised his head from his pillow, and screamed out in a voice so loud the entire ward heard him, "God have mercy on my soul!" And then he fell back, dead.

He had just turned forty. He had never had a complete success in his life. The four women he had loved all died in agony in front of him. Everything he touched turned into utter disaster. Yet today more people in the world read the poems and short stories of Edgar Allan Poe than the works of any other American author. Poe is our number one literary export, surpassing even Mark Twain. My father, who grew up in Hungary, told me that in Hungary as a young boy he had never heard of Shakespeare, never heard of Dickens, but by sixth grade he was reading the stories of Edgar Allan Poe translated into Hungarian. Ask anyone in France who was the greatest writer in the English language and he or she will answer Edgar Allan Poe. This would sound even more impressive if we could forget that the French also think that Jerry Lewis is the world's greatest comedian. In an ironic twist of fate that Poe himself might have appreciated, his works—like the delicate and ill-fated ladies he created—come to life again and again.

Charlotte Brontë *(1816–1855)*
&
Emily Brontë *(1818–1848)*

As we turn to the mysterious Brontë sisters—Charlotte Brontë, who wrote *Jane Eyre*, and Emily Brontë, who wrote *Wuthering Heights*—we begin by examining the name itself. *Brontë* is an unusual one, especially in the field of Victorian authors. The names of the other great authors of the Victorian period—Dickens, Tennyson, Browning, Thackeray, Meredith, Hardy—are all very English-sounding. But the name Brontë is exotic, foreign in sound. If you were to guess, you might suppose it is French, and you would be correct. But how much French blood flowed through the veins of Charlotte and Emily Brontë? Not one ounce. How can this be? To solve such a puzzle you must start with the sisters' father. His first name was Patrick, but his last name was originally Brunty. If you wonder what sort of name Brunty is, let me give you a clue: it had been changed from O'Brunty. It is, of course, an Irish name.

You may also wonder why I am ignoring the other Brontë sister, Anne. She did indeed write two novels—*Agnes Grey* and *The Tenant of Wildfell Hall*—but they are of a much lower order than those of Charlotte and Emily. The single most impressive feature of Anne's fiction is that it was written by the sister of two literary geniuses.

The father of these two literary geniuses was born Irish on St. Patrick's Day to dirt-poor parents who were tenant farmers. There seemed to be no future for him. But although Patrick Brunty was poor, he was brilliant. And he knew that if he was ever to rise in society, he could only do so in the Church of England. He decided to become a rector. He also knew, however, he had two formidable handicaps. First of all, his name, Brunty, just cried out poor Irish. It would have to be changed, and so it was. When Patrick was still a teenager, he picked up the newspaper one day and noticed that Lord Nelson, the great British hero of the Napoleonic era, had been given an honorary title, the Duke of Brontë. Patrick thought that name seemed exotic and would make people take notice. After all, how many people are allowed to place two dots above the final letter of their last name? So the entire family has always been known as Brontë. If you recollect the eeriness of both *Jane Eyre* and *Wuthering Heights*, and the importance of atmosphere and how it pervades the entire novels, you perhaps understand an Irish influence upon these two great authors.

Patrick's second handicap was being single. If he was going to be taken seriously, he needed just the right wife for a rector. Unfortunately for her, he found her, Maria Branwell. Her background was nothing like his. She came from Penzance in Cornwall, a region with one of the mildest climates in England. The two met, fell in love, and married. I think it is important that you understand the exact chronology of the Brontë marriage. They married in 1812. In 1813 their first child, a daughter, Maria, was born. In 1814 their second daughter, Elizabeth, was born. In 1816 their third daughter, Charlotte, was born. In 1818 their fourth child, another daughter, Emily, was born. In 1818 their fifth child, their only son, Branwell, was born. In 1820 their sixth child, another daughter, Anne, was born. And in 1821 Mrs. Brontë died, and who can blame her? Six children and one miscarriage in seven years of marriage. The year that poor Mrs. Brontë died was also the year Patrick Brontë was assigned to the parish that he would keep for life.

He had once said he wanted a London parish, but would accept a Manchester parish if necessary. But his church did not place him in London, nor in Manchester; the church gave Mr. Brontë one of the most desolate parishes in England, Haworth, in Yorkshire, in the far isolation of the northern moors. The parsonage was surrounded on three sides by the graves of the dead parishioners, a truly ghastly "neighborhood" for a young family. Not long after taking up his duties in Haworth, Brontë's wife died and left him a widower with six children, aged seven, six, four, two, one, and an infant. His first task was to find a caretaker for the family, and he called upon his dead wife's sister Elizabeth Branwell, who lived in Penzance. She gave up her comfortable life there and came to serve as housekeeper and substitute mother.

Patrick Brontë was an eccentric and exacting father, but his children took full advantage of one of his passions—a wonderful library. The four children could be found reading books from the earliest age. Now, you notice I said four children, even though there had been six in the family. But they didn't remain six for long, because the two oldest girls, Maria and Elizabeth, were sent off to a boarding school. Of course Mr. Brontë had little money to spare on education, but there were schools back then specifically for poor rectors' children. These schools were inexpensive; they were also nightmarish. The two Brontë girls were sent to Cowan Bridge School and suffered there under appalling conditions, eventually being taken home ill. Their release from the cold, hunger, and disease of Cowan Bridge came too late—both girls died within five weeks of each other. At the ages of eleven and ten, Charlotte and Emily lost their two beloved older sisters. For a detailed portrait of Cowan Bridge School, read the early chapters of Charlotte Brontë's *Jane Eyre*. Jane is sent to a school called Lowood, run by the villain Mr. Brocklehurst. According to Charlotte Brontë, Lowood's brutal conditions are an exact replica of those that killed her sisters.

One day Mr. Brontë came home from a journey and brought the four remaining Brontë children some beautiful wooden painted soldiers. He gave them to Branwell, who shared them with his sisters. Now, had these been normal children, they would likely have used the toy soldiers to play at war. Instead they went to the parlor, put the soldiers on the floor in various positions, and then pretended these soldiers were creatures from two fantasy kingdoms. The four Brontë children divided themselves into two writing groups, Branwell and Charlotte in one, Emily and Anne in the other.

Emily and Anne created a world called Gondal. It was a "science-fictiony" world where the rivers ran with milk and honey and all the trees looked like strange triangles. It was a beautiful, exotic world, very strange, peopled by the toy soldiers. Charlotte and Branwell invented a very different world, Angria. This fantasy world was what it sounds like, a pulsing, almost vicious world where the rivers ran red and a constant, strong beat was underneath. They wrote minutely detailed adventure stories of the soldiers who populated Angria. For over ten years, these four children expanded the two worlds through stories. But they didn't just write stories, they actually wrote books. Once an adventure story had been completed, the children would print the stories on little pieces of paper. They made sure the margins were even, right and left, just as in a printed novel, and when they finished, the little book looked like a tiny novel. Of course they needed a cover for their book, so they would raid the kitchen. Sugar came in blue cardboard boxes. They would pour the sugar into an earthen vessel, then cut up the stiff blue cardboard to make a perfect cover. They would put the title on the cover, with their names. They would use a little paste to glue it on, and presto, a tiny volume smaller than their palms. But they didn't compile just ten or even fifty of these stories—they wrote hundreds over the years. This was their training, as children, for the future novelists that at least three of them would become.

Mr. Brontë was not much impressed that his children were writing these vivid adventure books; his concern was with who would earn much-needed income once they left school. Charlotte was the eldest; the responsibility fell upon her. When she graduated from school, she began to seek employment. Charlotte was extremely bright, but she came from a poor rector's family. If a woman of that time was bright and yet poor, only one position was really available. If you have read *Jane Eyre*, you know what Charlotte became—a governess. I don't think we appreciate today what the position of governess was like in the Victorian period. Thanks to *Masterpiece Theatre* we have a romantic notion of a beautiful young girl employed in a wealthy home, tutoring darling little children. Charlotte tells us the reality—that being a governess was hell on earth. It was a wretched position. Darling, well-behaved children; were rare. Truly wealthy people didn't have a governess tutor their children, they sent their children to expensive boarding schools. Boarding school was a mark of status, a way to cement societal connections, as well as an educational experience. If, however, parents had a lot of money but had children who were such intellectual or emotional nightmares that no school would ever accept them, a governess was the solution. Occasionally one could find a good child, but only because the child was illegitimate (as Adele was in *Jane Eyre*) and therefore not eligible for a good boarding school.

The other problem the governess faced, probably a worse ordeal than not having decent students, was that the family would have nothing to do with her because she was considered too low in class to be part of their society. The governess actually worked for a living, and the family that hired her would have thought that was below their regard. But there was an upstairs *and* a downstairs in the family. Downstairs were the servants: the butler, the cook, the housekeeper, and the maids. They certainly wouldn't have found the governess too low to associate with—she was too high. Servants resented that "all she did" was tutor some brats for a few hours a day and thus earned three times what the kitchen maid earned by scrubbing pots. The family had nothing to do with a governess because she was too low; the servants had nothing to do with her because she was too high. It was a most painfully alienating position, unless the governess was beautiful. If you examine some of the family portraits that were painted of wealthy Victorian families, you will see in many portraits a rather ugly father, a plain mother, and three unattractive children. The sixth figure will be a beautiful and delightful young woman. You might think, "Well, at least they had one attractive child." They didn't. That's the governess. The upstairs family enjoyed having the beautiful governess because she was so attractive. The servants, the downstairs family, prized having a beautiful governess around because by just eating at the humble table of the servants this beautiful girl put everyone in a good mood.

But Charlotte Brontë was not beautiful; she was not even plain. A young man who saw her at a party wrote to his fiancée that night, "I met Miss Brontë tonight and I would have to say she would have to be twice as good-looking as she actually is to be considered homely." Charlotte Brontë was ugly: don't be fooled by the somewhat attractive picture I've included; Victorian portraits were notoriously flattering. She was about four feet ten, tiny, with a reddish complexion. I do not emphasize her ugliness in any invidious sense; I tell you she is ugly as a great compliment to Charlotte Brontë. Because she was so unattractive, when she would later invent her immortal heroine, Jane Eyre, created in her own image, she did something for Jane that no other author had done for a heroine. We know Jane is unattractive before we even open the novel. Why? The name of the novel is *Jane Eyre*. This was revolutionary at that time—no one had ever named a heroine Jane before. The name Jane always implied "plain Jane." Consider the names of the heroines of earlier novels: Clarissa, Evelina, Pamela . . . Just from the name Jane, readers knew she was going to be unattractive. And in the novel itself we are not left in doubt as to what Jane looked like. Her lover, Mr. Rochester, at one point says, "Though the world considers you ugly, I see beneath that façade." This is hardly what a young lady wants to hear from her beau in courtship. Charlotte Brontë has given us the first realistic heroine in English literature. As one critic wrote, "*Jane Eyre* is the story of an ugly duckling who grows up to be an ugly duck." There is no swan in *Jane Eyre* nor was there meant to be. Charlotte was unattractive and sullen, and therefore temperamentally unsuited to be a governess. She had no success as one, and she returned home.

We turn now to the second daughter, Emily. Was Emily unattractive? No, she was very attractive. She was five feet seven, tall for a young woman back then; she held herself regally, had a fine figure and an attractive face. How did she, in turn, fare on the governess market? We will never know because Emily was so eccentric in personality she was never considered governess material. Emily's problem was mental, not physical. She was excessively shy and withdrawn. We learn from Charlotte that when Emily was a teenager, she would spend five or six hours in her bedroom simply standing at the window and gazing out. That would be strange enough. But while she gazed, the white window blind was closed; she wasn't looking at the view of the moors, she was spending hours looking at simply this white window blind. Charlotte noted that if you passed close enough to Emily, you would see her mouth moving and you could hear her talking. She was inventing future characters for her Gondal stories, projecting those characters onto that white screen as we project characters onto a motion picture screen today. She was watching her creations and making up their dialogue.

Now we come to Branwell. Branwell was good-looking and brilliant in school; he could paint and fence and draw, sing and play musical instruments. Anything Branwell did he seemed to do perfectly. Adults found him delightful to be with. His peers looked upon him as a natural hero. All the Brontës were convinced that if their name was to live beyond their age, it would be because of this paragon, Branwell. But Patrick Brontë was so worried that Branwell would not choose the perfect profession that he begged his son not to make any decisions as to his future life too quickly—a ruinous delay.

Anne, the youngest, was neither as bright as Charlotte nor as attractive as Emily, but because she was both good-looking and had a good mind, she made a superb governess. The first family to employ her had a four-year-old little girl who was so wretchedly behaved that they had had six governesses in thirteen months. But Anne Brontë had such wonderful gifts as a governess that within six months she had turned the little demon into an angel, eager to learn. The parents were so delighted with Anne they doubled her salary and expressed their regret that as a female she could not tutor their troublesome son. The parents said, "If only you knew of a young man who could do for our son what you did for our daughter, we would hire him." Anne, ever conscious of her family's needs, responded that she knew of the perfect candidate—Branwell, of course. The parents immediately sent for Branwell to join the family with Anne.

Unfortunately, Branwell must have misunderstood his mission, because the first thing he did upon joining the family was not to tutor the young boy but to conduct a passionate love affair with the mother. Branwell was twenty, the mother was forty-eight; her name was . . . Mrs. Robinson. I am convinced that the author of *The Graduate* threw in this name for the few of us who could appreciate this very inside joke. When the father of the family, the Reverend Mr. Robinson, found out exactly what Branwell's tutoring encompassed, he of course fired Branwell; unfortunately he fired Anne as well, for as he said, "You have brought this viper into the bosom of our family."

We come to 1846, a troublesome year for the Brontë family in Haworth. All three daughters were once again at home, unemployed. Yet Charlotte, who should have been terribly depressed by the situation, was not. Her enthusiasm and initiative prompted her to a new idea: she and her sisters should put their storytelling gifts to use by writing novels. Branwell had yet to decide upon his life's focus but did not want to participate in this idea. What Charlotte proposed in early 1847 was that during the day all three of them would write their separate novels. At night each of them would read aloud the passages they had written so the other two could critique them. In a short time, she felt, each sister would have a work of her own, and they would have three separate novels to send off to publishers.

Charlotte finished her first novel before Emily and Anne had made a good start on their own. That first novel, not much read today, is titled *The Professor.* Why, Charlotte thought, shouldn't she send it out to see if it could be published before the other two were finished? She indeed sent it out—it came back rejected. She sent it out again—rejected. She sent it out again, and again, and again. She quickly accumulated five rejection slips. And then she sent it out for a sixth try. Actually *The Professor* is not a poor novel. One possible reason it was rejected so quickly by so many publishers is that Charlotte, though brilliant, was very provincial; she knew nothing of the publishing world. Believe it or not, when she would get the rejected manuscript back, she was in such a hurry to send it out to the next publisher that she never took off the rejection slips. By the time she sent it to the sixth publisher, he had to wade through five rejection slips before he could even read it. Of course he too rejected it. But this became the turning point for Charlotte Brontë, because although the sixth publisher, a man named Smith, rejected it, he wrote a personal note to Charlotte, which said, "If you ever write another novel, please send it to us first." This is hardly high praise, but to Charlotte Brontë, this unattractive girl from the moors who had never been encouraged by anyone, it was enough to fire her creative energy.

At this point it became imperative for the Reverend Mr. Brontë to go to Manchester to have an operation on his cataracts, and he needed one of his children to go with him, to serve as a nurse while he recovered. Charlotte, as the eldest, was the obvious choice. Think, for a moment, about the horrors of that particular operation in 1847. Anesthesia had not yet been developed. After the surgery, Charlotte had no time, by day, for anything but nursing Mr. Brontë. But at night, when Mr. Brontë's pain was so severe he was given morphine to sedate him, Charlotte could turn from her father's hospital bed to the little windowsill of the small window in the hospital room. She propped her journal against it and began to write the first chapters of the immortal *Jane Eyre*.

Upon returning from the hospital, Charlotte was so

quick, so inspired, that she finished this second novel at about the same time Emily and Anne were finishing their first. It was decided to send *Jane Eyre* to Mr. Smith. And we know what happened next. The manuscript arrived at Mr. Smith's office on a Monday morning at about 8:30 A.M. He had no appointment until nine o'clock, so he decided to begin reading *Jane Eyre*. At ten minutes to nine he stepped into the antechamber of his office and told his secretary to cancel all his appointments for the day: "I am reading a manuscript that is so superb it will make our name as a publisher of great fiction." And he was absolutely correct. From the day he read that manuscript right down through today, *Jane Eyre* has always been successful. It was a best-seller for years in Charlotte Brontë's age, and even today, it is always at the top of the classic novels that are sold to schoolchildren and to the general public.

Smith informed Charlotte that his firm would publish her novel. In his letter he asked what name she intended to use—what man's name? Charlotte, in her naïveté, didn't understand; her name was Charlotte Brontë, that was what should be used. Smith responded that of course they couldn't use the name Charlotte Brontë. There had never been a respectable novel by a woman. Hundreds of women used male pseudonyms in the nineteenth century to get published. But not Charlotte Brontë. She let Mr. Smith know she was not going to become a man to publish this book, but she cleverly solved the dilemma—and maintained her integrity. "I won't change my name to a man's," she said. "Change my last name from Brontë to Bell, and make my first name Currer. I want to be Currer Bell." Bell was a common name in the Haworth area. The publisher wondered, why Currer? And Charlotte told him the obvious: "Because the name Currer is neither a man's name nor a woman's name." It could be either. And when Emily's novel was published, it was under the name Ellis Bell. Anne's novels were by Acton Bell. Charlotte's compromise suited them all.

Jane Eyre was as popular as the publisher hoped it would be. You would think there would have been rejoicing at Haworth, but there was not. At this point Branwell reenters the Brontë story. Branwell—who had the potential to do anything, be anything—had finally decided on the two passions he would devote his life to: alcohol and drugs. He literally drank and drugged himself to death, in Haworth, as his family looked helplessly on. Just weeks before *Jane Eyre* was published, Branwell wasted away, the victim of his dissipation. At Branwell's funeral—for reasons understood only by herself—Emily decided to honor the memory of her brother by going barefoot to the cemetery. There was a terrible storm that day; the temperature dropped thirty degrees. Emily, shortly after Branwell's funeral, contracted a violent cold. The cold became consumption—tuberculosis—and within four months Emily was dying.

Her *Wuthering Heights* was published while she was still alive. As glowing as the reviews were for Charlotte's *Jane Eyre*, that is how devastatingly negative the reviews were for Emily's novel. The critics hated it; they called it the work of an immoral and amoral writer. They loathed the Heathcliff/Cathy relationship, failing to grasp the spirituality of the pair's doomed love. All they could see were all the deaths, the wretchedness, and the sadistic tortures that Heathcliff enacted to possess Cathy. Emily, on her deathbed, insisted on reading every review. And Charlotte tells us Emily read with a smile on her face, as though she knew that someday her creation would be appreciated. Not until the twentieth century did the critical tide turn and *Wuthering Heights* become known as a great novel.

Within six months of Branwell's death Emily was dead. And then another blow: Anne fell prey to consumption as well, immediately after Emily's death. The doctor told Charlotte the only thing that could save Anne was sea air, so Charlotte traveled with Anne to the seaside resort of Scarborough. Anne sank quickly, in a rooming house full of summer holiday-makers; Charlotte watched her last sibling die. She buried Anne there at Scarborough and returned, alone and desolate, to Haworth. She had lost her brother and her two sisters within thirteen months of the publication of *Jane Eyre, Wuthering Heights,* and Anne's novel, *Agnes Grey.*

How dark and gloomy Haworth now seemed to Charlotte. And although Mr. Brontë and his last remaining child suffered deeply, this tragedy hardly brought them closer together. One evening after father and daughter had sat quietly in the parlor, when both were ready to go upstairs to their separate bedrooms, they met at the bottom of the stairs. Mr. Brontë looked at Charlotte, shook his head, and said, "And you were the runt of the litter and weren't supposed to survive childhood." How did Charlotte survive? She fought her sorrow by writing two more novels. Her novel *Shirley* is not particularly worthwhile, but the other, the rather autobiographical *Villette,* is excellent.

And then, out of nowhere, the unexpected happened: Charlotte, at age thirty-eight, received a proposal of marriage. Her suitor was Arthur Bell Nichols, the curate for Mr.

Brontë. Mr. Brontë, at this point in his life, was extremely antisocial, but if there was one man he absolutely could not tolerate, it was his curate. What did Charlotte think of Arthur Bell Nichols? We know because of her journal; not only did she not love him, she didn't even like him. She thought he was pretentious, stuffy, and dull. Her father, of course, would absolutely forbid any such marriage. Yet when Arthur Bell Nichols begged Charlotte to marry him, Charlotte, after some soul-searching, accepted. Although she had no love for him, to be married to this man would at least give her life perhaps the newness, the warmth, that she craved. But unless her father withdrew his objection, there was no way she could marry Arthur Bell Nichols. Charlotte spent over a year insisting to her father that he allow her to marry this man. Finally, Mr. Brontë gave in. He told her he would not attend the marriage: "If you want to ruin your life and marry Arthur Bell Nichols, I will no longer stand in the way."

So Charlotte married Mr. Nichols. They honeymooned in Ireland, and Charlotte's estimation of Mr. Nichols altered completely. Charlotte, to her great joy, discovered that not only was Mr. Nichols incredibly intelligent, not only did he have the same sense of humor as she, not only was he inter-ested in nature in the same way as she was, but also he treated her like a queen. Finally she had met someone who loved her for who she was. As Charlotte said, she could not have invented a hero for one of her novels who would be more perfect for the heroine than her "lovely Arthur" was for her.

Shortly after the honeymoon Charlotte became preg-nant. The two things she had wanted most in life, a husband to love, and a child, were granted her almost immediately. She found out she was pregnant in September; she learned she had consumption in December; she was dead in March. The child, seven months inside her, died as well. On the last day of her life, pathetically weakened, she opened her eyes on her deathbed and saw her beloved husband standing over her with a grieving expression. She smiled and whispered, "Do not worry, Arthur, God cannot possibly part us now because we are so happy." They were her last words. None of the Brontë offspring lived past the age of thirty-nine.

Today Emily Brontë's *Wuthering Heights* is regarded as perhaps the greatest novel in the English language; many British and American critics say it is better than *Jane Eyre*. But as far as I am concerned, it is Charlotte, not Emily, whom we should admire the most of these two sisters. It was Charlotte, a homely woman from the bleak moors, who by publishing *Jane Eyre* gave us the first best-selling novel written by a woman. Her personal story is as romantic and inspiring as anything she could ever have conceived of writing in her fiction.

Elizabeth Barret Browning (1806–1861)
&
Robert Browning (1812–1889)

When we come to the poet Robert Browning, it does seem a shame to speak only of him, given that his wife, Elizabeth Barrett (who of course became Elizabeth Barrett Browning), was in her day even more famous than her husband. So I will indeed speak about both of these fascinating literary figures.

They are quite famous, but unfortunately they are not really famous for what they wrote, in the same way that a Dickens, a Shakespeare, or a Poe is. Elizabeth Barrett Browning, although she wrote numerous poems, is primarily known for one particular love sonnet, which of course begins, "How do I love thee? Let me count the ways." As for Robert Browning, people do not read him much at all today. He is known for a few famous lines, snatches of ideas embedded in poems that remain unread, lines such as "Grow old along with me! The best is yet to be," or "Ah, but a man's reach should exceed his grasp, or what's a heaven for?" In other words, these poets are not known for a large body of work, as John Keats is known, or Wordsworth, Lord Byron, or Coleridge. Keats, Wordsworth, Byron, and Coleridge are better known for their works because they wrote as Romantic poets; they wrote during the age of Romanticism, when poetry was the genre that the greatest minds of the age used to express their feelings and emotions. They were poets during an age when poetry was king.

But the Brownings wrote after the Romantics; they wrote during the Victorian period, so they are considered Victorian poets. The difficulty with that classification is that during the age when they wrote, the 1800s in England, poetry did not have the central position that it did in the Romantic era. The novel, the Victorian novel, was the most important vehicle for expressing thought during the Brownings' age. And it is the novelists who wrote during the lifetimes of the Brownings—Charles Dickens, Emily and Charlotte Brontë, George Eliot, Thomas Hardy—who are considered the most important writers. In fact, there is only one other Victorian poet we know well today—Alfred, Lord Tennyson.

Browning and Tennyson became the two greatest names in poetry during the Victorian age, and they were extremely different. Tennyson was far better known than Browning. Because Tennyson was poet laureate, Queen Victoria expected him to write poems for political occasions. The most famous one he wrote was "The Charge of the Light Brigade," composed during the Crimean War. But he also wrote "Idylls of the King," the beautiful Arthurian legend that he clad in such gorgeous poetry, "Crossing the Bar," his final poem, and "In Memoriam," which became probably the most famous poem of the period.

Browning was far more intellectual than Tennyson, and much more difficult to understand. He was an acquired taste. Because he wrote poems about incidents and people that require knowledge of history, particularly art history, his poetry today is rather like a crossword puzzle—it is full of references that have disappeared in the twentieth century. Even at the time Browning was writing he was constantly accused of being terribly obscure. His wife, reading a poem that he had written years before, came to him one day and said, "My dear Robert, I do not understand what you are referring to in this line. Would you explain it to me?" Robert Browning read his own poem, looked at the line, looked at his wife, and said, "My dear, when I wrote that line, only God and Robert Browning knew what it meant. And now God only knows!"

What I want to do first is tell you about these two people's fascinating lives, looking at the time before they met, and then continuing with the incredible story of their engagement and marriage. Let us begin with Elizabeth Barrett.

She was born in 1806 and was six years older than her future husband, Robert Browning, which was unusual in the 1800s. The most important person in her life before she met Browning was her father, Edward Barrett Moulton. His middle name, Barrett, was his mother's maiden name. He inherited money from his mother's family, and to get that money he had to change his last name to his mother's maiden name. Unfortunately, he had already been named Edward Barrett Moulton, so he ended up with the unwieldy name of Edward Barrett Moulton-Barrett.

Edward Barrett Moulton-Barrett, whom we will now just call Edward Barrett, was a ruthlessly dominating personality, and this nature would lead to the conflict between himself and his daughter Elizabeth when she fell in love with Robert Browning. Edward found a submissive, weak woman to marry, Mary; coincidentally he was six years younger than she was. They married and had twelve children, four girls and eight boys. Elizabeth was the oldest, and the favorite of

Edward Barrett. His marriage lasted twenty-seven years, and then Mary died in 1832.

The other important child in the family was the eldest son, Edward, and he and Elizabeth were close. He always called her Ba, which was short for "baby"; she always called him Bro, for "brother." It was clear that Elizabeth was a prodigy. From the age of four she developed a fascination with ancient Greece; by six she was writing poems about the subject. Her father paid to have them published when she was only twelve years old.

The Barretts were a strange family, unconventional. Edward Barrett was an agnostic, rare in the Victorian age. This was something that one certainly did not teach to children, but he did. We have a prayer that he taught to his children: "O God, if there is a God, save my soul, if I have a soul." Hardly your typical pious Victorian family. Elizabeth's personality from a young age was impetuous. She wanted to do everything quickly—learning, reading, talking, writing. At fifteen, although she had been told never to saddle her own pony because the saddle was so heavy, she decided to do it by herself. She stumbled as she was putting the saddle on her pony, and the heavy saddle fell on her spine. This caused a spinal injury that would torment her the rest of her life and caused her to become a semi-invalid. She had to lie flat on her back for so long after the accident that it caused a lung affliction that would eventually kill her.

Now let us turn to her future husband, Robert Browning. Born in 1812, he also came from a rather eccentric family. His paternal grandfather was notoriously tightfisted. When Robert Browning's father finally got his first job as a clerk in the Bank of England, his father, Robert Browning's grandfather, presented to his son a bill of all the expenses the family had incurred from the time of his birth, and he expected Robert's father to pay him back. On the bill was even the fee the midwife had charged for delivering Robert's father. Because Robert's father suffered from such stinginess, he made sure that when his son was born—the only child in the family—he would be given everything and never be expected to pay back anything. Robert Browning's father was a delightful man, as was his Scottish mother, and Browning enjoyed a warm, secure childhood. As an only child he was doted on from the time he was born.

He certainly was an unusual child. He kept a diary from the time he was seven, and we have one of his first entries: "I married two wives this morning." Here was a young man with a vivid imagination! Browning loved to read books from his father's vast library, and he decided from an early age he wanted to be a poet.

When he was in his early twenties, his first poem, "Pauline," was published. The poem was greatly influenced by the poet Shelley, and if you know anything about Shelley, you know he was the most emotional of the Romantic poets. "Pauline" was reviewed by John Stuart Mill, who began his career in writing as a reviewer of poetry. Robert Browning was dismayed when he read Mill's review; it would change the direction of his poetry for the rest of his life. John Stuart Mill wrote: "This writer seems to me possessed with a more intense and morbid self-consciousness than I have ever known in any sane human being." Browning was humiliated, and he vowed he would never again so reveal his true feelings and emotions.

Robert Browning, reeling from the harsh review from John

Stuart Mill, decided he should not be a poet, he should be a playwright; a playwright could hide behind his characters and no one would ever know what his true emotions were. He did not have the talent to be a playwright, but he had to write one bad play after another before he discovered this failing. A humiliation worse than Mill's review awaited him when a brutal drama critic said of his first play: "I saw Mr. Browning's drama under the worst possible circumstances; the curtain was up." He was frustrated—he knew he should be a poet, but he did not know how to express himself in the best way through poetry.

This brings us to 1836. Elizabeth Barrett was thirty years old and unmarried. She had been publishing her poetry, which had garnered favorable reviews and a reading public interested in her. She moved to 50 Wimpole Street, which became one of English literature's most famous addresses because of her elopement with Browning.

In 1840, Elizabeth and her beloved brother Edward were at Torquay. Mr. Barrett was in London, and he wrote asking Edward to come back home to help him. Elizabeth was so enjoying the seaside stay that she begged her father to let her brother stay through the weekend and then come home, and Barrett relented. The very next day Edward went boating and was drowned. For the rest of her life Elizabeth blamed herself, for keeping Edward with her. Some critics say that this tragedy made her poetry better and informed her writing with a philosophical base it did not possess before.

Recovering from the tragedy of her brother's death as best she could, Elizabeth had become beloved by the public. They knew that she was a semi-invalid and could usually be found on her couch composing, so they called her the Caged Nightingale. Myths began to spring up around her, making her poetry even more delightful to the public. She was interviewed by numerous magazines anxious for details of her existence. Her great love was a cocker spaniel, Flush. A reporter came to Elizabeth Barrett's home one day, seeking information for an article about the beautiful semi-invalid poet, and he was of course invited to meet the dog. The reporter, in his article, observed that Elizabeth Barrett and her beloved Flush looked similar. But unfortunately, in the article the reporter not only said that the owner looked like the dog, but also specified in which way: "Both have prominent round eyes, a high rounded forehead, and long hanging silken ears." That certainly gives you an odd picture of Elizabeth Barrett's appearance.

Elizabeth Barrett read a poem written by Robert Browning called "Pippa Passes" that has the famous line in it "God's in his heaven—all's right with the world." She liked the poetry very much. The general public was still not interested in Browning, and he was finding it difficult to be published. But two years later, in a poem that Elizabeth Barrett published, she mentioned Robert Browning and compared him to William Wordsworth and Alfred, Lord Tennyson, praising him and saying what a fine poet he was. Browning read this and realized it gave him the opportunity he had been thinking about, which was to write Elizabeth Barrett and tell her how much her poetry meant to him. And so in 1844, when he was thirty-two, unmarried, and she was thirty-eight, unmarried and an invalid, he wrote to her.

On January 10, 1845, he sent Elizabeth Barrett a short letter that ended, "I love your verses with all my heart, dear Miss Barrett," and he was so bold as to ask if they could meet sometime. She only wrote back, "In spring we shall see," putting him off, but not telling him no. One of the reasons she put him off was that her father, Edward Barrett, had become an absolute tyrant. He never wanted to be separated from his beloved daughter and even went so far as to use her guilt in the death of her brother to keep her in her place. What their relationship was psychologically is hard to guess, but we do know that he vowed he would never let his daughter marry. Now there appeared a possibility that she might fall in love, because on Tuesday afternoon, May 20, 1845, from three to four-thirty, she invited Robert Browning to visit, which he did.

The visit went awry from the moment he walked in the door, because Flush the cocker spaniel ran up to Robert Browning and bit him. Browning patiently decided to ignore this welcome; his main reason for being there was to introduce himself to this woman whom he knew, at first sight, he wanted to marry. He certainly found out soon enough that Elizabeth Barrett's father welcomed him even less than Flush did.

Elizabeth returned Browning's interest, but she was not strong enough physically or psychologically to break away from her father. Robert Browning realized this, but he believed firmly that this was the woman he wanted to marry. Over the next year, he worked carefully to strengthen Elizabeth and get her strong enough to leave that household and elope with him. A regular marriage was out of the question because her father would not allow it, so the only hope was subterfuge. Browning also saw that Elizabeth had become an opium addict because the drug had been given to her in large quantities to ease the pain of her spinal injury. The first task he set for himself was to wean her from the opium. She slowly became strong enough to be carried up and down the stairs of her house when her father was absent. Finally she became strong enough to climb the stairs herself and venture outside.

Robert Browning sought the help of Elizabeth Barrett's maid, Lilly Wilson, in fostering the invalid's strength. In the meantime Elizabeth was certainly falling head over heels in love with the handsome poet, writing sonnets to him, though she did not let him read them. Finally, in September 1846 they realized they must act, because Mr. Barrett had decided the house needed to be painted, and all his children would accompany him down to the country while the house was being prepared. He left, and Robert and Elizabeth took this opportunity to escape.

Taking the maid with them, they eloped; after the marriage they sailed to Italy. They knew that once they had been married, so against Mr. Barrett's wishes, there was no hope that they could live together with him. Indeed, when Mr. Barrett discovered what his daughter had done, he wanted all traces of her obliterated from the house. Any poems he had of hers were destroyed, any pictures put away forever. When people said to him, "It seems you would rather have her dead than alive," he responded, "No, I would not want my daughter to be dead rather than alive, but I would want her dead if the choice were between being dead or alive and happy as she is now."

Robert and Elizabeth arrived safely in Italy. They decided to make Florence their home because of its beauty and because it was cheap. They had little money, for although Robert Browning was still writing poetry, the public still did not eagerly read it. It was his wife who was famous—behind his back many called Robert Browning "Mr. Elizabeth Barrett Browning."

Now that they were married, Elizabeth at last showed her husband the love sonnets she had been writing steadily to him from the time they had first met. And when he read these sonnets, he recognized that they were her finest poems. He insisted, over her objections, that they should be published, but neither wanted the public to know they were Elizabeth Barrett Browning's poetry. Robert's pet name for her was "his little Portuguese," so they decided to publish these love sonnets and call them *Sonnets from the Portuguese* so it would sound as if they had been translated from some obscure poet in Portugal. When they were published, however, most readers recognized that the poet must be Elizabeth Barrett Browning. Today the one sonnet that begins, "How do I love thee? Let me count the ways," is by far the most famous thing she ever wrote.

The couple was happily ensconced in their home, Casa Guidi, in Florence. They were thrilled to be with one another, and of course what they wanted more than anything else was a child, but because of Elizabeth's frail health they thought it was impossible for her to conceive. Finally, in 1849, two and a half years after they were married, a son was born. Because both of them were poets, what better name to give the child of two writers than Pen. They called him Penini, which in Italian means "little pen."

Once Pen was born, the Brownings decided that because there was now a grandchild for Edward Barrett, they would return to England, try to visit her father, and make amends. It was a big mistake. Not only did Edward Barrett refuse to meet them, but also when he heard they were in England, he, through a messenger, sent her every letter that she had written him. Even though there had been no communication from him, she had faithfully corresponded with her father from the time of the elopement. Not only were all her letters returned to her, but not one of them had been opened. She and Browning realized the rift would never be healed; she had forever lost her father because she had married the man she loved.

They devoted their energy and effort to their son. He was a beautiful and precocious boy, and Elizabeth Barrett Browning could not help herself, dressing him in velvet and lace and plumed hats. This would become a problem for Pen, because as he grew up he somehow felt that the world owed him a living, that the world owed him adoration. He eventually became a painter and sculptor, but he would always be second-rate. He could imitate things pretty well, but he had no original thoughts. Because he was so spoiled as a little boy, he never was able to grow up and realize he must face the world on its own terms.

Robert Browning continued to write, and although the public was still fairly unreceptive, he knew he was finding his strength. He published a volume of poetry, *Men and Women*, which is superb. In this volume he settled upon the kind of poetry he could write effectively. The form he specialized in and brought to genius was called the dramatic monologue. No one wrote dramatic monologues better than Robert Browning, so let me just say a word about this kind of poetry. You remember that once John Stuart Mill had told him that his feelings were too strong, that they needed to be suppressed, and Browning decided to hide himself. The best way to hide himself, he concluded, was behind other characters.

The form is called a dramatic monologue because, as the word *monologue* implies, one person alone is speaking. It is called *dramatic* because the poet chooses a crucial, character-revealing moment in this person's life. Usually the name of Browning's poem is the name of the character who is speaking, and the character is generally a figure from history, usually Renaissance art. "Andrea del Sarto" is one of the famous dramatic monologues; "Fra Lippo Lippi" is another. They are somewhat obscure in that you need to know about the historical personage, but what Browning does so well is that, as you hear the character speak, his poems seem as though you are eavesdropping on one side of a conversation. And as the character speaks, that character reveals in the poetry far more about his personality than he or she ever wanted to. Just by listening to a Browning character speak you are able to judge him as an immortal soul and as a human being, and pass judgments—usually against the character. It is a very intellectual form, and no one was able to pack more psychological realism and power into a poem than Robert Browning. My particular favorite is "My Last Duchess." The narrator is a subtly vicious man who is looking for a second wife. As he speaks, the horror of what he has done to his first wife is gradually revealed, though he does not really think he is giving that away.

In 1857, Elizabeth Barrett Browning published a long verse novel called "Aurora Leigh." It is a poem, but it almost reads like a novel. It was a tremendous success. An interesting thing about Elizabeth Barrett Browning's poetry is this: if you read that poem now—and most of her poems—they do not have the same effect they did during her lifetime. Today they seem dated; they really do not seem all that powerful. And what is even more interesting about Elizabeth Barrett Browning is that during her lifetime she hated the indifference the public showed to her husband's poetry, and she began to resent how much the public loved her own poetry. An astute critic, she realized that although she was a good poet, her husband was far better. She predicted that his poetry would live into the future in a way hers would not, and that turns out to have been absolutely correct. Today we consider Robert Browning one of the greatest English poets, while Elizabeth Barrett Browning is simply a very good poet.

Shortly after she wrote "Aurora Leigh," which was considered her masterpiece, all the years of lung problems and spinal problems came together, and by the late 1850s she was sinking fast. On June 29, 1861, at the age of fifty-five, she died. On that last evening Robert was at her side. She opened her eyes and he said to her, "Do you know me?" She responded, "My Robert, my heaven, my beloved, God bless you." She shut her eyes, then opened them one more time. Robert said, "How do you feel?" She gave a radiant smile and said, "Beautiful," and she died. The moment she breathed her last, Browning removed an Etruscan ring that he had given her, which she had always worn, from her finger. He put it on his watch chain, where it remained for the rest of his life. They had had fifteen happy years together as husband and wife in Italy. She was buried in the English cemetery in Florence, where you can find her grave today.

Pen, now eleven, was motherless. Robert Browning, now having to rear him alone, worried about his son's dependent nature and realized he needed to earn a greater income because this artistic son of his would likely never be able to function on his own. Fortunately for Browning, the public was finally beginning to appreciate his poetry, particularly in America. Suddenly numerous Browning societies, which you can still find today in America, sprang up all over the United States. Because Browning's poetry was so difficult and obscure, the purpose of the Browning societies was for people to sit, read some lines aloud, and then say, "What do you think he meant by this?" And people would look for references in their art histories and say, "Well, I think he is trying to say this about this historical figure."

Before Elizabeth died, the two of them had loved to walk about Florence; they would frequent outdoor bookstalls, because they could purchase marvelous books, just as you can today, cheaply. One day when Robert and Elizabeth were strolling through one of these outdoor book markets, his eye was attracted by an old book. It was bound in yellow vellum, cost today's equivalent of 40¢. He bought this book and discovered it was about a triple murder that had taken place in Rome in 1698. The book told of an evil count who murdered his estranged wife and foster parents, after accusing this poor woman of falling in love with a priest. Browning became fascinated by this tale of murder, and he turned it into his own masterpiece poem. He decided he would write nine different dramatic monologues, each told from the point of view of a different person involved in the tragedy: the woman who was murdered, the count who murdered her, the priest who was unjustly accused . . . these nine characters would tell their sides of the story. He called it *The Ring and the Book*. It took him four years to write it, from 1865 until 1869, and when *The Ring and the Book* came out in 1869, it was immediately recognized as the work of a genius.

Even Queen Victoria, who was passionate about Alfred, Lord Tennyson, and who had pretty much ignored Robert Browning, now recognized that she had a second genius poet writing in her reign. Her acceptance of Robert Browning finally established him in England. She claimed she kept *The Ring and the Book* at her nightstand, a shrine of sorts since her beloved husband Albert had made that piece of furniture.

There is the wonderful story (though, alas, probably apocryphal) that when Victoria died in 1901 and they removed the nightstand from Buckingham Palace, they discovered that Albert had been somewhat lacking as a furniture maker. One leg of the nightstand was obviously too short, for resting beneath it to balance the piece was *The Ring and the Book*!

Browning's son, Pen, was still unsettled and dependent, and his father began to think perhaps he should marry again, even though he was still completely devoted to Elizabeth. Perhaps he should marry someone wealthy, to make sure his son would be well protected. He did propose to one woman, Lady Ashburton. She was rich, a widow, and pretty. But when he proposed, he was rejected, and it is little wonder why. Robert Browning was painfully honest; he said to her in his proposal, "Though my heart is buried in Florence, I must think of my son and make sure he is well provided for." Hardly a romantic effort.

He was really quite grateful when she turned him down, because had they married, he would probably have felt terrible guilt. His one everlasting love, Elizabeth, was always in the forefront of his thoughts. In his journal he once quoted the great Italian poet Dante, who also had a love of his life, Beatrice, though she was someone he would never marry: "Thus I believe, thus I affirm, thus I am certain it is, that from this life I shall pass to another, better there where that lady lives of whom my soul is forever enamored." Clearly Browning's soul would be forever enamored by Elizabeth Barrett Browning, and he remained faithful to her memory for the rest of his life.

By now his best years as a poet were behind him. He had become so popular, so accustomed to being invited to wealthy homes and sharing meals and giving entertainment by talking about his poetry, that one critic said about his final years, "Browning dinnered himself away." Rather than working on his poetry, he was enjoying too much the life of just being a celebrity. His son, Pen, married a rich woman from New York when he was thirty-eight, and Browning realized that no matter how mediocre an artist Pen was, he would always be provided for. This relief from a father's burden freed Browning in one sense; he died not long after. You would of course expect that he would be buried next to his beloved Elizabeth in Florence. But he was not, because by the time of his death he was so renowned as a poet that the English wanted his body brought back on a barge from Italy to England to be buried where the greatest artists are buried, in Westminster Abby.

And so today Elizabeth Barrett Browning is pretty much known as the wife of Robert Browning, and the one who penned those immortal *Sonnets from the Portuguese*, where anybody can find a spiritual soul mate in those beautiful rhymes. Robert Browning's reputation, on the other hand, has continued to grow. Many people who like him as a poet see him as a philosopher and religious teacher, because in his poetry the doubts that troubled other Victorian authors, such as Tennyson and Dickens, are resolved due to his basic optimism. People who want to be uplifted by literature turn to Robert Browning in a way they cannot turn to someone like Charles Dickens, who presented so many gloomy predictions about what was going to happen to society. Browning is viewed as a relief, an escape from gloom to where you can still be inspired. I think Elizabeth Barrett Browning would be proud today to realize that what she predicted, that her husband's neglected reputation would rise, has come true.

Charles Dickens

(1812–1870)

I admit I sometimes feel guilty lecturing upon Charles Dickens, because of all the authors we study in school, he really doesn't need much more publicity. Other than William Shakespeare, his is the most recognized name in the history of our language. Yet Dickens does suffer from a problem in reputation that no other author seems to have.

The problem is not, of course, that we don't know about Charles Dickens; the problem is that we have the wrong idea about him. By this I mean that he is the only author who, for eleven months out of the year, we can ignore as we go about our business; then, come December 1, we cannot avoid Charles Dickens if our lives depend on it. Come December we are *Christmas Carol*ed ad infinitum (and some would say ad nauseam). If you have a little theater group in your town, in December—for the thirty-seventh time in a row—they will perform *A Christmas Carol*. You may pick up a newspaper in December and see advertisements featuring caricatures of Ebenezer Scrooge wearing everything from headphones to toenail polish. If you turn on the television, there will be seven different movie versions of *A Christmas Carol* to choose from. In December, all we can ever think about in literature is *A Christmas Carol*, and then come January, Dickens is gone again, not to reappear for another eleven months.

Now, I would be the last person to say that *A Christmas Carol* does not deserve the tremendous reputation it has today. Many people call it the greatest expression of the Christmas spirit in secular literature, and I would hardly disagree. Charles Dickens, however, would undoubtedly be frustrated at the thought that, more than a hundred years after his death, he is known only for that one small short story he tossed off in six weeks of a writing career that lasted for more than thirty years.

If you know much about Charles Dickens, you should be thinking, "But wait a minute. Isn't he the same author who wrote *Oliver Twist, Great Expectations, A Tale of Two Cities?*" Of course he is. It is rather impressive, more than a century after Dickens is gone, that he is known for such enduring works. And yet Dickens would still not be happy if he thought he were known in our day for only those four, because he wrote fifteen major works, and believe it or not, people in America and England knew all fifteen equally well. Every novel and story he wrote was devoured on both sides of the Atlantic. Yet today he is known for just the four I've mentioned. What has happened to his reputation?

Unfortunately, of Dickens's major works, all but four are eight hundred pages long or longer. The four works Dickens wrote that are less than eight hundred pages are *A Christmas Carol, A Tale of Two Cities, Oliver Twist,* and *Great Expectations.* Today, we do not read the best of Dickens or the worst of Dickens, we read the least of Dickens. We pick up a book of his, and if it's eight hundred pages, we toss it aside. We don't have time.

Even if you did read every book Dickens ever wrote, however, you still wouldn't have a clue to his greatness, because Charles Dickens's life is far more fascinating than any book he ever wrote, yet people know virtually nothing about his life. There *is* an exception to that ignorance. A large group of students at my university know all about Charles Dickens's life; they are in my freshmen composition course, in the fall. On the first day of class I announce to my students that I am a Charles Dickens expert and we will be studying Dickens in this section. My students don't even blink. They've all seen a late-night movie version of *A Christmas Carol* and figure, "What else is there to know about this particular author?" I wait about three weeks, then announce to my students that I want them to read a typical Dickens novel. Since the typical Dickens novel is over seven hundred pages long, we won't be doing *A Christmas Carol* or *Tale of Two Cities*. In fact, I always assign the same typical Dickens novel to my freshmen—*The Life and Adventures of Martin Chuzzlewit*, which is 942 pages long. Even my colleagues at my university say it is cruel and unusual punishment to assign a nine-hundred-page Dickens novel to freshmen. But I'm not stupid. I always make the assignment the day after the drop-and-add deadline, when students cannot wriggle out of a class unless they're willing to pay a hefty fee.

Why do I assign a novel like *Martin Chuzzlewit* to freshmen? In self-defense I maintain I do not do it to be cruel. If you have ever taught English at the junior-high, senior-high, or college level, you know why I choose *Martin Chuzzlewit*. I assign it because I worry—just as high school English teachers worry today—that the students won't read it—they will head, of course, straight to the Cliff's Notes. But there are no Cliff's Notes to *The Life and Adventures of Martin Chuzzlewit* because nobody's read it but me and I'm not talking. My students have no hope. They have to read every page of this novel.

I'm an old-fashioned English teacher. I give a quiz every Monday. Since there are no Cliff's Notes, unless students read the book, they won't be able to pass. I wait until they have finished the entire novel before I start lecturing on it and on Dickens, because I feel it will mean more to them after they have read the novel. So the day after they have finished *Martin Chuzzlewit*, I begin lecturing on Dickens. I always open my first lecture by stating, "Charles Dickens's life was far more interesting than any book he ever wrote," and my students look up at me with an expression that says, "God, I hope so," having slogged through the nine hundred pages.

But even if you like Dickens, you will be hard-pressed to ever think that his books are more influential than his life. What is the most interesting thing about Charles Dickens? It is probably this: Charles Dickens earned $68 million as a writer, and that $68 million makes him the top-grossing author of all time that we still study in school. No one—not Faulkner, not Hemingway, not Shakespeare—earned $68 million and is regarded as a classic author in school. How did Dickens earn that $68 million?

That will be told in a few more pages. But the first question is *why* would Dickens become obsessed with earning such a fortune? The answer rests with his father, John Dickens. Had John Dickens given his family financial security, then Dickens would not have spent his entire adult life trying to earn more and more money. But John Dickens was a failure; he was a feckless father.

If I asked you what the adjective *feckless* means, you would probably answer, "Having no feck whatsoever." That's true, but more specifically it means irresponsible, and it was John Dickens's fecklessness that would change his son forever when Charles was twelve.

Dickens grew up thinking that he came from one of the wealthier families in the city. He noticed that his parents gave lavish parties with lots of food, wonderful drink (particularly lemon punch), and all sorts of money expended on gifts. Dickens thought he was living the life of a rather upper-crust, upper-class little boy. But on that terrible day in 1824, there was a loud knock on the front door. Charles Dickens's father opened the door, and there stood the biggest, meanest, ugliest policeman Dickens had ever seen. The policeman said, "Are you John Dickens?" And Dickens's father said, "Yes, I'm John Dickens." And the policeman said, "Then I am arresting you here, on the spot, for debt. You must come with me to the debtors' prison immediately."

What did Dickens's father do? Even in that hour of absolute grief, Mr. Dickens was always conscious of whether he had an audience; and he passed this on to Charles wholesale. He turned around, saw his twelve-year-old son sitting on the floor, burst into tears, and said, "The sun has set on our house forever. We are ruined!" And he was led away by the policeman. Mr. Dickens was nothing if not theatrical, and off he went to debtors' prison.

However, not only did John Dickens leave, but soon the entire Dickens family was thrown into debtors' prison. Actually, it's unfair of me to say they were thrown into debtors' prison. You weren't *thrown* into debtors' prison; you moved into debtors' prison. Because debtors' prison in

Dickens's day really wasn't a prison at all. What it was would be in our day a low-income apartment complex. The only way you'd never confuse debtors' prison with a low-income apartment complex was that you'd notice an iron gate all around the complex, and you didn't have the key to get out.

That brings up the question, how did you get out of debtors' prison? You got out of debtors' prison when you paid off your debt. But there is that catch-22: they wouldn't let you out of debtors' prison to do anything until you paid off your debts. Instead the British Crown, in its great wisdom, gave you two options. Plan A was that if you dropped dead while you were in debtors' prison, all your debts were forgiven and you were free to go. But alas, you were dead, so this was not the popular option. The popular option was B. If you had children, you looked over your brood and you picked out the one child you thought could most efficiently earn a living. Because your children, although in debtors' prison because they slept with you, were not confined there. They were free to go to school or work.

And so when Dickens was only twelve, he had to go out on his own, drop out of school, and rent a room so he could get to work early the next morning to support the entire family and earn enough money to get them out of debtors' prison. Dickens learned early in life a lesson he shouldn't have learned at all. Dickens was convinced, even at age twelve, that if people are going to like you, you better have status, and the only way to have status is to have money.

For the rest of his life he would be haunted by the mere six months he worked at a shoe polish factory to earn the money his imprisoned father could not. In fact, he was so ashamed that he never told a soul about it his entire life. It wasn't until after Dickens's death, when his best friend, John Forster, published his biography on Dickens, based on his personal papers, that it became known. This humiliation of being among the working poor at age twelve would give him the creativity and drive to insure that by the time he was only twenty-three he would already be among the working rich.

The idea that would lead to his $68 million began to emerge when he was twenty-three. When Dickens was twenty-three, he was a nobody. He had a job that was so boring (a parliament reporter) that at night, he said, to keep his sanity he would simply wander the streets of London, and he would sketch. He didn't sketch with a pencil, however, he sketched with a pen. He wrote essays, sketches on people and places that caught his eye.

For example, let's say that he was walking down Piccadilly Circus and he saw a tree that had been blown over by the wind for so many decades that it looked like an old woman, all hunched over. Dickens would create a literary sketch about this tree that looked like an old woman. Who would pay an author to publish such a sketch? Nobody would. But if you were an unknown like Dickens—a twenty-three-year-old upstart—you would send the sketch to your favorite magazine; if the editor liked it, he would publish your sketch. The magazine didn't pay you anything; your reward was seeing your words in print.

Now, the one thing you never saw in print was your name, because if you were an unknown like Dickens, you couldn't use your own name on the sketch; you had to invent a pseudonym. Dickens thought up literature's most memorable disguise—he decided to call himself Boz.

Dickens borrowed the name Boz from his youngest brother, who was seventeen years younger than Dickens.

This brother was so adorable that his parents regretted the first name they had given him. They had named him Augustus, yet Augustus or Gus seemed inappropriate for such a cute child. They decided to nickname him Moses. Now, few of us would rank Moses in the top five of a list of cute names, but in Dickens's day, there had been a popular novel, *The Vicar of Wakefield* by Oliver Goldsmith, that had a minor character—a cute little boy—named Moses. Many literate parents thenceforth nicknamed their cute children Moses.

Everybody called Dickens's youngest brother Moses, except for Dickens's youngest brother, because he was just beginning to talk and he couldn't get out more than a syllable. So rather than calling himself Moses, he called himself Moz. But he had been born with a chronic sinus condition and his nose was perpetually stopped-up. He couldn't pronounce *M* to save his life. So *Moz* came out sounding like "Boz." Dickens took Boz from his adenoidal younger brother and put it on every sketch he sent out to magazines.

By the time Dickens was twenty-three, numerous publishers had accepted a total of thirty-six different sketches by him. Everything he sent out was published. Did this make Dickens happy? No, he was disgusted, because he wasn't being paid anything. He then came up with the practical idea of sweet-talking a publisher, John Macrone, into bringing out all thirty-six sketches in a book. So Dickens's first book was not *A Tale of Two Cities* nor *A Christmas Carol;* his first book is *Sketches by Boz*, because he was not "Dickens" yet. And was this the book that launched

Dickens's $68-million career? Hardly. I will let Dickens himself tell you how successful this book was; he wrote in a journal, "My first book, *Sketches by Boz*, fell stillborn from the press." *Sketches by Boz* sold poorly, yet its publication was the smartest thing Dickens ever did.

In his day—1836—if a publisher brought out a book that didn't sell, he could still make a decent profit on it. All the publisher had to do was send a complimentary copy to other booksellers, with an accompanying note that said, in effect, "This is one of our hottest best-sellers, but we respect your firm so much we want you to have a complimentary copy." Now, every bookseller in England knew what this meant: "We cannot sell this turkey. Please, take it off our hands," and every bookseller would willingly comply. If a publisher was burdened with a book that didn't sell and was willing to give it away to other booksellers so it could go on the shelf, he received from the British government a tax credit for each book. So although *Sketches by Boz* didn't sell to anyone, it was on every bookseller's shelf. Tit for tat—they knew they had to take in this turkey so when they had a turkey of their own, they could send it on and receive the tax credit. So *Sketches by Boz* was mailed out to other booksellers, who took a quick look at it and said, "Oh, no, not another book by some clever young hack kid." They would put these books on the very top shelf in the back of their bookstore where it wouldn't take up valuable space, and it would simply gather dust and die a quiet death.

But that is not what happened to *Sketches by Boz*. Unbeknownst to Dickens, six months after *Sketches by Boz* was published and fizzled, the finest illustrator of that era, Robert Seymour, walked into the publishing house of two

young, unknown, rather incompetent publishers named Mr.
Chapman and Mr. Hall. Chapman and Hall were about to go
bankrupt. They never claimed any good authors among their
literary stable, and they never published books that sold
respectably.

Seymour approached the penurious publishers with a
request that seemed heaven-sent. He had just finished a picture book and wanted Chapman and Hall to publish it. Of
course Chapman and Hall were ecstatic; any book with
Robert Seymour's name on the title page would be an
instant best-seller because of his reputation. It would save
their firm. But they couldn't understand why the great
Robert Seymour—who could have had Queen Victoria's
own publishers, had he wanted them—had come to these
two unknowns, Chapman and Hall.

What Chapman and Hall didn't know was that Robert
Seymour was an alcoholic, a drug user, and a compulsive
gambler. These vices had gotten him into such deep debt
that he needed 85 percent of the profits on his next book
just to break even. He knew too that no self-respecting publisher would give him 85 percent of any profits. Chapman
and Hall were known to be in dire circumstances, so he told
these two young men, "I'll let you publish my picture book,
but I need 85 percent of the profits. Is it a deal?" Chapman
and Hall had never had 15 percent of anything; they considered the offer generous and were ready to sign, but Mr.
Chapman did say, "By the way, Mr. Seymour, what is this picture book you've written about?"

Seymour described his work thus: "I've invented an athletic club, a sports club, but it only has four fat, old men in
the club and they're not athletes at all. They try to skate on

the ice—they're so fat they fall through. They try to shoot a bird—they're so incompetent they shoot someone's rear end off by mistake. I've drawn one hundred and fifty pictures of these fat and funny sportsmen, and that's my book. What do you think?" Well, Chapman and Hall thought it was the silliest thing they'd ever heard of, but they told Seymour in no uncertain terms that it was brilliant. They knew the name Robert Seymour on the title page would guarantee a bestseller. But it was Robert Seymour's next words that changed the history of British literature:

"Perhaps if we wrote humorous captions underneath my pictures, it wouldn't be just a picture book, it would be a joke book and we could charge double. Do you know of some clever young man we can hire for a little money to write amusing captions?" Chapman and Hall did not know of anyone—which is why they were going bankrupt. But, Mr. Hall tells us later, he was not about to tell Robert Seymour that they didn't know of some young, funny writer because they were afraid they would lose his business.

Mr. Hall decided on the spot, in desperation, that he would pray to God for a name to give Robert Seymour. As his eyes went up to heaven to pray, they passed the top shelf at the back of the store, and right at the front of that back shelf, in a red binding, was *Sketches by Boz*. Mr. Hall looked right at Robert Seymour and said, "Oh, yes, we are intimately connected with a delightful young man, a good friend of ours who would be perfect, but we just need a week to get back in touch." Which of course meant they needed a week to find out who in the world this "Boz" was. Seymour agreed to wait and left the shop.

As soon as he was gone, Chapman and Hall raced to the

bookshelf, took down *Sketches by Boz*, and frantically, fruit-lessly searched for a name they could contact. But of course Dickens couldn't put his name on the book; it only said "Boz." And so, as the joke goes, for the next week they ran all over England crying, "Who the dickens is Boz?" Finally Chapman and Hall decided that if they went to the publisher of *Sketches by Boz* and offered him a bit of money, perhaps he would share the author's name. Well, of course Macrone was only too happy, for very little money, to tell them the fateful red-bound book was by some writer named Charles Dickens.

Thus literary history was made on February 8, 1836, when Robert Seymour, Mr. Chapman, Mr. Hall, and Charles Dickens all met to sign the agreement for the joke book that Seymour would draw and Dickens would caption. Dickens insisted that they all meet at his home. He was insecure and wanted the meeting to take place where he felt most com-fortable. As soon as they had arrived, Dickens asked, "Now tell me, Mr. Seymour, what is your idea for the picture book?" and Seymour launched into his description of the antics of the sports club. Everybody assumed Dickens would rejoice, "Isn't that wonderful? Where do I sign?" They did not, however, know the twenty-three-year-old Charles Dickens, who wanted control in everything he ever did and wanted it even now. Dickens said instead, "May I have five minutes in my study to consider this proposition?" He walked into his closet (he didn't have a study in his apart-ment, but he didn't want them to know that). If we can believe Dickens, he took a candle into a closet area, wrote for five minutes, came out, and gave a list of five demands to Mr. Chapman and said, "If these five demands cannot be met, I do not wish to work on your project."

You would assume that Chapman, Hall, and Seymour would in unison have said, "Who do you think you are, Dickens, giving us these ultimata! Do you realize there are young men who would pay for the privilege of working for the great Robert Seymour?" But Mr. Chapman wisely read the list of demands and found one ultimatum so brilliantly conceived, they knew they would side with Dickens. What was this fateful ultimatum, this condition that would change British literature?

Dickens's idea was breathtaking in the simplicity of its innovation. Rather than publish Seymour's idea of four fat, old men as a joke book, release it as a novel, which Dickens would write and Seymour illustrate, and charge a hefty price for it. But—and this was the key—they would soften the blow to the reader's pocketbook by bringing out the novel once a month, three chapters at a time. Dickens said, "Ask readers to come to the bookstore in January and pay us one shilling. They give us a shilling and for that amount they will be given chapters one, two, and three of our novel. Then they will have to come back in February, put down another shilling, and get chapters four, five, and six. And they are going to have to come back again in March, put down another shilling, and get chapters seven, eight, and nine. I will make this novel so long, readers will be buying it for two years. We finally get all of their money, they finally get all of our book."

Mr. Hall was pessimistic that such a radical notion would work and explained the finances of publishing to Dickens. "It costs us a minimum of three shillings a copy to produce any book, even this new once-a-month, three-chapter-at-a-time idea you have. You just told me to sell your book for one shilling a copy. When I sell your book, I lose two shillings each time."

Dickens said, "No, I've done my homework and there is a way we can make a fat profit on one shilling." When I give this lecture to my students I pause here and point out that Dickens *always* did his homework—and he earned $68 million dollars. I don't know why I bother; it goes right over their heads. He walked over to his bookshelf and pulled off a book—any book would do—and said, "When someone buys a book, is it not true that whether the book has eight pages or eight hundred pages the reader is not paying for the pages?"

Mr. Chapman agreed. "Of course. Pages are made out of cheap paper pulp. They cost us almost nothing, so the price of the book is not determined by the pages."

Dickens said, "Isn't it also true that when someone buys a book, what he is actually buying is the front cover, the back cover, and the spine, because they are made out of wood? The wood is expensive and determines the price of the book." Chapman and Hall agreed.

And then Dickens said, "Why can't we invent a new kind of book for my once-a-month, three-chapter-at-a-time idea? This book will have the covers made out of the same thing as the pages—cheap paper pulp. We could call it paperback." Thus Dickens, at twenty-three, invented the mass-market paperback book, but this was not what made him rich. That is still to come.

The publishers said, "Let's pretend we invent this paperback book. We could then make a profit on one shilling, but we will still go bankrupt. Everyone will come the first month and buy the first three chapters. Some of them will come back the next month and buy the next three chapters. Maybe some of them will come back the third month. But no one is going to come back every month for two years." Chapman and Hall maintained the public would get bored with the long, strung-out process and would quit reading. The publishers, however, would be obligated to keep on publishing Dickens's chapters even though no one was buying them.

Dickens was already one step ahead of them. "I guarantee readers will be throwing money at us, more eagerly at the end than in the beginning, because in each monthly installment on the last page, in the last paragraph, something incredible will happen." He went on to describe what he meant. "At the end of chapter three I'll have my hero start walking up a very steep cliff, but a formidable root will be growing out of that cliff. My hero, absentminded and near-sighted, will trip over the root and fall off the cliff. But my hero has forgotten to cut his fingernails for five years. As he starts to fall off the cliff, with his last ounce of energy he will grasp a fingerhold. So, in the second-to-the-last sentence of chapter three, he will be hanging at the cliff by his nails alone. And in the *last* sentence of chapter three I'll have someone start walking up that same cliff, but the reader won't know if that person is the hero's friend, who will pick him up and save him, or if he is the villain, who will slash off the hero's fingers and send him crashing to his death in the ocean below." Dickens delivered his last flourish: "You know how they find out? The readers come back and put down their money in February and buy chapters four, five, and six."

With that flash of inspiration, Dickens invented the form that every one of his novels would take. He never published an entire novel first; he always published them once a month, three chapters at a time. He also thus invented *General Hospital, The Young and the Restless, The Bold and the Beautiful*—all of daytime TV but the talk shows. Charles Dickens was the first person to come up with the idea of suspense to link together a work of art. He did not call this principle "soap opera." He had a much better name for it, "procrastinated suspense," and that is exactly what it is and has remained for all these years.

Chapman, Hall, and Seymour himself thought Dickens's inspiration was an idea of genius. The next step was to give this novel approach to the novel a title. Dickens offered, "Why don't we call the sporting club the Pickwick Club? And we want to title the novel so people will know it is coming out for the first time in a new, cheap form of paperback publication. I want to call the novel *The Pickwick Papers*." And they did.

Was *Pickwick Papers* a success? I would say so—it was the best-selling novel of 1836. And thanks to Dickens's idea, it was also the best-selling novel of 1837 because it was still coming out in 1837. In 1900 a survey found that the best-selling novel of the entire nineteenth century was *Pickwick Papers*. And by now you probably think you know exactly why it sold so well: because Dickens had invented the paperback and the soap opera—but you would be wrong.

As clever as those two innovations were, *Pickwick Papers* sold so many copies not due to what happened before it came out, but to what happened after. You see, for the first time people had to go to the bookstore every month and buy three chapters at a time, over and over. Yet what had they to show for two years of buying *Pickwick Papers*? Nothing.

Dickens and the publishers made sure the paper the novel was printed on was of such poor quality it fell apart if you read it too hard. The readers did not care—they were only paying a shilling, they did not expect paper of quality. What bothered them was this: when they had finished *Pickwick Papers*, they were left with nothing but flimsy, cheap paperbacks.

There were no public libraries at this point; the first public libraries came in the 1890s. The only library was in your house in a room reserved for books. When you finished a novel that you loved as much as *Pickwick* (and people *had* loved it, thought it was the funniest thing they had ever read), you put your novel on your mahogany bookcase and displayed it proudly. But now readers had a new problem. All they had from *Pickwick* was this pile of paperback trash. They tried to put the paperback *Pickwick* up against their beautiful edition of *Pride and Prejudice* or their leather-bound *Ivanhoe* and it looked terrible. What were they to do?

Dickens, with his big heart, came to the rescue. In September of 1837, when the last three chapters of *Pickwick Papers* were published, everyone rushed to bookstores because they were eager to see how Dickens tied the novel all together in the end. But after they had bought the last three chapters of *Pickwick*, they noticed, on the other side of the bookstore, piled high to the ceiling, leather-bound, gilt-edged, silk-ribbon–markered editions of *The Pickwick Papers* in hardback. Here was a handsome keepsake, a presentable addition to their bookshelves. So everyone bought the expensive hardback edition of *Pickwick* when they bought the last three chapters of the paperback. Charles Dickens is the only author we know of who sold the same book to the same people twice. They had to buy it in parts because they wanted to know what happened next. Then they had to buy the hardback, because they wanted it to display. But we are not finished; if you ever wondered how Dickens could invent anyone as greedy as Ebenezer Scrooge, read on. . . .

Once the hardback edition came out, Dickens began to wonder, "Now that readers have bought the hardback of *Pickwick*, what will they do with the cheap, three-chapter parts they have been buying for two years?" He knew what they were going to do, they were going to throw them away. People did not throw them away, however, because a few days after the hardback of *Pickwick* came out, a salesman would knock on the door and ask, "Have you bought the beautiful leather-bound edition of Charles Dickens's *Pickwick?*" and you would say, "Well, yes, so I am not going to buy another from you." And the salesman would say, "Oh, no, I do not want to sell you another book. But what are you going to do with the cheap parts of *Pickwick* that came out originally?" "Oh," you would reply, "I'm going to throw those away. I don't need them, because I have the display copy." "Oh, no," remonstrated the salesman, "don't throw them away! May I buy back each installment of *Pickwick Papers?*" He would pay you almost nothing for them, but whatever he paid was profit, because you had been going to toss them.

Now why would Dickens's firm buy back the cheap three-chapter parts of *Pickwick Papers?* Profit. They bought back the chapter parts, ripped off the front and back covers of each installment, put them together in chronological order, and sewed them into a gorgeous leather spine with a thin twelve-karat gold band around the edge. This "new" version was sold as *The Collector's Edition of Charles Dickens's*

Pickwick Papers, and it was advertised, "Printed on the original paper, when this world-famous novel first appeared." You may think, "Well, surely no one was gullible enough to buy the collector's edition. For goodness' sakes, they had bought it in parts, they had bought it in the hardback, why would they need it?" You would be too hasty. The collector's edition was hideously expensive, but anyone who could afford to buy it, bought it.

You, the reader, bought the collector's edition, but you didn't take it home—you already had one there—you took it to your bank and put it in your safe-deposit box. Dickens was now a world-famous author, and you had the original printing of when *Pickwick Papers* first appeared. You had an original work of art. You left the collector's edition in your safe-deposit box for a few years and it steadily gained in value as an investment in original art. Anyone who could afford to buy the collector's edition always bought it.

You realize, of course, what this means. Charles Dickens is the only writer to sell the same book to the same people three times: once in parts, once in hardback, and once in the collector's edition. It was a moneymaking scheme like no other. Dickens was only twenty-four years old and he had written the best-selling novel of all time. People thought *Pickwick* was so funny, they approached Dickens in the street to beg, "Please, consider writing another novel. Will you?" And Dickens would say, "You know the first day of next month? Go to the bookstores, my next book will be there." Dickens also told them his next novel was titled *Oliver Twist*. People heard the name *Oliver Twist* and thought, "*Oliver Twist*? That's the silliest name I ever heard—this novel will be funnier than *Pickwick*."

Readers rushed to buy the first three chapters of *Oliver Twist*, and what did they find to laugh about in chapter one? They found a beautiful, well-bred woman, obviously pregnant yet with no wedding ring, crawling to a workhouse in a rainstorm. And what was the big joke at the end of chapter one? She died giving birth to this instant orphan, Oliver Twist. By chapter two poor Oliver is apprentice to a coffin maker; in chapter three little Oliver is so ill-fed at the workhouse that he has to utter what became the third-most-recognizable line in British fiction: "Please, sir. I want some more."

(In case you're wondering, "What is the second-most-recognizable line in British fiction?" it goes, "It was the best of times, it was the worst of times." Charles Dickens. And in case you are insatiably curious and want to know the most-recognized line in all of British fiction, it goes, "God bless us, everyone." Watch for it at Christmastime. Dickens has the top three lines most recognizable in all British fiction.)

Readers couldn't believe how abused poor Oliver was; they also could not wait to buy the next three chapters, to see how little Oliver is further maltreated. They finished the novel and they observed to Dickens, "You know, I have never cried so hard over any novel as I cried over *Oliver Twist*." And Dickens—not modest—pointed out, "Well, that is odd. In my first novel, I made you laugh harder than you have ever laughed. In my second novel, I have made you cry harder than you have ever cried. I have run the gamut of human emotions in two novels, both of which are world best-sellers. And I am only twenty-six."

But Dickens is not famous today for how he peddled his novels; few people even know the story I have just told you.

No, Dickens is known to students by the few short novels of his they read and by the few biographical facts doled out in school: by age eight, we might know all about his poverty-stricken childhood; by age sixteen we may know all about his angry social conscience due to the industrial revolution; and by age twenty we're trying to forget all of it as fast as we can.

What truly gives Charles Dickens his immortality is neither the life he lived nor the commercial genius that spurred enormous sales of his works. His immortality rests on the inimitable characters he created in his novels. And his method of creating those characters was unique. Do you realize that Dickens never gives us a believable character in a realistic setting, speaking as real people would in actual life? In one way, all of Dickens's characters are complete nonsense. Look at his most famous character—you know him as well as I do: Ebenezer Scrooge from *A Christmas Carol*. Is Scrooge realistic? Hardly. No one in real life is as stingy as Scrooge is at the beginning of *A Christmas Carol*. Furthermore, no one in real life is as Santa Claus-y as Scrooge at the end of *A Christmas Carol*, and no one in real life ever went from being that miserly to that benevolent so speedily, with the help of four ghosts in his bedroom overnight on Christmas Eve. That's not how this world has ever operated.

And if Scrooge is unrealistic, look at Dickens's second-most-famous character. You know him too—Tiny Tim, also from *A Christmas Carol*. Is Tiny Tim a good example of what a real five-year-old child is like? I'll let you decide. You may remember the famous scene in *A Christmas Carol* when Tiny Tim and his father, Bob Cratchit, come home from church on Christmas morning. Mrs. Cratchit meets them at the door and says, "Well, Father, how was our son, Tiny Tim, in church on Christmas?" And Bob Cratchit says, "Oh, Mother, he was good as gold, even better." "Really?" says Mrs. Cratchit. "What happened in church?" "Well," Bob Cratchit says, "you remember how late it was, Mother, when we finally got off to Christmas service?" "Oh, yes," Mrs. Cratchit says, "it was late." "Well," Bob Cratchit says, "by the time we got to church, we were so very, very late that everybody was already seated. So as we came down the aisle to get into our pew, everybody turned around to look at Tiny Tim because that wooden crutch of his made so much noise. So I looked at him too and I asked if the attention bothered him. And our son replied, 'Oh, no, Daddy, I love it. Everyone will look at me and see that I am a cripple and realize that they are not a cripple, so they will have a better Christmas. God bless us, everyone.'"

Most of us know real five-year-olds, and we know what they are really like. You walk in a room; they say, "What did you bring me?" If the answer is "Nothing," they do not care if you go out and vanish forever. Have you ever known a five-year-old who prayed to be crippled on Christmas so others could look at him and feel uplifted? And yet, and yet—there *is* something recognizable about Tiny Tim, Ebenezer Scrooge, Oliver Twist, David Copperfield, Uriah Heep, Miss Havisham, Lucy Minette, the Artful Dodger, Fagin, and every other unbelievable character in Dickens. As we read a Dickens novel, somehow his characters seem more real to us than people in our own lives. How does Dickens get away with creating characters as unbelievable as these, and yet we eagerly accept them?

He does not give you realistic characters. Tiny Tim is not realistic at all. Instead, Dickens makes sure that his characters, rather than being real people, are walking, talking, living, breathing personifications of a universal feeling. Scrooge represents stinginess in everything he does. We have all felt stingy; we can identify with a Scrooge. Tiny Tim is not simply a five-year-old child; he represents the victory of benevolence over handicap.

You might wonder, "Why would Dickens have an entire character representing overcoming a handicap? I am not handicapped, I cannot identify with Tiny Tim." But of course Dickens knew that that is not true at all; he knew that all of us are handicapped in some way. Most of us are not physically handicapped, but Dickens understood very well that all of us are to some degree mentally handicapped—by attitudes, by fears, by minds that run in unproductive ruts over and over. Dickens knew that because we are human beings, we are often at the mercy of our worst emotions and therefore feel very disabled. But of all the characters Dickens created, the best one I can use to illustrate Dickens's technique of emotional personification is not in his most famous work, *A Christmas Carol*. This character is from *Great Expectations*, and I am referring to that maddening, pathetic, unforgettable woman he named Miss Havisham.

For those of you who have not read *Great Expectations* this past week, let me give you just a little background on Miss Havisham. Miss Havisham was a wealthy young woman who was happily engaged to a young man. But on the morning of her wedding day, as she was dressing for the ceremony, at exactly twenty minutes to nine she received a devastating message from her fiancé, jilting her. Do you remember what Miss Havisham did? The moment she received news of her abandonment she stopped all the clocks in her house, at twenty minutes to nine, never to run again. She closed all the drapes to ensure daylight would never enter as long as she lived. She had already put on her wedding dress; for the rest of her life, she never removed that garment. She had had one wedding shoe on and was about to put on the other when she received the message—for the rest of her life, she hobbled about with one shoe on and one shoe off. The wedding cake had already been placed on the banquet table for the reception; she vowed no one would remove that cake, for the rest of her life. This was the only vow she could not keep, because when we come into the story fifty years later, the cake is being moved, crumb by crumb, by the spiders and mice that have nested in it all the decades. In other words, when Miss Havisham received the news of her jilting, she stopped the clock literally and metaphorically for the rest of her life.

Now, none of us is likely to meet a Miss Havisham in our life. Her behavior is not normal, it is not anything you would see in any human being, but that does not make it unrealistic. It is only unrealistic in that no one would ever *behave* thus, but it is exactly realistic to what happens to all of us emotionally, internally, mentally, in our feelings when we are devastated in some way. If Scrooge represents stinginess and Oliver Twist represents neglect and Tiny Tim represents overcoming a handicap, Miss Havisham represents a much more complex emotion, something that unfortunately happens to all of us, usually more than once in our lifetime. She is a living, breathing personification of rejection. All of us have been rejected. Do we then behave as Miss Havisham does? Do we stop all the clocks, draw all the drapes, and wear the same clothes? No—yet, what we do immediately after we are rejected is similar; what we do, of course, is withdraw. We do not literally stop the clocks, we metaphorically do. The hurt is sometimes so painful we cannot move on; we want to get underneath the covers and never come out again. We are so hurt and so humiliated that a person we love does not return that love that, although we do not behave in Miss Havisham's exaggerated way, we carry out in a small way what Dickens's characters do in a big way. And we feel it as hugely as his characters do.

But what makes Miss Havisham so brilliant is not just that she captures the immediate response we have to rejection; she also captures what inevitably happens to us after we have been rejected for a while. What do we do when we have been rejected? At first we do withdraw, we are depressed; we do not want to see anyone. But eventually we tell people we are close to about how awful this person has been to us, how terrible we feel, and our friends (if they are patient) sympathize. But eventually we get bored with the process, and our friends get bored too. Rejection eventually becomes boring because there is nothing you can do: you are not going to get the person back and how long can you talk about it?

Then, after a little while, we start thinking about this person we loved so much. We start thinking about the despicable thing this person did to us, and suddenly we are not depressed anymore. Suddenly a brand-new emotion sweeps over us, an emotion that is much more fun. Suddenly there is only one thing we want in life in order to die happy: we want revenge! We do not want to hurt the person as much as the person hurt us—there is no fun in that—we want to hurt the person *more!* We want that person to learn once and for all that he or she cannot get away with rejecting someone as lovable and wonderful as we are.

But as Dickens teaches us in *Great Expectations*, the great irony is that we can never avenge ourselves on someone who does not care about us. You cannot hurt someone who does not care. So you have to seek revenge, if you can, in an indirect way, a way that we call today, with our sociological and psychological jargon, passive-aggressive behavior. And this is where Dickens, in creating Miss Havisham, shows himself to be so brilliant. Just as we do, she becomes depressed at first, but eventually she begins to hate her ex-fiancé. She is wise enough to realize she can never avenge herself upon the young man himself because he does not care. What does she do? She goes out and buys a child, Estella, and raises her as her daughter. But perversely she raises Estella for one reason only. She makes sure the girl has no heart, never feels love for anyone. Miss Havisham realizes this little girl is going to be beautiful, and that when Estella becomes a lovely young woman, handsome young men will fall wildly in love with her, and she will break their hearts. In her own warped way Miss Havisham will have achieved her revenge on the one young man who broke her heart. She uses Estella as a vengeful tool to make sure young men are as miserable because of her daughter as she was miserable because of the young man. Of course it makes no realistic sense, but we believe every detail of Miss Havisham because we have felt as she felt.

Many critics today carp at Dickens for his extreme personifications. They say Dickens never explains what the character is thinking and why. Dickens was far too subtle for such explicitness. He took the *inside* of a character's mind, the psychology, and he put it on the *outside;* he made the setting and the symbols what we remember. That decaying wedding cake, that tattered dress, the mice, the spiders, the gloom, the stopped clocks—those symbols enlighten us far more effectively than hundreds of pages of psychological analysis. Symbolically Dickens put the psychological mood of Miss Havisham in all the bizarre things around her.

You may wonder why Dickens gave her the rather dull, upper-class name of Havisham. Why not symbolically name her? Ah, but he did. Miss Havisham wasted her life in revenge, using other people to exact retribution, and it was the most narcissistic thing she could have done. Dickens teaches us by her sad ending that this is not what you should do. She lived her life as a lie, a sham. He named her for what she was: "have a sham," Havisham.

Ultimately, the secret of Charles Dickens is that his characters will live forever because they never lived in the first place. They were not real when he invented them, they are not real today. They will not be real in the twenty-fourth century, but I would bet Dickens will be read in the twenty-fourth century because his characters represent unchanging human emotion and feeling. In this way, his characters are similar to Shakespeare's because they are timeless. Like Shakespeare, Dickens bursts through the age in which he lives. This Dickensian imagination, which we call grotesque, by its very nature of being so exaggerated represents a realism that we feel inside ourselves in a way that no "realistic novelist" could ever achieve. This is why Charles Dickens remains today as great a novelist as Shakespeare was a dramatist.

George Eliot

(1819–1880)

Her name, of course, is what people today remember George Eliot for, since almost no one reads her now. Because George Eliot was a woman and knew that in the Victorian period if you wanted to be published, you had better disguise yourself as a man, she changed her name in publication—certainly not in real life—from Mary Ann Evans.

I think one of the reasons she is not read much today is because so many of us had to read *Silas Marner* when we were in high school. Though *Great Expectations* and A *Tale of Two Cities* are probably not the best books to assign young children to have them appreciate Dickens, it is a given that *Silas Marner* is not the work to give to a teenager to spark appreciation of the Victorian novel. *Silas Marner* is a gem of a little story; I recommend that when you have exhausted the list of Victorian novels, you give *Silas Marner* another look. As an adult reader you will find it full of fascinating details that as a young person you could not possibly appreciate.

I want to begin our look at George Eliot by mentioning her birth year. It is not remarkable in itself, but it tells you something interesting about the Victorian novel in general. George Eliot was born in 1819. I emphasize that date because when you look at the greatest Victorian authors—Dickens, Thackeray, Trollope, Charlotte Brontë, Emily Brontë, and George Eliot—those six brilliant novelists were all born within eight years of one another. Thackeray was born in 1811, Dickens in 1812, Trollope in 1815, Charlotte Brontë in 1816, Emily Brontë in 1818, and George Eliot in 1819. It does seem that in the history of both poetry and fiction, when you look at the eminent writers of a particular age, their birth years are clumped together. Then there will be a period of ten to thirty years when no one writer who is ever remembered beyond his or her period is born, and then there will be another ten-year period when all the giants seem to come. It happened earlier in this century when Ernest Hemingway, William Faulkner, Eugene O'Neill, and F. Scott Fitzgerald were born within five years of one another—then nothing. We have been in a nothing period for a long, long time in twentieth-century American literature.

We have John Updike, who is rather good at short stories and reviews but certainly not a George Eliot or a Dickens. We have Saul Bellow, who wins all sorts of awards but clearly is neither broadly popular nor popular much with critics. So, like soil, there seem to be fallow and fertile years for genius.

The fact I wish to emphasize regarding George Eliot is that no other Victorian novelist had to overcome so many social and personal handicaps to be a writer. Her origins were overwhelmingly unlikely to produce a woman of independent intellectual, almost agnostic doctrines. She was born in the county of Warwickshire, the same county where Shakespeare was born. Her father was of the rural low middle class. He managed a squire's estate, and the squire was not of the upper class to begin with. In 1819 the caste system of rural England determined one's life; if you were born low middle class, you would probably die low middle class. If you were a woman born in this rural area, your place was in the home. You would make the small name you could make by either nursing people in the home or being mother or wife of the people in the home, and you would die appreciated but unknown.

Eliot came from a small but devoted family. She was devoted to her brother, who was three years older than she was. She had a conventional education in an extremely religious atmosphere, because when George Eliot was growing up in the 1820s, rural England was experiencing an evangelical revival.

I need to discuss evangelicalism, briefly, because its religious force would shape George Eliot, and she would, in some sense, fight against but never rid herself of this force. The evangelicals gained such prominence in England in the nineteenth century because in the eighteenth century the Anglican Church had become deist in not a passionately religious time. Everyone accepted God, but people did not think about Him in an everyday sense. He was the ultimate gentleman of a gentleman's club called the world. He had invented the world; he left it alone. The comparison that was often made was that God was a watchmaker. The world was the watch; He created it, He started it ticking, He went on to something else. And then revivalists like John Wesley began to preach, and evangelicalism was born. Evangelicalism was at its height when George Eliot was growing up in rural England. Above all, she felt the evangelicals were suspicious of anything fun: no drinking, no card playing, no levity, no dancing, and no humor. In the rural areas especially they were very, very Puritan. On the positive side, as George Eliot said, the evangelicals did good deeds, but they tended to do them with a vengeance. You could count on an evangelical to always help the little old lady across the road whether the little old lady wanted to go across or not.

Above all, evangelicals believed that a child must be dutiful. The definition of duty was respect for and obedience to your parents. The key word is *parents*. You cannot be a dutiful parent; you can only be a dutiful child, because you must revere someone older and more important than you are. George Eliot was the ultimate dutiful child because her mother died when she was very young and so she became housekeeper for her father. She sewed, she cooked, she milked the cows, and she looked after her father as a wife would have looked after him in all the ways that are domestic. But she was much more than dutiful—she was brilliant. She had a magnificent intelligence and there was no one to care. Her mind was enormous but that was of no importance to her daily duties. It did not make her a better sewer, cook, dairymaid, or "wife" to the father. So, what good was it?

The only thing she could do to advance her thinking was to read. She translated Italian, learning it by herself. She translated German, by herself. She taught herself piano. Amazingly, though, she was so dutifully evangelical that she gave up novels. She did not read novels after the first six months of trying them when she was twelve because she thought they were wicked and naughty. A woman who would become one of the great novelists in the English language denied herself the pleasure of even reading them as a child.

Fortunately her father finally moved from the tiny village she was born in to Coventry, and although Coventry is not London or Manchester, back then it was the major city of the rural Cotswolds area. Here she met intellectuals for the first time. Now, let's get straight what we mean by intellectuals, because, as you will find out, George Eliot is regarded as *the* intellectual among nineteenth-century novelists. An intellectual is a person who feels as much at home with ideas as with tangible things. That is why so few people are intellectuals. They discuss ideas as most of us discuss people. What we do as gossip, they do at an intellectual level, thinking about things that you cannot see or touch—beauty, justice, and truth. An intellectual finds these as real as most of us find things that are concrete. The intellectual lives in the abstract.

Eliot visited a friend in the neighborhood one afternoon and noticed an American stranger in the parlor by the name of Ralph Waldo Emerson. Here was a girl from Coventry actually listening at the feet of Ralph Waldo Emerson, one of the great transcendentalists. This exposure to brilliant thinkers fueled her imagination as well as her intellectual capacity, and so she was nourished in spite of everything.

This exposure to the stimulating heights of thinking caused her to question her religious beliefs; her intellectual capacity forced her to give up evangelical orthodoxy. She became a freethinker. She could not go back to evangelicalism, and she stopped going to church—more than that, she stopped believing in traditional Christianity. She started to contemplate whether the God of the Old and New Testaments ever existed, but because she could no longer be sure of orthodox religion, she hung on to the duty and morality that the Old Testament and the New Testament had taught her more strongly than had she been an unthinking, small-minded, evangelical Christian.

It became important to Eliot to teach others through fiction about morality and duty. These principles are what she wrote about in all of her works. God may have been dead to her, but what He was taking with Him when He left, she would grab back and make the cornerstone of her thinking for the rest of her life.

Her father became terribly ill, and Eliot felt guilty; she thought her freethinking might have caused it. She gave up friends and her reading to nurse her father through a long, slow, painful illness because she was, still, a dutiful daughter. When he died, she was thirty-two. She was extremely unattractive; it seemed she would never marry. She had no visible means of support, either from parents or from an occupation or from friends. What did she do? She did the unthinkable. She moved by herself to London and decided to become a professional writer. You may imagine the kind of courage it took for a solitary woman, brought up in a tiny rural town, to go on her own to London to earn her living. She had translated pieces from German and Italian into English, and people had told her how brilliant her style was. She thought she might be able to succeed, even alone. She would not be alone for long. She had strong mental powers, but like a typical woman of the Victorian period she depended upon a forceful male personality for confidence and incentive. She was brilliant enough to stand alone, but she lived in an age when if you were a brilliant woman, you had better latch onto a man who would give you confidence and status.

She was not the sort of woman that men would flock to, but she, starved of love for thirty-two years, would fall in love, not with handsome men, but with intellectual equals.

She first fell in love with Herbert Spencer, a brilliant

philosophical and sociological thinker of the nineteenth century. Because of her writing skill she had found work reviewing operas for magazines; Spencer, in turn, wrote intellectual essays on opera. Their work took them to opera, theater, and concerts together. He was not at all physically attracted to her and warned her in no uncertain terms, "Do not, under any circumstances, fall in love with me."

The letters they wrote to each other are painful to read, but you need to read at least one of them to understand the weakness as well as the strength of George Eliot. After he had been so cruel to her and said, "Don't you dare fall in love with me," he wrote her a letter and apologized for his lack of tact. She wrote one back saying that she would never have dreamt that any man could fall in love with her, so he certainly did not need to apologize for that, but she could not help herself in falling in love with him. In the letter, she declared her strong feelings for him and she asked for love. She said, "All I am looking for is companionship." She promised she would not attach herself in a way he would find unsightly, but she needed a commitment that he would not just abandon her. She said, "I do not ask you to sacrifice much. I would be very good and very cheerful and never annoy you. But I find it impossible to contemplate life under any other condition. Those who have known me best have always said that if I ever loved anybody thoroughly, my whole life must turn upon that feeling and unfortunately, I find that they said this truly. You curse the destiny which has made the feeling concentrate itself on you, but if you will only have patience with me, you shall not curse it long because you will find I can be satisfied with very, very little, if only I were delivered from the dread of losing it." Rather a sad thing to have to write the man you want to be your lover. Needless to say, their relationship did not continue long; Spencer immediately abandoned her.

Then she met the man who would be with her for the rest of his life, George Henry Lewes. Lewes was another abstract intellectual thinker. He was a big, burly, unattractive man whose wife had deserted him for another man because she wanted to have the other's children. Lewes was such a kindly soul that he did not divorce her; he allowed his wife to live with another man and have his children. You did this in the Victorian period if you loved your wife and really did not want to lose her. There was a term for it, *annexing*. You annexed your wife to have children with someone else, but you simply did not get a divorce.

When Lewes met George Eliot, they were attracted to each other, physically and intellectually, but since no divorce was possible, Eliot and Lewes left together to live in Germany. They could not live together thus, they felt, in England; in Germany, perhaps they could. George Eliot's brother, the one man she respected and craved the love and affection of more than anyone else in her life, vowed he would never speak to her or see her ever again while Lewes lived. They were now considered moral outcasts in England because this *is* the height of the Victorian period. They eventually decided that they might as well come back to England—they were ruined anyway, no one who was respectable would see them. Why continue to live in Germany, where she had to translate everything for her husband? Why not return to England and live in sin there? So they did.

At this point, when she was thirty-seven, for the first

time Eliot tried her hand at fiction. She had previously written nothing but nonfiction reviews and prose. In 1856 she
wrote her first short stories and brought them out in a book
called *Scenes of Clerical Life*. She knew that if it was by "Mary
Ann Evans," it would have no sales, so she changed her name
to George Eliot. She picked George to honor George Henry
Lewes, and she said she chose Eliot, which I have always
been rather fond of myself, because "it was a good, mouth-
filling, easily pronounced word."

Scenes of Clerical Life was a success; because she was such
a skilled writer and creator of fictional characters, people
found it wonderful. Everyone said that a new author had
come on the horizon who would challenge Dickens and
Thackeray. Dickens heard about this and decided he had
better read this man and give the book a review. Although
over twenty-five reviewers had reviewed *Scenes of Clerical
Life*, Charles Dickens was the only one who accused George
Eliot of being a woman. He was the only one bright enough,
through reading alone, to intuit Eliot's identity.

People did eventually know who she was, and they did
not care because they bought her works anyway. The wonderful thing about people realizing, "Well, maybe she is a
woman," is that, at this point in the Victorian period, most of
the short stories written by women were written by women
who had no idea what real life was about. They were women
from wealthy homes, writing saccharine, sentimental fiction.
People had thought that women should be allowed to write
because they assumed these women had no money and were
writing to earn a living. Well, George Eliot saw through it.
She realized these women were wealthy, because they obviously knew nothing about life; they were of the pampered

upper class. George Eliot was so annoyed by what these women were doing to fiction (though she still felt she should write as a man), she wrote an essay called "Silly Novels by Lady Novelists." There is a wonderful sentence when she is trying to tell the world that these are not poor women struggling to feed their families by writing these stories: "It is clear that these women write in elegant boudoirs with violet colored ink and a ruby pen. It is equally clear that they must be entirely indifferent to publisher's accounts,"— in other words, they do not care about money—"and they are inexperienced in every form of poverty except poverty of brains."

When she was forty, she tried her hand at a novel, *Adam Bede*. It not only was a success; it was a best-seller. The sales of *Adam Bede* trailed only those of the novels of Charles Dickens and William Thackeray. It was so good and sold so well because she was the only novelist of the nineteenth century who had forty years of preparation before her first novel. Her maturity was obvious in a novel that seems extremely moral, brilliant, and from the pen of someone who had lived. Do not forget: her first twenty years were spent in English rural life. She would write about this kind of life her entire career. She had become sophisticated enough to look back at the rural life in which she had been raised from a broad moral perspective. What she was most brilliant at—better than Dickens or Thackeray—was showing conflict in placid lives. Her analytical and philosophic thinking make her unique in the history of the Victorian novel.

She wrote *Adam Bede* in 1860 and followed it the same year with *The Mill on the Floss*. There is no better novel, in the first half, for showing a bright, not particularly attractive little girl being reared in a country atmosphere when looks are everything and brains are nothing for a woman. It is Eliot's *David Copperfield*, her life disguised. That was followed by the one work we all know, *Silas Marner*. Then came her historical novel *Romola*, then *Felix Holt* in 1866. Her masterpiece, *Middlemarch*, was written in 1872, and finally in 1876 came *Daniel Deronda*. They were not all best-sellers, but they were all revered for their intellectual approach to writing.

She was leading the kind of life she wanted until 1878, two years after her last novel, when George Lewes died. They had attained a kind of respectability by the time he died. Intellectuals would come to their table on Sunday. She was such a brilliant woman, and she was so well liked and respected, that even people who cared about respectability eventually warmed to them both.

One year later she did the unthinkable. She had a friend, twenty-one years younger than she, named Johnny Cross. She married him a year after George Henry Lewes had died. Not only did she give up Lewes's memory rather quickly after his death, especially for the Victorian period, but also she had all those years made a statement against marriage; she had lived with Lewes in disgrace. Yet here now was this younger man, and she falls in love with him and marries him. But we can perhaps figure out her motive. Now that she was legally married, her brother would finally speak to her. Six months later, going to a concert that she was to review, she caught a chill and died the next day. She was sixty-one.

There you have briefly the life of George Eliot, but that really does not inform you as to what makes her so different from everyone else who wrote during that era. I think if you had to define what formed George Eliot as a novelist, you may say this: she could be called the first modern novelist. She was the first highbrow novelist, the first intellectual. In other words, she always analyzed and generalized experience. Her mind was not inspired by what she felt or what she fancied; her mind was inspired by what she thought. She was an instinctive abstract thinker. The other great Victorian novelists wrote their novels because something in their personal experience compelled them: domestic life (Dickens and Thackeray); the oddities of London (Dickens); or the violence of their personal feelings (Charlotte and Emily Brontë). Those writers were inspired by what they felt. Their strong feelings kindled a spark of imagination, and then instinctively their feelings embodied themselves in characters, dialogues, and scenes. For example, after *Pickwick Papers* became such a best-seller, a critic asked Dickens, "How in the world did you come up with *Pickwick Papers*?" Dickens gave the simple answer "I thought of Mr. Pickwick." In other words, for Dickens, Mr. Pickwick came into his head pretty much as he would have come into a room in real life. Dickens thought about him, found him fascinating, and wanted to show him off to the rest of us—he found Pickwick delightful and wanted to share him.

Not George Eliot! She was interested in discovering why and how things happen. She did not invent a character, as Dickens did, then invent what was likely to happen to him given his personality. She thought of what happens to people in real life and then evolved a character who would demonstrate what happens when you go down the wrong path. You see the enormous difference? The first approach is pure inspiration. George Eliot's approach was to think about the tragedies and comedies of lives—how people end up in situations we can all identify with—then to invent a character to duplicate it.

Plot was not important to her; the morality and the moral of the story were. In George Eliot's novels—as opposed to those of Dickens, Thackeray, Charlotte and Emily Brontë, Thomas Hardy, Elizabeth Gaskell—you do not find strokes of fortune, coincidences, sudden inheritances, long-lost wills, children who had been switched at birth and thought they were Oliver Twist but were actually Lord So-and-So. She is the first novelist not to depend on those manipulated conventions. Dickens and the others borrowed these conventions from Victorian melodrama. On the stage there were always lost orphans and girls who thought they were Cinderella but turned out to be princesses. Authors felt they needed exciting action to keep people reading. George Eliot knew she did not need exciting action to keep people reading. All she had to do was tell them about something they already knew about—life—and put it in beautiful prose.

In the novel I love most, *The Mill on the Floss*, Maggie Tulliver, because she is so ugly and everyone makes fun of her hair, cuts it off. She then has to go downstairs and meet her aunts and uncles. Her brother—like George Eliot, she has an older brother—comes up and looks at her and ridicules her, warning her of the anger she will face when her parents discover what she has done. Of course she had never thought about that. She only knew that they did not really like her hair that much, so why not chop it all off? Then it dawns on her what will happen, the punishment she is going to face. And of course, she goes downstairs and is punished. George Eliot realizes that we will read this as adults and smile and think, "Isn't that sweet." But George Eliot the intellectual wants us to remember that when we were children and we did something risky or forbidden, we took the consequences, the punishment, deeply, deeply to heart:

> Very trivial, perhaps, this anguish seems to weather-worn adults who have had to think of Christmas bills, dead loves and broken friendships, but it was not less bitter to Maggie who had chopped off her hair. Perhaps it was even more bitter than what we are fond of calling antithetically the "real troubles of mature life." "Ah, my child, you will have real troubles to fret about by and by," is the consolation we have, almost all of us, had administered to us in our childhood and have repeated it to other children since we have grown up. We have, all of us, sobbed so piteously standing with tiny bare legs above our little socks when we lost sight of our mother or nurse in some strange place. But we can not longer recall the poignancy of that moment and weep over it as we do over the remembered sufferings of five or ten years ago. Every one of the keen moments in childhood has left its trace and lives in us still. Such traces have blended themselves irrevocably with the firmer texture of our youth and manhood. And so it comes that we can look on, at the troubles of our children, with a smiling disbelief in the reality of their pain. Is there anyone who can recover the experience of his childhood, not merely with a memory of what he did and what happened to him, of what he liked and dis-

liked when he was in trousers, but with an intimate penetration, a revived consciousness of what he felt then when it was so long from one summer to another, what he felt when his school fellows shut him out of their game because he would pitch the ball wrong, or on a rainy day in the holidays when he didn't know how to amuse himself and fell into idleness and then into mischief, from mischief into defiance and from defiance into sulkiness, or when his mother absolutely refused to let him have a tailored coat that semester although every other boy of his age had gone into tails already. Surely if we could recall that early bitterness and the dim guesses, the strangely perspectiveless conception of life as a child that gave that bitterness its intensity, we should never, ever again pooh-pooh the griefs of our children.

Eliot gives us an insight that we all tend to forget and that she expresses so beautifully in chapter 7 of *The Mill on the Floss*. Do not ever think childhood hurts are less than an adult's. Fortunately God has given us the capacity to forget how awful we actually felt. She knows so well how to create an image, as when she is trying to describe what miserable experiences we have in childhood: "Haven't all of us sobbed so piteously, standing with tiny bare legs above our little socks when we lost sight of our mother?" The image, not just of the little legs, which is good enough, but of the tiny socks above the shoes is gripping and poignant. We have all been there.

George Eliot knew how to revive memories, but do not think she was not as good a humorist and a satirist of people's pretensions as Thackeray or Dickens. For example, in *Scenes of Clerical Life* she creates a character named Miss Rebecca Linnett, who is not an evangelical; she is not even very religious. But when a handsome rector comes to town and she thinks perhaps she has a prayer of snagging him, he misinterprets her ardor for evangelical zeal and is constantly giving her books on saints' lives and brilliant pastors. She has absolutely no interest in them, but she is trapped; she has to read them and discuss them with him. Consider this insightful put-down of Miss Rebecca Linnett when George Eliot describes what she does when she is forced to accept the rector's books:

> Miss Linnett had become a reader, therefore, of religious books because of Mr. Tryon's interest, and as she was in the habit of confining her perusal to the purely worldly portions of the book, which bore a very small proportion to the whole, she could make very rapid progress through a rather large number of volumes. On taking up the biography of a celebrated preacher that he had forced upon her, she immediately turned to the end to see what disease he had died of, and if his legs swelled as her own occasionally did, she felt a stronger interest in ascertaining any earlier facts of the history of this dropsical saint. Particularly of interest was whether he had ever fallen off a stagecoach, whether he had married more than one wife, and in general, any adventure or repartee recorded of him previous to the time of his conversion. She then glanced over the letters and diaries, and wherever there was a predominance of the words Zion, River Jordan and the Book of Job, she

> turned quickly past these passages to the next page, but any passage in which she saw the promising nouns smallpox, pony, books and shoes, and in particular Yorkshire pudding, she read and re-read with great interest.

Truly that is a delightful, but kind, put-down of a woman who thinks she is in love with religion when she is actually in love, it turns out, with this man's legs.

Let me end by sharing one more passage from George Eliot's writing. It portrays a character taking a journey through England by coach, passing wealthy market towns with no industry. Any other novelist would have described the journey as a vivid outing, but George Eliot as an intellectual cannot help herself; she must describe the scene in terms of what people are thinking about:

> There were trim cheerful villages, too, with a neat or handsome parsonage and gray church set in the midst. There was the pleasant tinkle of the blacksmith's anvil, the patient cart horses waiting at his door, the basket maker peeling his willow wand in the sunshine, the wheelwright putting his last touch to a blue cart with red wheels, here and there a cottage with bright transparent windows showing pots full of blooming balsams or geraniums, and little gardens in front, all double daisies or dark wallflowers. At the well, clean and comely women carrying yoke buckets and toward the pre-school, small Britons dawdling on and handing their marbles in their pockets of unpatched corduroys adorned with brass buttons.

That portion sounds just like Dickens and could have been written by him, but the last paragraph could not have:

> The land around was rich in barley. Great corn stacks stood in the yards, for the rich burners had not found their way hither. The homesteads were those of rich farmers who paid not rent, or had the rare advantage of a lease and could afford to keep their corn 'til prices had risen. The coach would be sure to overtake some of these rich farmers on their way to their outlying fields or to the market town, sitting heavily, stately, on their well-groomed horses or weighing down one side of an olive green gig. They probably, these farmers, thought of the coach with contempt as an accommodation for people who have not their own gigs or who, wanting to travel to London and such distant places, belong to the trading and less solid part of the nation. The passenger on the box could see that this was the district of protu-berant optimists, sure that old England was the best of all possible countries, and that if there were any facts which had not fallen under their own observation, they were facts not worth thinking about. This was a district of clean little market towns, and by God, these farmers were proud of it.

That is pure George Eliot, because she cannot help getting inside the minds of the farmers who are incidental to the main characters. Just as an aside we get a brilliant thumbnail sketch of what these self-satisfied upper-middle-class farmers think of the outside world. Everything has to be analyzed, and it makes for profound and delightful reading.

Emily Dickinson

(1830–1886)

When we examine Emily Dickinson's unique contribution to American literature, the best way to begin is to realize what she was not. To illustrate my meaning, let me give you the names of the most famous American poets during her lifetime, which was in the middle of the nineteenth century, and let me mention one or two of their most famous works.

The authors and their works that were most popular during her lifetime: William Cullen Bryant, "Thanatopsis"; Ralph Waldo Emerson, "Concord Hymn"; Henry Wadsworth Longfellow, "The Courtship of Miles Standish"; John Greenleaf Whittier, "Snowbound"; Oliver Wendell Holmes, "Old Ironsides"; Walt Whitman, "Oh Captain! My Captain!" Now, consider the poetry of Emily Dickinson—you can understand immediately how different she was as a poet from what was demanded of poets during her lifetime. What were the crucial hallmarks of nineteenth-century poets? Above all the poets were male. Emily Dickinson was a female poet in an age dominated by men. Second, popular poems depended on a powerful title. Many poets of the day spent almost as much time thinking about the title for a poem as they did working on the poem itself, because this helped sales and helped readers grasp the poem's meaning. Emily Dickinson did not give titles to her poems; the first line is usually used as the title. Her poems are simply numbered from what we believe was the earliest poem to the latest poem, and we refer to them in numerical order. Third, readers in Emily Dickinson's time wanted long poems. The average length of published poetry written during her lifetime was 110 lines, almost epic in length. The average length of an Emily Dickinson poem? Fourteen lines. This may explain why she is so wildly popular today in America: any poet who specializes in poetry as short as fourteen lines is going to be embraced by our rapid-paced society. Fourth, in Emily Dickinson's era poets were regarded so highly that their poems were expected to be elevated in tone and almost biblical in cadence. Emily Dickinson's poems rely on simple, hymnlike rhythms. Finally, readers wanted their poets to be prophets and teachers, turning out what we call didactic poetry. Fortunately for us Emily Dickinson was not trying to teach us at all. Most of her poems express a beautiful feeling or experience:

> I'll tell you how the Sun rose—
> A Ribbon at a time—
> The Steeples swam in Amethyst—
> The news, like Squirrels, ran—

Her poems are gorgeous in their evocation of nature and its beauties. Teaching was not her aim. To truly show you how different her poetry was, let me offer a contrast. The two most recognized lines of poetry written by an American poet during her lifetime are the following:

By the shores of Gitche Gumee,
By the shining Big-Sea-Water

Longfellow's "Song of Hiawatha," of course. These lines certainly don't sound like anything Emily Dickinson would ever write. She undermined all the expectations of what poetry should have been. Her vision was unique.

There is a further difference. As opposed to the famous poets of her era, who were widely published and renowned, Emily Dickinson was unknown. Only seven of her poems were ever published during her lifetime; she was reviewed in print once. The reviewer simply said, "These poems are obviously the work of an oversensitive, coy, ill-disciplined, well-bred, hysterical spinster." Imagine how depressing it would be to be a poet with the genius of Emily Dickinson and to read this and only this about your poetry.

What sort of existence served as the environment for Emily Dickinson's poetic vision? Emily Dickinson lived one of the most unremarkable lives, in terms of important events, of any literary figure we know of. To us her life seems dull on the surface, but there were fathomless depths underneath.

She was the middle of three children; she had an older brother, Austin, and a younger sister, Lavinia. She was born in 1830 in the small but intellectually vigorous town of Amherst, Massachusetts, where she spent almost her entire life. The only time she ever left was to travel to Boston as an adult for a serious eye problem. Her lawyer father, Edward Dickinson, was one of Massachusetts's most distinguished men; for a time he was a member of the House of Representatives in Washington. We know little about her mother, but Emily Dickinson did make this reference in a letter to a friend: "My mother does not care for thought." We have only glimpses of a loving but rather shadowy and ineffectual maternal figure. We do have a sense that Emily Dickinson was close to both her parents, and although her father was an authoritarian Victorian paterfamilias so typical of the mid-1800s, when he died, she offered one of the most beautiful statements one could make about someone beloved who has passed away. At his death she wrote a friend, "I am glad that there is immortality, but I would have rather tested it myself before entrusting someone so precious as my father to it." Although quite a bit of biographical material is available on Dickinson, her poetry always speaks so brilliantly about the states of her immortal soul that familial influences seem beside the point.

Emily Dickinson had an excellent education for a woman of that era. She attended Amherst Academy for what we would consider her high school years, then continued her schooling at the recently formed Mount Holyoke Female Seminary. She did not stay even a full year and withdrew partly due to ill health and partly due to her father's desire to have her at home while Austin was away at law school. It is ironic: if you receive literature from Mount Holyoke today, you would swear that Emily Dickinson must have been born on campus, lived her entire life on campus, and is probably buried underneath the library. I have never seen a college that got more out of one alumna than Mount Holyoke does today with Emily Dickinson.

When Emily Dickinson was in her twenties and thirties, a religious zeal spread through New England, and everyone seemed to become caught up in the fervor—everyone except Emily Dickinson. She was by no means irreligious; she simply could not deny her doubts regarding the evangelical doctrine. She could not, would not, compromise her religious integrity by being swept along with numerous enthusiasts, whatever the pressure of teachers, family, and friends. By the time she was thirty she had ceased attending church: "Some keep the Sabbath by going to church—I keep it staying at home . . ."

Her sister, Lavinia, like Emily, never did marry, but her brother, Austin, did. He married the sisters' friend Susan Gilbert, and the couple moved next door to the Dickinson home. Emily became extremely close to her sister-in-law; Susan had a kindred love of poetry, and Emily frequently turned to her for her opinion and guidance. Susan was a prominent yet ultimately disappointing part of Emily's life, as we shall see. Susan was temperamental and high-handed, and her friendship with Emily would not survive, for several possible reasons. Certainly one strong cause was a scandal that enveloped the Dickinson family and titillated Amherst.

Some time after Susan and Austin Dickinson married, a young couple, David and Mabel Loomis, moved to town. Loomis had been hired as a teacher at Amherst Academy; Mabel was determined to make her mark as a sparkling socialite in Amherst. Both couples had much in common, and they became close friends, socializing frequently. But at some point Austin and Mabel became far more than friends—Austin Dickinson began a passionate, thirteen-year love affair with Mabel Loomis. Eventually the affair became common knowledge in Amherst; the lovers' relationship continued, and the marriages continued as well. You can imagine that when Susan found out that her husband was having an affair with Mabel Loomis, her already prickly nature found an outlet in bitterness toward Austin's accommodating sisters. The path between the two Dickinson households, worn so well by Emily and Susan, became overgrown with weeds.

After decades of intensive creativity and increasing reclusiveness, Emily Dickinson contracted Bright's disease (a kidney malfunction) during the last year of her life and died in 1886 at the age of fifty-five. Perhaps the most fascinating part of Emily Dickinson's life actually occurred immediately following her death. Once she had passed away, within a week of her death, her sister, Lavinia, went into Emily Dickinson's room and found a locked sewing box, where Lavinia knew her sister had kept the poems that she had written during her life. When the box was opened, Lavinia was shocked to discover over a thousand poems, tied neatly into little booklets or written on scraps of paper, on the backs of recipes, wherever paper could harvest the brilliant rhythms of her mind—1,775 poems!

Lavinia desperately wanted the poems published, in a complete edition if possible, but she did not have the wherewithal nor the talent to know how to edit these poems, all of which were in Emily's idiosyncratic handwriting, or how to go about getting them published. But she knew of someone who did—Austin's wife, Susan.

As Lavinia feared, Susan wanted no part in bringing Emily's poems to public attention. Lavinia, desperate to publish the poems, turned to Mabel Loomis. Mabel, because she loved poetry and had esteemed Emily highly, agreed. In 1890 a small volume of the poems was published. It became immediately popular as readers in increasing numbers discovered Emily Dickinson's unique voice.

Not until the 1950s were all her known poems published, due to the animosity that developed between Lavinia
and Mabel Loomis. Both became increasingly eccentric and
litigious as they aged, each of them determined that the
complete works of Emily would not be published by the
other. Not until the third generation was it finally understood that Emily Dickinson's works were far too important
to be suppressed because of a family bitterness that had
gone on for sixty years.

I think we should find it all the more remarkable that
Emily Dickinson was able to write almost eighteen hundred
poems when we realize she was deprived of three of the
most important stabilizing elements of a poet's life, elements
that allow most poets to feel they are worthy of writing
poetry. First, during Emily Dickinson's lifetime, the certitude
of an orthodox religious faith gave one's life a stability that
encouraged poetry of great conviction. Emily Dickinson,
however, never had a conventional religious faith to sustain
her. Secondly, most of the established male poets married;
they had spouses and children who supported them emotionally. Emily Dickinson never married; she never had a sustained love relationship. She had suitors, but her belief in her
own poetic gift was matched by a conviction that marriage
and children would distract her from the drive to create.
And third, most of the remarkable poets of the age—
Emerson, Longfellow, Whittier, Holmes, Whitman—gained a
wide audience, eager to read what they would write. But
look at Emily, essentially unpublished, unrecognized.

So what *did* she have? She had her uncompromising
sense of herself as a poet, a sense that led her to sequester
herself more and more. She never ventured from her father's

house or her beloved garden. She dressed all in white. She hid from curiosity seekers who came to the door: "The soul selects her own Society . . ." The result was her reputation, enduring to this day, as a depressed and highly eccentric New England spinster.

A niece of hers said to her one day, "You realize, Aunt Emily, that people do talk about you. They feel sorry for you, that you spend so much time in your room alone. It must be terrible to be so deprived." What Emily Dickinson answered is significant. She smiled at her niece, then pantomimed herself at her bedroom door. She pretended she held a key, and in pantomime she locked her bedroom door from the inside. "Just one turn of the wrist, Mattie, and then freedom." In other words, she did not lock herself in her room writing poems because she would have preferred mingling with people but was too shy and felt she had nothing to offer. On the contrary, she had made a deliberate, conscious decision to withdraw from life because she knew her genius lay in images and beautiful words. Life was too precious for her. She knew what her gift was, and she decided she would spend it the way she enjoyed most—by herself in her room, with a dictionary, creating some of the most brilliant and original poems ever written. She wrote the purest poems we have because she never wrote with the intention of publishing. She wrote with the intention of pleasing her most important audience, herself.

Because her poems are so short, Emily Dickinson is the only author whose individual works I can actually offer in their entirety. The first poem is quite often included in high school, and even junior high school, English literature anthologies. It concerns the most important invention of

Emily Dickinson's lifetime—the train. She lived from 1830 until 1886; in that time the "iron horse" brought radical changes to rural Massachusetts. In fact, Emily's father had fought energetically to have the train come through Amherst. Emily was fascinated by the monstrous power of this new industrial marvel. In this, one of her most accessible poems, she played upon the image of the train as a horse:

> I like to see it lap the miles,
> And lick the valleys up,
> And stop to feed itself at tanks;
> And then, prodigious, step
>
> Around a pile of mountains,
> And, supercilious, peer
> In shanties by the sides of roads;
> And then a quarry pare
>
> To fit its ribs, and crawl between,
> Complaining all the while
> In horrid, hooting stanza;
> Then chase itself down hill
>
> And neigh like Boanerges;
> Then, punctual as a star,
> Stop—docile and omnipotent—
> At its own stable door.

A superficial reading of this poem might give the impression that, well, here's Emily Dickinson, delighting in how novel, how "animal," the train is. But this is not what she intended at all. First of all, this poem is not a positive view of a train. How do we know she wasn't favorably impressed with the train? In this poem, what does this train actually do? How many passengers were on the train? None. How much cargo was it carrying? Cargo isn't mentioned at all. Where is the train going? It starts in one place, it makes a vast circle, and it ends up right where it began. It is a train that has no purpose. Does it actually do anything? Yes; it blows its own horn and makes a great deal of noise, even though it is perfectly worthless and useless.

Emily Dickinson sent this poem to a friend in a letter. The friend wrote back saying she had really enjoyed the poem about this silly train that doesn't really do anything but makes a lot of noise and brings attention to itself. Emily's caustic reply: "I'm so glad that you reminded me that this is a poem about a train, because given that it doesn't do anything, it just makes a lot of noise about who it is, I always tend to forget if I wrote this about a train or a man."

So we have this clever poem, satirizing the train. Why would she be against trains? The train represented material progress. Its invention showed great ingenuity, but Emily as a poet was not interested in material reality. Material advancement had nothing to do with spiritual reality or aesthetic reality, and so to her the train wasn't worth much. But what is the most intriguing element of this poem is this: when the train was first invented, what so amazed people was that just one car did the work—the engine. No matter how long the train was, all the other cars did absolutely nothing, but because they were coupled to the engine, when it moved, it pulled the others along. Emily Dickinson decided to see if she could write a poem whose structure was the same as a

EMILY DICKINSON

train's: the first "car" would do the work, and all the others
would be coupled to it. But poems aren't made of cars, they
are made out of clauses and phrases and sentences and
words, so she cleverly has one main clause at the beginning
of the poem: "I like to see it lap the miles." That's the
"engine," and the rest of the poem just tags along. Just as a
train is linked together by huge iron couplers that have all
the cars linked one to one, her poem uses the most common
coupler in our language—*and*. Her poem is one main clause,
"I like to see it lap the miles," and everything else is pulled
along behind.

The next poem needs a little explanation. Although it is
not about cooking at all, I want you to keep in mind that
Emily Dickinson loved to bake. What she disliked was the
cookbooks she had to use. In the mid-1800s most cookbooks
were written by men; what bothered her about these cookbooks was how stupid men must have thought women were.
Just as in today's cookbooks, at the beginning of the recipe
was a list of ingredients: a half a cup of flour, a quarter teaspoon of salt, a teaspoon of vanilla, two teaspoons of sugar,
etc. But then the directions for the recipe would read something like this: "Take the half a cup of flour and add the two
teaspoons of sugar. When you've added the half a cup of
flour and the two teaspoons of sugar, then put in the teaspoon of vanilla. Once the half a cup of flour and the teaspoon of vanilla and the quarter teaspoon of salt are added,
then whip in three eggs . . ." In other words, men thought
women were so mentally weak that when they wrote recipe
books for them, they wouldn't trust that the women would
go back to where the recipe ingredients were listed in the
proper amounts; they kept repeating the amounts ad nau-

seam. Emily Dickinson kept this repetition in mind in one of her more famous poems about the imagination:

> To make a prairie it takes a clover and one bee,—
> One clover, and a bee,
> And revery.
> The revery alone will do
> If bees are few.

In other words, if you wish to build a prairie there are two ways of doing it. Either you get a clover and a bee and you sit down for a hundred years, and after a while all the clovers and the bees get together and eventually you have a prairie. But if you want a shortcut to a prairie, you do what Emily Dickinson did. You go up to your bedroom, you lock the door, and you envision a prairie that never was, and through revery—through imagination—you create a prairie. So we have a concise poem about imagination; it's a recipe, really, to make a prairie.

The next poem we will explore is one of her most famous:

> Success is counted sweetest
> By those who ne'er succeed.
> To comprehend the nectar
> Requires sorest need.
>
> Not one of all the purple host
> Who took the flag today
> Can tell the definition,
> So clear, of victory.

EMILY DICKINSON

As he, defeated, dying,
On whose forbidden ear
The distant strains of triumph
Break, agonized and clear.

Initially it seems Emily Dickinson is saying, "If you want to understand success, there are two ways. Either you understand it because you have become successful, or you are not successful at all. And because you lack success you sense instinctively what you lack, and so you understand success because you never achieved it. Then she brings in the soldier. The soldier who truly understands success—victory—is the one who is dying, who has been defeated; he hears the victor's trumpet and he recognizes that success is beyond his grasp.

But I don't think that is what she is saying; I think she is making a much more remarkable point. She is stating that the *only* way to know the definition of anything is not to have it. The only way to really understand, to appreciate, something is to be utterly deprived of it, and in your deprivation and your longing for it, you will understand it. When you achieve success, you then tend to take it for granted. Only when you don't achieve it and you long for it do you know what it is. Of course Emily Dickinson lived her entire life this way. This is one reason she locked the door to the bedroom, so she wouldn't be tempted to experience the messy business of "life" firsthand because then it can't be imagined any longer.

When I speak on Emily Dickinson in high schools, I give this example to illustrate her point: Suppose it's time for the senior prom, and in a class you have a young man who is the

179

ELLIOT ENGEL

high school hero. He's on the football team, he's handsome, he's a brilliant student—everything he does is perfect. He is attractive in all ways. When it's time for him to go to the prom, he has a choice between two girls as his prom date. He may select either the perky, adorable, popular cheerleader, or he may choose the unfortunate girl who always sits in the back of the class, the one who is extremely unattractive, who has never been asked out. Whom *does* he take to the prom? If this is a realistic situation, we may assume he takes the perky cheerleader. The question I pose is this: Who knows what it is like to go to the prom with the high school hero—the perky cheerleader, or the poor girl who is not asked out at all? If you are Emily Dickinson, your answer is, the only female who understands what it is like to go to the prom with the hero of the high school is the unattractive girl, home on that night crying her eyes out because she didn't go.

Then why doesn't the perky cheerleader understand what it is like to go to the prom with the high school hero? She actually goes, so of course she should know, correct? *No!* She hasn't a clue, because when she indeed goes out with the high school hero, what does she discover? He has bad breath, worse morals, and cares about nothing but himself. . . . Unfortunately she went to the prom with the hero and discovered there is nothing heroic at all about him. But that poor unattractive girl crying in her bedroom is thinking about what it must be like to be that cheerleader and go out with this absolute paragon, a young man who is perfect in every way. And because she can imagine what such a date would be like, because she doesn't have to go out with him and discover that he is a pig, she knows exactly what it is like to go out with the campus hero. In her imagination he—and the prom—will always be perfect. Emily Dickinson teaches us that if you really want to understand something, nothing is purer or "truer" than our imaginations.

The last poem, perhaps her most beautiful expression of this same theory, is this one:

> I never saw a moor,
> I never saw the sea;
> Yet know I how the heather looks
> And what a billow be.
>
> I never spoke with God
> Nor visited in heaven;
> Yet certain am I of the spot
> As if the checks were given.

Some of you, if you know this poem, may say, "Wait a minute, that's not how it was written in my book." And you're correct; usually it is written:

> I never saw a moor,
> I never saw the sea;
> Yet know I how the heather looks
> And what a *wave* must be.

Emily Dickinson never wrote "what a wave must be," she wrote, "what a *billow* be." *Billow* is the perfect word because its sound—so round, so forceful—sounds likes a wave. It is a very poetic word. Why then do many books print "what a wave must be"? Mabel Loomis, who edited Emily's first edition of poetry, thought that Emily was a good poet but that she had some good ideas too. When she saw *billow*, she thought, "Well, no, she doesn't mean *billow*, she means *wave*," so she changed it. Fortunately we have Emily's manuscript to prove what she wrote.

The last point I wish to make about Emily Dickinson is not just how prolific her genius was, but how brilliant she could be in so few words. Her poems are not only exquisite, they are brief. One other literary work, written at just about the midpoint of Emily Dickinson's life, has that same virtue of being short and memorable. In 1863 Abraham Lincoln wrote the Gettysburg Address. If any work of prose has the power of Emily Dickinson's poetry, it is the Gettysburg Address; it too uses a minimum of words to magnificent, memorable effect.

> A word is dead
> When it is said
> Some say—
> I say—
> It just begins
> To live
> That day

Oscar Wilde

(1854–1900)

When I give lectures on other authors—Dickens, Shakespeare, Mark Twain—and I talk about the lives and careers of these men, I worry sometimes that people are learning about the authors, but they are not reading the authors' works. Thus they are not understanding the genius of the authors. I do not have that worry with Oscar Wilde, and that is because as Oscar Wilde himself put it, "I put my genius into my life, only my talent into my writing." Even Wilde believed that his greatest genius was the life he lived, so when you discuss the life of Oscar Wilde, you are really getting to the core of his greatness about as quickly as any other method would do. And certainly, years and years now after Wilde died in 1900 we really think of him not for any one particular work. His play *The Importance of Being Earnest* comes to mind as the one famous work we still know him for today, but it was his life—the tragedy of it in particular—that we recall.

In looking at Oscar Wilde you must begin with his parents, because if we consider him an eccentric genius, once you hear about Oscar Wilde's parents, you understand that he came by his eccentricities legitimately. Let me begin with his mother. He certainly got his writing talent from her; she was well known as an Irish poet during her lifetime. She was six feet tall and loved to wear outlandish costumes, always with a headdress festooned with jewelry and feathers that made her appear all the taller. She was born with the name Frances, but she insisted that everyone call her Francesca Speranza. Francesca Speranza always wanted everyone to know that she was not only writing Irish verse in favor of Ireland against England, but she wanted her verse to be so contagious that the Irish people would catch her fervor and somehow make their country better because of it. She repeated so often that she wanted her poetry to be contagious that her enemies called her Francesca Speranza Influenza Wilde. In any case, she was an extraordinarily unforgettable woman.

Wilde's father was even more well known. Sir William Wilde was a doctor who specialized in both the eye and the ear. He was so famous as an eye and ear surgeon that even today when a doctor is doing a mastoid operation on the ear, the cut that is made is called the Wilde incision. Unfortunately, he was dragged into court during the middle of his career because a young woman he had operated on said that he had raped her while she was chloroformed. He lost this trial, so there was thereafter a scandal attached to his name.

When Oscar was born, his mother, of course, would not name her child merely Oscar. "His name," Francesca said, "must be Oscar Fingal O'Flahertie Wills Wilde." He had an older brother, Willie. As you can imagine, he too was inundated with four names—mercifully, everyone called him just Willie. Wilde was born on October 16, 1854, in the middle of the Victorian period, which he not only would come to hate, but which all his work would try to overthrow in terms of the morality that the Victorians were so proud of.

We do not know a great deal about Oscar as a child, but the first example of his writing tells us an enormous amount about what an unusual child he was. It is a letter he wrote to his mother from summer camp when he was only thirteen, a thank-you note:

> Darling Mama, The hamper came today and I never got such a jolly surprise. It was more than kind of you to send it, though the flannel shirts you sent are both Willie's, not mine. Mine, you may remember, are one quite scarlet and the other that divine lilac shade. By the way, have you written Aunt Warren on the lime green notepaper that we finally selected from the stationers? All my love, Oscar.

This is not the typical note you might get from a happy camper, age thirteen. This note tells us that Oscar developed strange and exotic tastes at a young age. He was an excellent student, as you would guess, and he went on to Trinity College in Dublin. Trinity was the college you went to if you wanted to rise intellectually in society. In fact, we can follow the fortunes of Oscar Wilde's reputation by going to Trinity College today and looking at a plaque near the administration office. When Wilde became famous for plays and for *The Picture of Dorian Gray*, Trinity was so proud to have him as an alumnus that they put his name in huge, gilt, brass letters on a plaque. But when he later went through the sordid trial that was such a scandal to the late Victorians, Trinity painted out with black paint those gilt letters. Just recently, because Wilde's reputation has now been restored so many years after his death, they have regilded the letters.

At Trinity, Wilde developed into an aesthete. We do not use that word that often today—let me define it for you. It simply means one having an acute sensitivity to the beautiful, especially in art. Wilde decided as an undergraduate that he would devote his life to the pursuit of beauty. We think he probably made this conscious decision because of a wonderful teacher, Reginald Mahaffey. Mahaffey was a professor of ancient history, particularly interested in the Greeks. Mahaffey gave Oscar Wilde not only his career but his hobbies as well, because Mahaffey spent as much time enjoying claret, cigars, old silver, and furniture as he did in researching the Greeks. He loved to be surrounded by beautiful things. He also was a wonderful talker, as Wilde would become, and like Wilde he tended to exaggerate everything. In fact, it is said Mahaffey once told his colleagues, "I was only caned once in my life and that was for telling the truth." Another colleague chimed in, "Well, it certainly cured you, Mahaffey."

So at Trinity Wilde developed the lifestyle of an aesthete and became a collector of all things beautiful. There he decided on the symbol he would always use to describe his aesthetic life: the lily. People asked him, "Why did you pick the lily?" and his answer should have been obvious: "Because it is the most beautiful and useless thing in the world."

When he finished at Trinity, he understood that Ireland was not the place for him, though he had been born in Dublin. Dublin was too small, too parochial, for an aesthete such as himself. At twenty he decided he needed to go to Oxford to explore the areas of his personality that he felt he could not develop in the claustrophobic and confining atmosphere of his native Ireland. He rid himself of his Irish accent and got himself admitted to Oxford. He did well in school whether he studied hard or not, but what he loved most to do, thanks to Mahaffey's training, and spent most of his days doing was furnishing his rooms. He would get one type of furniture and appropriate accessories. He would have these for a couple of months, then call his friends in, get advice, and completely redecorate his rooms in another style. Wilde said at this time what would widely be quoted as early evidence of his great wit. After he had refurbished his rooms for the fifth time, he noted, "I find it harder and harder every day to live up to my blue china." That bon mot sums up fairly well the values that Wilde became known for.

He was also experimenting outside his rooms, because he contracted syphilis from a woman prostitute. I mention this not because it affected his health at the time—it did not— but because the most recommended treatment for syphilis at that time was to take mercury internally. The (useless) mercury treatment turned the teeth black, and this was awful to Oscar Wilde. If you have ever seen a portrait of Oscar Wilde, I think you would admit that no matter how witty he was, he was not a particularly good-looking man; he was extremely upset about his black teeth. It is said that, for the rest of his life, when in close conversation with anyone he would always put his hand over his mouth as he spoke; he did not want people to have to look at his unsightly black teeth.

He did well at Oxford, but he had no idea what he would do for a career. It is one thing to say you are an aesthete; the problem is how to make a living out of appreciating things beautiful. He decided he would either have to become a poet or write literary criticism. The one thing he did know how to do was spend money and spend it lavishly. He took time to fall in love with a woman named Flo Balcombe. She did not marry him; she went on to marry another Irishman, Bram Stoker—who wrote *Dracula*. Wilde set up his living quarters in London, constantly refurbishing his rooms of course. At this point he met a seductive beauty who had also come to London to make a name for herself, the actress Lillie Langtry. He was immediately attracted to her. Anytime he saw her out walking, he would take innumerable lilies and thrust them at her feet because he wanted to surround her with the very beauty that he felt she was surrounded by always, because of her looks.

He tried to write a few plays, but in his mid-twenties he was known throughout the city primarily as a wit. His greatest art was the clever retorts he would make at parties. He loved nothing better than to have a witty answer to what someone else said. At a party on one rare occasion, someone made a comment and another person came back with such a witty retort that Wilde, for one of the few times in his life, was jealous. He turned to one of his friends and said, "Oh, how I wish I had said that." His friend said, "You will, Oscar, you will."

His "career" was floundering when he was rescued by, of all people, Gilbert and Sullivan. We know of Gilbert and Sullivan because of the magnificent light operas they wrote at the end of the nineteenth century. They had written an opera called *Patience*, a satire of the aesthetic movement, and since Oscar Wilde was one of the great figures of this movement, they created a character in the opera by the name of Reginald Bunthorne. Bunthorne carries lilies; he makes clever retorts—when this character came onstage, everyone knew immediately whom he was supposed to be. *Patience* was wildly successful, and the producer, while in America with a new production of *Patience*, came up with the idea of asking Oscar Wilde if he would like to come to America on a lecture tour, because now he was famous. Even though Wilde had never been to America, had never written anything that was read in America, Americans were suddenly fascinated by this man who *was* Reginald Bunthorne. The producer asked Wilde if he would lecture throughout America on the topic "The Beautiful."

It was not in Wilde's wildest dream to go to America and give lectures, but he decided such a venture might establish him more quickly than anything else, and so off he went. He did prepare his lectures carefully, but he knew what the public wanted. What he had to say would be of some interest to the public, but what the Americans really wanted was to see, in the flesh, one of these "aesthetes." They would wonder, what will he look like, what will he wear? Wilde tells us he spent four times as much time planning his wardrobe for the performances he would give as a lecturer than he did on the lectures themselves, and that was probably the right thing to do. He was particularly impressed by finding in London a "befrogged and befurred green overcoat." He knew this coat would cause an immediate sensation, and it did.

He came to America in January 1882 at the age of twenty-seven, and things could not have gone better. He arrived in New York by ship so late one night that passengers could not clear quarantine until the next morning. But the New York reporters knew that Oscar Wilde—Reginald

Bunthorne—was on that ship, so they took a ferry out to the ship while it was still in quarantine. They wanted to interview Oscar Wilde to garner all the witty comments they were sure he was going to make. They asked Wilde numerous questions, but for the first and last time on the tour Wilde was not prepared with any witty answers. When they asked him, "What did you think of crossing the Atlantic?" the only thing Wilde could say was that he "was quite disappointed with the Atlantic Ocean." Much to Wilde's shock, in the society page of *The New York Times* the next day, the headline was "Mr. Wilde Is Disappointed with the Atlantic Ocean."

Wilde understood the Americans were going to be a perfect audience, because although two days before the headline had been "Mr. Wilde Is Disappointed with the Atlantic Ocean," forty-eight hours later, in the "Letters to the Editor" column of *The New York Times*, a reply said, "To the Editor: I am disappointed with Mr. Oscar Wilde," signed "The Atlantic Ocean." This was the kind of wit that Wilde had himself, and he knew he was in a country that could appreciate it and throw it back at him. After this everything went swimmingly. When he came through customs the next morning, the customs officer, as was his duty, asked Wilde, "Sir, do you have anything to declare?" Wilde's answer: "I have nothing to declare except my genius." Everyone could make fun of Oscar Wilde, but they could not take their eyes off him. Wilde realized any publicity was good publicity, and he decided that derision, in its own way, was a tribute as well.

You really have to admire Oscar Wilde, at his young age, for what he did on this lecture tour. People like Dickens,

Thackeray, and Mark Twain had gone before Oscar Wilde, but when they'd lectured in America they'd picked their cities carefully: Boston, Philadelphia, New York, Washington—the centers of sophisticated audience. Not Wilde; he was there to make a splash. So he too did Boston and Philadelphia and New York, but only Wilde went on to do cities in Illinois, Nebraska, all the way to California, lecturing through Kansas, Iowa, Colorado, New Jersey, Missouri—even some places that were not even states yet. There was no place Wilde would not go to give a talk to Americans, to tell them what it is to appreciate the beautiful in life. And because he was an author, though he was not famous for it yet, everyday people would thrust manuscripts at him and ask him to read them. Every manuscript that Wilde ever received was returned to the person by mail, with copious comments Wilde had made. He took this job seriously; he understood the needs of the public and he was at their beck and call.

If I can choose one anecdote to sum up his American trip, it would be this: He went to Leadville, Colorado, to talk to miners down in a mine. When he found out that he was going to be talking to silver miners, he decided that he would give a lecture on the great Renaissance silversmith Cellini, who lived in the 1500s. Wilde decided Cellini would be a subject these miners could appreciate. He gave a brilliant talk, underground in the silver mine, on Cellini, and when he was finished, one of the miners asked, "Well, how come you did not bring this fellow Cellini with you?" Wilde laughed in a kindly way and said, "Well, you know, Cellini has been dead for some time." And another miner yelled out, "Really? Who shot him?" Wilde never condescended to his audiences. He took them seriously, they took him seriously.

The tour was a triumph of courage and grace for Oscar Wilde. Now people in America, from the upper class of Philadelphia to the lowest miner, understood aestheticism and what it was to be an aesthete in a way they could never have understood before.

Upon returning to England, at twenty-eight, Wilde still did not know what he would do for a career. Rumors started to spread in London about Oscar Wilde, that he was frequenting the wrong crowd, that he was seeing too many young men, no young women. His friends warned him that if he did not want to suffer the wrong reputation, he had better find himself a wife immediately. A wife would save him from the moralists; a rich wife would save him from the moneylenders. I would not say, however, that he took the idea of having to get married all that seriously, even from the beginning. A sister of one of his friends, he decided, would make a good wife. Her name was Charlotte, but she ultimately refused him. As soon as he received her letter turning him down, Wilde wrote back to Charlotte, "I am so sorry about your decision. With your money and my brains we could have gone very far."

The next woman he proposed to, Constance Lloyd, unfortunately for her did not turn him down. Constance was five feet eight, extremely tall for back then, a good match for Wilde's six feet three. She was pretty, three years younger than Wilde, and could have made a normal man a good wife. Probably the first clue that the marriage was in trouble is that from the time he proposed until the wedding itself, the one thing Wilde spent all of his emotional and intellectual energy on was designing the gown that Constance would wear at the wedding.

The marriage did give him respectability, virtually overnight. Soon Constance was pregnant, and she gave birth to two sons, in 1885 and 1886. This was a disappointment to Wilde, because he had wanted daughters, and because when Constance was pregnant, he found her swollen body distasteful. He lost enthusiasm immediately, he said, for playing the role of husband. Long before he married Constance it was clear that he was attracted to a style of life that had to be kept extremely secret in Victorian England. Most people certainly know today, if they know anything about Oscar Wilde, that he was homosexual. To be homosexual and to be as flamboyant as Wilde was and is a recipe for disaster in any age, but drastically so in the Victorian age. Supposedly a young man by the name of Robert Ross seduced Oscar Wilde in 1886. Shortly after that he told Constance about the syphilis that he had contracted years before. He also told her, "From this point on I must be celibate because I do not want to risk your health." Their marriage became one in name only.

Wilde began to spend much of his time among bright, intelligent, wealthy young men; they became his disciples. He always had a group of young men gathered about him. They were probably gay as well, but what attracted them to Oscar Wilde were his audacious wit and his unconventional ways. These disciples would spend afternoons at his feet as Wilde would throw out one brilliant idea after another for short stories and poems. Wilde was such a generous sort that many of these young men, who would go on to be second- and third-rate authors themselves, would steal his ideas and turn them into literary works that were eventually published. Rather than being offended, Wilde was magnanimous; it pleased him to read a poem written by someone else that had been his own idea. But one day he threw out an idea about a story that he realized was so clever and could be so important in defining for him what he wanted to say to Victorian England that, for the first and only time, he asked his young friends not to use this idea until he had a crack at it.

The idea? A good-looking young man leads a terribly dissipated life, but this dissipation never shows in his person. He continues to look youthful and handsome. However, in his closet there is a portrait, and every time this man indulges in a night of dissipation, the face on the picture ages and becomes more hideous. This idea became Oscar Wilde's first great published work, *The Picture of Dorian Gray*, a novella published in 1890. It was a sensation. In fact, most critics say the publication of *The Picture of Dorian Gray* ushered in what we now consider the decadent nineties of the nineteenth century, as other writers followed him in reacting against the Victorian era.

Everyone was reading *The Picture of Dorian Gray*, and one young man, Lord Alfred Douglas, flattered Wilde by saying he had not only read the novella nine times but could also quote passages, long passages, from memory. For the rest of his life—for better . . . actually not for better at all, almost always for worse—Wilde's fortunes would be tangled with those of this young man.

Lord Alfred Douglas was the youngest son of the Marquis of Queensbury. If that name sounds familiar to some of you, it is because the Marquis of Queensbury invented what we consider modern boxing. He was a great sportsman. He believed in rules and he thought up the weight stages: the welterweight, the heavyweight, and the featherweight.

This son that Oscar Wilde fell head over heels in love with, this Lord Alfred Douglas, on the surface appeared to be a rather good-looking, wealthy young man. But anyone who knew him could have told Oscar Wilde from the beginning that this young man was spoiled, reckless, insolent and, above all, fiercely vindictive. Wilde saw none of this; he was enamored and inspired by Lord Alfred Douglas. Beginning in 1891 and for the next few years Wilde wrote plays. He wrote *Lady Windermere's Fan* in 1892; it was a big hit. He then wrote *A Woman of No Importance* in 1893—which also did well.

In the meantime, he and Lord Alfred Douglas were being extremely reckless. It was bad enough that they were involved with one another, but they really did not even try to hide their relationship at all. They took hotel rooms together, yet they never used the less public entrance. It was easy to see in the early 1890s that this affair would end in disaster for Oscar Wilde.

The Marquis of Queensbury, wanting his son to graduate from Oxford, set the tragic events in motion. The son would never have graduated from Oxford on his own because he was not particularly bright and had absolutely no discipline. The Marquis saw that not only was his son failing in his education but he was also keeping company with this despicable man with a terrible reputation, Oscar Wilde. The Marquis blamed Wilde for his son's educational problems. Tensions became inflamed, and yet while all this was coming to a head, Wilde wrote his finest work, *The Importance of Being Earnest*, in 1895. By now Lord Alfred Douglas was using Oscar Wilde only to get back at his tyrannizing father; that was really the only attraction that Lord Alfred Douglas felt.

The Importance of Being Earnest was a tremendous hit. Even the Prince of Wales came to the premiere and thought it hilarious. But at the height of Wilde's fame the Marquis of Queensbury decided that his son's affair had to stop. He went to Wilde's club and left a letter for Oscar Wilde on the main table, where all the members of the club came to pick up their mail. Anyone could have read the letter, addressed to "Oscar Wilde, posing as a Sodomite." Needless to say, Wilde was upset when he saw this note and realized the men at his club had seen it as well. Yet Wilde would never have done anything about it but for Lord Alfred Douglas, who began to bait him, insisting, "You must get back at my father." And Wilde, of course, realizing he was in no position to get back at anybody given the kind of life he was living, said, "What do you mean?" And Douglas answered, "I want you to take out a slander and libel suit against my father in court!"

Well, of course this would have been absolute madness. No jury in Victorian England would ever side with Oscar Wilde against a father who seemed to be protecting his son from a degenerate man. But Lord Alfred Douglas kept pushing: "If you loved me you would take out this suit. If you do not, it tells me what you think about me." Finally Wilde went against all common sense and took out a suit against the Marquis. And so came the traumatizing trial by jury in April of 1895, with Oscar Wilde going into court to sue the Marquis of Queensbury for publicly libeling him. Oscar Wilde undoubtedly knew he could never win the case.

The first trial did not take long at all. The jury quickly found the defendant, the Marquis of Queensbury, innocent of the charge. Everyone knew what was going to happen next. The Marquis of Queensbury immediately took out a suit against Oscar Wilde and had him arrested for indecency.

Wilde could have packed his bags and taken off for France or Spain, and that would have been the end of the matter. But Wilde, either because he possessed a foolish courage, or because he felt he could do no wrong and that he was so witty and charming he could convince anyone of anything, did not flee. He decided to fight, and he did so well in the first trial against him that the jury came back with no decision. The court immediately proceeded with a second trial, but at this point people were tired of Oscar Wilde, and they did not want to think any more about this disgusting case. The Marquis of Queensbury made sure that chambermaids from hotels were called in to describe the condition of the bedsheets, even though Oscar Wilde was saying that love between men is simply platonic. All was dragged as deeply into the gutter as it could be. By the third trial Oscar Wilde was a broken man. The jury returned in less than an hour and a half with a guilty verdict.

The judge loathed Oscar Wilde and sentenced him to the most severe sentence possible, two years of hard labor. Hard labor, indeed, meant the breaking of rocks that we think of today. When Wilde heard his harsh sentence, he simply cried, "My God! My God!" and was led off.

This disaster was the end of Oscar Wilde's writing career and the end of him as a respected public figure. At the time his trial began, *The Importance of Being Earnest* was doing well. The day after the trial's opening, Oscar Wilde's name as author of the play was removed from the billing. Once the jury came back the first time with a hung jury, the play's royalties to Wilde were stopped. Puritanical England sanctioned such an unjust practice. For him to pay a lawyer he had to sell most of his possessions. The last item sold was the blue china that he had alluded to when he was just beginning his star-crossed career.

Prison was complete torture to Wilde. He hadn't the strength for the kind of physical hard labor demanded of him, and it broke him. It would literally kill him; he did not die in prison, but he would not live long after his release. Even when his mother died, he was not allowed to go to the funeral or to visit her in her last days.

Wilde came out of prison a changed man. He did write in prison, a philosophical work in the form of a letter to Lord Alfred Douglas. This lengthy cry from the heart he called *De Profundis*, which was published posthumously. He also wrote a poem called "The Ballad of Reading Gaol," in an old-fashioned kind of rhyme. It is well worth reading even today.

No one would have anything to do with Oscar Wilde; the humiliation and degradation of the trial had rendered him untouchable. Lord Alfred Douglas, one of the most worthless figures in literary history, would have nothing to do with his former companion. He did, somewhat, while Wilde was in prison, and when Wilde came out, Douglas thought there might still be something gained by an association with him. They reunited briefly, then split. It was the worst thing for Wilde to do, to go back to someone like Douglas. But as Wilde once said, "I can resist everything but temptation."

He left prison in 1898 and lived only two more years. He could not remain in England because he was shunned by every level of society, so he began a wandering existence in Europe. It is said that in the United States, in 1896, nine hundred sermons were given in churches against Oscar

Wilde specifically. He began to drink heavily. Even at this point his wit did not fail him. When people asked him why he drank so much, he answered, "I have discovered that alcohol, taken in sufficient quantity, produces all the effects of drunkenness." Drunkenness was about the only escape left to him. His wife, Constance, had divorced him and died at the young age of forty, the year that he was set free from prison. He was denied all access to his sons.

Homeless, he wandered the streets of France. On one occasion he encountered Nellie Melba, the great opera singer. When Wilde was at his height in the early 1890s, they had attended the same parties and were equally famous. But now it was very different. When he spotted her going into the entrance of the opera theater in Paris, he approached her and said, "Madam Melba, you do not recognize me anymore. I'm Oscar Wilde and I'm going to do a terrible thing. I am going to ask you for money." He was reduced to begging now from the very people with whom he had been on equal footing when his star was rising in the early 1890s.

The Marquis of Queensbury died. An extremely wealthy man, he left Lord Alfred Douglas, his son, £20,000, which was a fortune. All of Wilde's former friends pleaded with Douglas to at least give Oscar something. When nothing was forthcoming from Douglas, Wilde wrote him, asking to be advanced some money. Douglas finally broke off all communication by writing Wilde, "You are wheedling me like an old whore, Oscar. Quit bothering me about the money."

At the end of 1900, a friend took Wilde in, in Paris, because he could no longer afford the little rent he had been paying when he was living alone. When people asked him why he could not keep at least his little apartment, he said,

"Because I am dying beyond my means!" He ended up in a shabby garret, so ill he was confined to bed. The syphilis that had weakened his body originally and the terrible hard labor he was put through in prison had combined to destroy him.

One of the last things we learn about Oscar Wilde is that he was characteristically upset by his final surroundings. His deathbed was in a room of shocking poverty. All things that had been beautiful to Wilde were gone. One of the last things he said came when he looked up at the wallpaper in the little garret room: "My wallpaper and I are fighting a duel to the death. One or the other of us has to go!"

A few of the friends who still had anything to do with him came to visit him on his deathbed. He died on November 30, 1900. Now Lord Alfred Douglas suddenly remembered his dear, dear friend. He not only came to the funeral, but friends reported that at the graveyard he jockeyed himself into the position of prime mourner so he would be closest to the grave as the coffin was lowered. He nearly fell into the grave because he wanted to be so close that everyone would know he was the most grief-stricken of those Oscar Wilde had left behind.

Alfred Douglas lived for forty-five more years. He married and then divorced an heiress. He decided after Wilde was dead that it was his duty to write a book to expose and besmirch the Wilde myth. He had even tried to have published the love letters that Wilde had written him when Wilde was in prison. Because he had known Wilde so well, he figured there might be some money to be made by excoriating Wilde long after Wilde could defend himself.

And so we come to the end of the sad saga of Oscar Wilde. It is a tragedy because, like all tragedies, it was brought on by the main character himself. Wilde's great faith that he could move the masses any way he wished was his downfall. He should never have brought the case against the Marquis of Queensbury, and then when he lost it, he should never have appeared in court as the defendant when Queensbury brought suit against him. And once the trial was over, although he would live for four more years, he was the walking dead. Nothing else would come out of Oscar Wilde's pen that truly reflected his great wit and wonderful love of life.

I think we should go back to that trial for one other comment Wilde made. In the middle of the trial, when Wilde was trying to explain to the judge and the jury why he was involved with Lord Alfred Douglas, the Marquis of Queensbury became so furious that he leapt out of his chair and shouted, "You are in the gutter and you are dragging my son there too!" Without missing a beat, Wilde looked at the Marquis and responded, "We are all in the gutter, sir, but some of us are looking up at the stars." The wit and openheartedness of Oscar Wilde can still sustain and inspire us, in spite of the life that he decided to lead.

Mark Twain

(1835–1910)

It might surprise most people to learn that English professors can be unanimous in agreement about *anything* regarding literature. It might surprise people even more to learn that these professors will say that Mark Twain is the greatest writer who ever picked up a pen in the history of the United States of America. As Americans we're always interested in who's number one in the field of sports. Well, in the field of American literature, Mark Twain has always been considered our greatest writer and probably always will be.

Now this might strike most people as rather peculiar. In his entire career Twain only produced one book that is regarded today as absolutely first-class world literature, the relatively short novel *Huckleberry Finn*. Yes, *Tom Sawyer* is equally famous, but both public and critics agree that it is a lesser work of fiction with a disagreeable hero. So how can a man who, in a rather long life, produced only one work of stupendous literary merit be called the greatest writer in the history of our country?

Mark Twain is our premier author because during his distinguished and colorful career he gave American literature two priceless gifts. What are these two gifts? Well, if I told you right now, this glimpse of Mark Twain would soon be over. You're going to have to be patient for a bit while I give you first what I consider fascinating and invaluable background information.

The first thing to tell you about Mark Twain is something you probably already know: his date of birth and the state he was born in. (And I don't mean the state of infancy . . .) Most people know where he is from because he sets his most famous works of fiction there: Missouri. And because he is so associated with Missouri, most people probably think that he had a nostalgic fondness for his home state. He did *not*. He detested his home state. Twain gives us two clues as to his true regard of Missouri. First, he left Missouri when he was eighteen and he never, never went back—unless he was paid handsomely to do so. The other clue is what he once wrote: "There are three proper ways to pronounce my home state. If you are born in my state, you pronounce it 'Misour*ah*'; if you are not born in my state you pronounce it 'Misour*ee*'; but if you are born in my state, and you have to live your entire life in my state, you pronounce it 'Misery.'" Subtle, yes? Actually this antipathy was not Missouri's fault. Twain's dislike of his home state had nothing to do with his state but everything to do with his home.

Twain came from a family we probably wouldn't want to be part of, either. As a depressed old man, Twain once wrote to a high school friend: "I hate to admit this, but I knew from my earliest memories that my father did not really love my mother. Fortunately, my mother did not really love my father either, and since they had this in common, the marriage went on forever." This lovelessness was sad enough, but an even worse burden, as far as Twain was concerned, was that his father never could make a decent living.

Then, when Twain was only twelve, his father dropped dead, literally, in front of him, and so at this young age Twain had to put himself to work to put food on his mother's table. The four other siblings were all called upon to support the large fatherless family by finding odd jobs. According to Twain, he got the oddest and worst job in the state of Missouri: assistant editor of the Hannibal, Missouri, newspaper. He had grown up in the dusty little town of Hannibal, which is right on the Mississippi River, and there at age twelve he is already an assistant editor. You might think, "Well, rather impressive for a twelve-year-old!" It was not—it was a nightmare. What exactly did the assistant editor of the Hannibal, Missouri, daily newspaper do in 1847? Twain had to get up at four-thirty every morning, to be at the newspaper office at five. He had to chop wood outside the office door, bring it in, throw it in the fireplace, and heat up the entire newspaper office by five-thirty.

Why did the senior editor want it warm by five-thirty? Because the editor lived in a fancy apartment attached to the newspaper office, and when the editor put his feet on the ground first thing in the morning, he wanted it warm. Not only did Twain have to heat up the newspaper office by five-thirty, he then had to go into the editor's bedroom, get the editor up, help the editor dress, cook the editor's breakfast, serve it, clean up after, mop out the entire newspaper office, and meticulously clean every nook and cranny of the editor's private apartment with a feather duster. This took him until almost eight. He had worked almost three hours as nothing more than a houseboy, and his real job hadn't even started yet. His real job was to print the paper. The newspaper editor wrote it, but had no intention of getting his fingers dirty with ink by printing it. Twain had to print the paper.

How big was the Hannibal daily newspaper? Not very big, only six pages long. How hard would it be to print a six-page newspaper? Twain said it was almost impossible because they had no automated printing presses back then in Hannibal. So, how *do* you print a newspaper if you don't have a printing press? Twain said he had to stand in front of fifty-two cases. Each case was a little wooden box, narrow and deep, and each of these cases had thousands of tiny little tin letters in them—tintype. There was a case each of *A*'s, *B*'s, *C*'s, *D*'s, all the way down to *X*'s, *Y*'s, and *Z*'s. There were fifty-two cases and not just twenty-six because the bottom row of cases had the small letters and the upper row of cases had the capital letters. (And that's why, even on a computer today, we still call capital letters "upper case," because in Twain's day, you had to reach up into the case and pull them down.)

To print the newspaper Twain had to pull out every letter of every word of every sentence of every paragraph of every page of the newspaper. There were only six pages, but there were about twenty-one hundred words per page. The task would have taken forever even under good circumstances. Twain's circumstances, however, were daunting, because he couldn't just pull out a letter, put it in the press, and print it. On the contrary, he never knew if the letter he wanted to pull out would actually be there, because the newspaper worker who had put the letters back in the cases the night before was always dead drunk. The job didn't pay enough for a sober person, Twain said, so they hired a drunk off the streets who would come in late at night, throw up the letters in the cases, throw up his dinner onto the floor, and leave. Every morning Twain would have to come in and clean up this stinking mess before he could even stand in front of the cases. Twain never knew when he pulled out a letter if it would be the right one; he had to look at each letter before it went to print. And if you've ever seen a letter on a piece of type, you understand his problem. On a piece of type the letter is backward, the mirror image of the actual letter. It does not become right-side-to until it is printed, and by then if there is an error, it is too late to correct it.

With most of the letters Twain had no problem because most letters in our alphabet look the same forward or backward, but two letters in the English language are actually backward mirror images of each other, and that drove him crazy. Which letters? A small *q* is the same letter as a backward small *p*, and of course, a small *p* is the same letter as a backward *q*. So when Twain reached in to get a *q*, he had to remember, if it looks like a *q*, put it back, it's wrong, it's backward, it's actually a *p*. But if it looks like a *p*, it's actually a *q* because it's backward, it's correct, put it in the press and print it. Twain once wrote in an essay: "I hated the printing business, because no matter how careful I tried to be I could never mind my 'p's' and 'q's.'" That is where the famous expression comes from. Some critics say that the expression can be traced back to the late 1700s but all agree that it was Twain who made it famous.

(I think one of the great joys of being an English professor today is that when I teach a Twain novel at the university, I always tell my students this story, and I always say, "And that's where the famous expression comes from." And they always look at me and say, *"What* famous expression?" Not only are young people not minding their p's and q's today, they never even heard the expression.)

Twain had to stay at this dreadful job until he was eigh-teen, when an opportunity to escape seemed to offer itself. Living next door to him was a friend he had had from child-hood, Michael. Michael ventured to South America to make his fortune. Upon his return he knocked on Mark Twain's door and said, "Sam"—because as you surely know, Mark Twain is a pen name; Twain's real name, of course, is Samuel Clemens—he knocked on Twain's door and said, "Sam, I'm back from South America, and I have a way we can each make about a million dollars if you'll quit the printing busi-ness and join up with me." Well, of course Twain wanted des-perately to get out of the printing business, and who wouldn't wish to make a million dollars? Twain said, "This sounds hopeful, what is it?" Michael said, "Well, you know what is happening in Massachusetts, don't you?" Everyone knew that the whole state of Massachusetts was then virtu-ally on strike. During this time of industrial revolution, man-ufacturers had brought brand-new machinery into Massachusetts, but had not trained the workers how to use it. Laborers were victimized by serious accidents caused by the powerful new machinery, and the entire state was in chaos and on strike.

Michael said, "I've brought back something from South America. We will sell it to the workers of Massachusetts, and not only will they go back to work, but they will become the most productive workers on earth!" Twain said, "This sounds too good to be true; what have you brought back?" And Michael said, "When I was in South America, I spent five days on a plantation in Chile, and I noticed something very strange there. I noticed that the servants on this plantation worked eighteen hours every day, without a rest. They had one small break for water, one small break for food. Otherwise, they worked eighteen hours in a row, went to sleep, woke up refreshed, and worked another eighteen hours. Can you just imagine how much work they would accomplish each day?

"On the last day I went up to the plantation manager and I asked him, 'How do you get these servants to work eighteen hours every day?' And the manager said, 'Oh, that is no secret here in South America.' The manager walked over, picked up a big leather pouch, opened it up, and had me look inside. All I could see was a fine, white, powdery substance that looked like snow.

"The plantation manager said, 'Every morning when our servants are awakened, we take the tiniest pinch of this magic white powder and we put it up the right nostril of the servant. We take another little pinch, put it up the left nostril, and ask our servants to breath it in. They then work eighteen hours in a row, big smiles on their faces—never get hungry, never get tired, never complain.' I asked him, what *is* this magic powder that puts everyone in such a good productive mood? And the plantation manager said, 'It grows wild here on a plant called *coca*.'"

Obviously what Michael had stumbled upon was pristine, unadulterated South American cocaine. Remember, the time is 1853. You can be sure no one in backwater Hannibal, Missouri, had any clue as to what this substance was. At that time cocaine was not known as a dangerous drug; it wasn't known at all. Michael certainly seemed to be onto something, since thirty years later, in 1886, this same coca was used as a key ingredient in Coca-Cola—look how well that little business has done. So it is no surprise that Mark Twain, in his naïveté said, "You mean we acquire this magic white powder, bring it up to Massachusetts, sell it to the workers, they return to work, and we become heroes? It sounds like a fine idea, but I have one question. What is my role in all of this?"

And his friend Michael said, "Oh, that's easy. I was able to buy half a ton of this white powder, although I did have to pay ninety-five dollars for it. Because I was rushed in leaving, it is still on the docks in Chile. I want you to take a riverboat to New Orleans, sail down to South America, rent a freighter, load the powder on it, and take it up to Massachusetts. Then we go into business." Twain thought that this was such a promising idea that almost immediately he boarded a riverboat to New Orleans, from where he expected to travel to South America and bring the magic powder up to Massachusetts. Had he done that, he would probably never have become an author.

What happened to alter American literature forever? Twain embarked on the riverboat and it took him down to New Orleans, but as fate would have it, the riverboat he boarded was captained by Horace Bixby, one of the finest riverboat captains on the waterways. So legendary and impressive was Bixby that when the riverboat arrived in New Orleans, Twain abandoned his entrepreneurial journey to South America. Instead he begged Horace Bixby to teach him how to be a riverboat captain as well. Why the change of plan? Why would Twain toss away the idea of a million-dollar scheme? He did it simply because Horace Bixby happened to mention that a riverboat captain earned $250 a month. Of course, today $250 a month is not an extravagantly large sum of money. But in Twain's day that $250 a month would equal over $150,000 a year today. In Twain's day, a riverboat captain was the third-highest-paying job in America.

Why would anyone pay someone that much money just to be a riverboat captain? It appeared that all one did was go up and down the Mississippi all day, docking and delivering goods. But a riverboat captain earned every penny, because he had to make at least half of his deliveries at night, in the dark. This was how the middle part of the country was supplied with trade goods; a riverboat couldn't just stop when the sun went down. And what was so difficult about making deliveries at night on the Mississippi River? There could be no light on the boat at night, because the only kind of portable light was a big metal lantern. Lanterns, of course, have flames. If just two sparks, Twain tells us, would leap out of that lantern and land on the deck of a boat, the boat had a sure chance of catching fire. Riverboats were made out of extremely dry timber and were highly flammable. To avoid the danger of fire on the river, the order was, "You can have *no* light on your boat at night."

Well, if you had no light on your riverboat, exactly how far ahead of you could you see on the Mississippi at night? Twain tells us: "Five inches." Unless it was foggy—then it was two-inch visibility. That meant at night you could put your hand right up in front of your face and it would disappear. "You were not legally blind," Twain said, "you were completely blind," as if someone put a blindfold around your eyes.

If, then, you cannot see anything on the river at night and you are required to make ten or twelve deliveries to obscure, tiny riverside docks, how could you possibly do it? There was only one way. As a prerequisite to becoming a riverboat captain and being paid the third-highest salary in America, all you had to do was memorize the Mississippi River. The entire river. Every bend, landmark, sandbar. How big is the Mississippi River? It is 2,357 miles long. Mark Twain had to know, precisely, that at mile 830, yard two on the east bank, there was a sandbar. Had Twain not memorized where that sandbar was exactly, he would strike upon it in the black of night and maroon his riverboat. His cargo, which was always perishable, would rot and he would be out of business.

So did Twain have to memorize 2,357 miles of Mississippi riverbank yard by yard before he could become a captain? No. As Twain said, "That would have been a picnic." What was the catch? The Mississippi has an east bank, and, obviously, a west bank. And that west bank doesn't look a thing like the east bank. Not only did Twain have to memorize 2,357 miles of Mississippi River going up in the east, he then had to memorize a different 2,357 miles going down in the west: 4,714 miles of Mississippi River to memorize yard by yard, to pass the test. It took him two years, studying every night, Christmas, New Year's, weekends; he did nothing but study and memorize the river. He didn't mind this laborious task because after two years of agony, he would have the third-highest-paying job in America. He was so bright and diligent that he passed the riverboat test on the first try, and he emerged a qualified pilot, on his way to being a richly rewarded captain.

But he never earned that exalted salary. According to Twain, he never earned anything. And why not? His maiden voyage on the Mississippi began April 10, 1861. Only a few days later the Civil War erupted. Because the Mississippi

River runs north and south, one of the first acts passed by the Yankees said, "All traffic on the Mississippi River may continue to go north. No traffic may now head south." A few hours later, the Confederates passed an injunction that said, "All traffic on the Mississippi River may continue to go south, no traffic may head north." With the river thus off-limits, Twain was out of a job before he even started it. As he wrote in his journal: "I have spent two years memorizing every yard of the Mississippi River only to discover that unless you are going to be a riverboat captain this information will *not* come in handy in any other profession."

By the way, he is not being completely honest here. He would put this knowledge to great use in *Life on the Mississippi*. And Twain might have mentioned that the river did give him his pen name, Mark Twain, which he was using by 1870 with his earliest essays. He claimed that those two words were the most beautiful sounds ever heard on a riverboat, and that was because of the constant measuring of the water's depth on board. The crew member in charge of measuring would throw overboard a rope that was calibrated in fathoms. A fathom equaled six feet. If the rope went down only six feet, the crew member would yell to the navigator, "Mark one"—meaning mark down one fathom deep. All on board would groan when they heard this because one fathom of water was too shallow for them to dock the boat.

But if the rope went down twelve feet—two fathoms—the man would yell, "Mark twain"—*twain* being the measurement term for "two." Now everyone would cheer. Twelve feet would be deep enough to dock the boat, which meant those on board could now leave the boat, visit their "girl-friends," get drunk, shoot up the town, or engage in other delightful shore pastimes. Because the words *mark twain* were synonymous with "good times ahead," Twain adopted them and thus immortalized them.

In 1861, Twain thus found himself in limbo. The only occupation he had a knack for was reporting, though he hated newspaper work. He was finally given a job on a paper in far Virginia City, Nevada; soon he was so effective at his work that it seemed inevitable that he should land a position with the finest newspaper in the West, the *San Francisco Chronicle*. Twain headed for San Francisco and applied for a job. Unfortunately, the only job available was that of society page editor. Equally unfortunately no one *loathed* society more than Mark Twain. He detested the wealthy and abhorred those who graced the social pages. Because he was reared poor, in an out-of-the-way place, he thought if you were very social, you had to prove to him you weren't stupid as well. But as this was the only job open, he applied for and got it.

As soon as Twain signed his contract, the *Chronicle* editor informed him that the editor's wife was the president of the Women's Club of San Francisco, and she would be giving Mark Twain most of his stories. This was not an auspicious sign. Every day the editor's wife gave him one fluffy, inane story after another, all about social teas and charity balls, until soon Twain considered quitting. Then one day the editor's wife brought Twain what she eagerly announced was a monumentally big story. What's more important, her husband, the editor, had told her that if Twain wrote the story up, it would be the headline not only on the society page but also on the front page of the paper. Twain was intrigued. He got out pencil and writing pad and waited for the editor's wife's grand news. She said, "Last night the Women's Club of San Francisco held a charity ball, and we raised one hundred dollars"—which was a fortune back then—"all of which we are sending back east to decorate the graves of the Union and Confederate soldiers." This was 1864 and the war was still on. Twain said, "I see. Now what's the interesting story?" "That's it!" she said. "Write it up. It's going to be the headline on the front page tomorrow."

So Twain wrote up the story just as she told him on regulation reporter paper for the next day's *Chronicle*. But to vent his disgust at such inanity he took another piece of regulation reporter paper, and on this one he wrote a parody of the Women's Club fete. The first paragraph was the same: "Women's Club of San Francisco raises $100 at a charity ball and *says* they are sending it back east to decorate the graves of soldiers." But the second paragraph went, "The *Chronicle*, however, has a scoop. We have learned that they are not actually sending the money back east, to decorate soldiers' graves. Instead they are secretly sending it to a large plantation in the state of Alabama where black women and white men are bred together to produce a superior slave to work in all the homes of the wealthy throughout the South!"

This was in the absolutely worst possible taste. Twain didn't care because he'd written it up as a joke for a fellow cub reporter. The reporter would read it, enjoy a cheap laugh, and throw the parody away. As you might expect, events did not work out that way. Twain did put the bona fide article right on his desk where it was supposed to be to be collected for the next day's paper. And he placed the joke article in the cub reporter's cubicle, assuming that when he came in, he would read it and discard it. But the cub reporter didn't come in that day because he had the Asian flu. Late that night the copyboy, who was illiterate, went around collecting the articles to be printed in the newspaper. Had he seen the joke article in the cubicle, and the real article on Twain's desk, that would have confused him. He would have taken it to the night editor, who of course could read, and the confusion would have been solved. Unfortunately for Twain, the joke article remained where it was in the cubicle (since the reporter didn't come in), but what about the real article? Twain had indeed put it on his desk, but he had neglected to put a paperweight on it. He had also left his window open, there had been a windstorm, and the real article had blown behind the door. Nobody saw it.

Imagine San Francisco's shock when the city awoke the next morning to read, as the *Chronicle*'s headline on the front page, that the Women's Club was supporting a breeding farm of black women and white men in the state of Alabama! The Women's Club, as you may imagine, was not amused. Not only did the women insist Twain be fired, but Twain claimed they kicked him clean out of San Francisco and added, "Had those women had just a little more power, they would have banished me from the United States entirely."

This was the greatest humiliation of Twain's professional career; he could hardly expect to get a job as a reporter anywhere after such a fiasco. The only thing he could think of to do was to head for the Sierra Nevadas, not far from San Francisco, where gold had been discovered six months previously. Twain took miner's supplies and his high hopes, and off he went to the mining camp known as Angel Camp.

There was no gold—only mud; he found nothing except hard luck. He had virtually no money, and he was so depressed that he said later that it was the only time he actually tried to commit suicide. He would become possessed by depression again as an older man, and many times more he would think about suicide, but this was the only time he made the attempt. One night in the mining camp, he took a loaded gun, put it in his mouth, and pulled the trigger. As Twain said, had he been just a little more accurate a shot, he could probably have hurt himself. We have to assume that this impossible though hilarious episode falls under his category of "whoppers."

He survived, obviously, but remained deeply depressed. His brother sent him just enough money to have one shot of whiskey a week to try to drink himself into oblivion. One night, Twain was in the saloon of Angel Camp when a stranger came in at the stroke of midnight. Twain was the only person in the bar. The stranger looked at Twain and said, "It's late, I'm bored, and you're the only person in the saloon. I'll buy you a shot of liquor if you'll sit there and listen to a rather long story I just heard." Well, Twain wants the drink, so he says okay. The man buys him the shot of liquor and then starts to tell the story.

We don't know exactly what the man said to Twain, but we do know that Twain had in his pocket—because he had been a reporter—the stub of a pencil and a dirty scrap of paper. And as the man tells the story, Twain writes down seven famous words: "Frog, Bet, Jump, No Jump, Lose Bet." Why do I call these "famous words"? Because after the man told him the story, Twain goes back to his hut—he lived in a hovel at this mining camp—and half-drunk he writes up the story in his own unique style. The name of this story is "The Celebrated Jumping Frog of Calaveras County." He called it Calaveras County because that's the county in California that the mining camp was in.

If you don't know this story by Twain, you're not missing much. It's about a frog who jumps farther than any other frog in the world, so the owner of this jumping frog gets filthy rich, because he bets his frog against all other frogs in jumping contests and always wins. But then one day a clever stranger comes to town, and when the owner of the famous jumping frog is out of the room, the stranger opens up the jumping frog's mouth and pours in buckshot. Then when the owner comes back, the stranger says, "Let's have a bet. I'll bet my jumping frog against yours and we'll put all our money on it." The stranger's frog only jumps half an inch. But the famous jumping frog just sits there and belches out black pellets because it's full of lead. The stranger wins the bet. Now that's the entire story. You would not confuse it with *Romeo and Juliet* or *Moby-Dick*. And yet, in some ways, it is the most important story ever written in American literature. How come? Because, as you may suspect, it has in it the two gifts that Twain gave American literature that are so important that they have made him our number one author.

First, believe it or not, "The Celebrated Jumping Frog of Calaveras County" is the first story written in America that allows its characters to talk like Americans. What does that mean? It means it is the first story with American dialect. Before Twain wrote this story, earlier great American authors made their characters sound as if they were out of a drawing room in a Charles Dickens novel. Because England was the center of world culture during this period, every American author before Twain modeled his characters' speech on English characters so that they all sounded as if they were British. But Twain said this was ridiculous. We in America don't sound like the English in real life, so why should we sound like them in our stories? Twain said, "My rule is, make your characters sound exactly like where they are from. For example, if you have a character from Maine in your story, give him a Yankee accent. If you have a character from Alabama, give him a Southern accent. If you have a character from Oregon, give him a Western accent. If you have a character who is a member of Congress, make him sound like an idiot." Some things don't change in a hundred years. He always made his characters speak *American*—that's his first gift.

But to be honest, that's not why he is our greatest author. It is the second gift in this story that makes him immortal. Believe it or not, "The Celebrated Jumping Frog of Calaveras County" is the first story written in America that was written *to have a sense of humor.* It is our first *funny* piece of literature. And you need to get something straight. When did Twain write this story? In 1870. When did we start writing in America? In 1620. We had been writing 250 years and had never produced a great funny story. I'm not saying we didn't have great literature before Twain. Goodness knows, *The Scarlet Letter* was written before Twain. There are many good things you can say about *The Scarlet Letter,* but you can't say that it's funny. Before Twain, "great" generally meant "serious." Twain gives us an American sense of humor. As everyone knows, the Puritans founded this country. They had a somber outlook. They thought that levity was the work of the devil. And for almost two hundred years, this mentality was the American mentality. But in 1870, writing a funny story, Twain drags us kicking and screaming into the sunshine of American humor. Giving us our sense of humor in literature will probably always keep Mark Twain our greatest writer.

However, this story didn't actually do much for Twain's reputation. Every newspaper in America seemed to pick it up, but unfortunately, once people read it, everybody remembered the frog but nobody remembered Twain. Sometimes the newspapers didn't even put his name in the byline. He is depressed to realize that he now knows he can be funny, and he knows what brings out his greatest humor, but he's unknown to the reading public. So he moves to the East Coast and decides he needs to write something that will not only be funny but definitely associated with *him*.

He also knows that his greatest humor is evoked by society. He was always—as I told you—against good society. Wealthy people made the perfect butt for his satire, but he can't think of a topic to write about—until he sees a little advertisement in a newspaper in Massachusetts. It states that an Episcopal minister is taking a group from his congregation to the Holy Land—just as they do today—for a tour. Twain looks at that and thinks, "Gosh, what could be more wealthy or more stuffy than a group of Episcopalians going to the Holy Land." Twain thought, "If only I could get on that tour, disguise myself as a stuffy Episcopalian, and write up nasty satiric letters." He knew of some newspapers in New York, particularly in Brooklyn, that would even pay him to write such letters because the New York people couldn't stand Massachusetts, particularly wealthy Massachusetts Episcopalians. So, with the secret backing of the newspapers, he goes on this trip with the Episcopalians to the Holy Land and discovers, to his delight, that they are far wealthier and far more stuffy then he could ever have hoped for. He writes back the most hilarious, satiric letters against them to the New York papers. I won't overwhelm you with many examples, but I can give you the best one.

The highlight of this trip—and it was advertised in the papers—was an outing the participants were going to take across the Sea of Galilee. The day of the outing dawned sunny. The stagecoach let them off at the very edge of the Sea of Galilee, where they saw an Arab who had this little boat. The Arab came up to them and in broken English said, "And now it's time for your twenty-minute trip across the Sea of Galilee. That will be eight dollars per person." Well, $8 per person in Twain's day is about $230 per person in our money, and Twain thought, "Not even these wealthy Episcopalians are going to shell out what is the equivalent of over two hundred dollars for a twenty-minute trip. But the father got out his wallet: eight dollars for him, eight dollars for the wife, eight dollars for the kid. Nobody complained." However, that's not how Twain wrote up this incident. He was much more succinct. All he said for the newspaper was "The Arab boatman was charging $8 a person for the trip across the Sea of Galilee. Is it any wonder that Jesus walked?"

Now today, that's pretty funny, but back in Twain's day it was utter sacrilege—and the New Yorkers ate it up! They thought it was hilarious. Twain gets back, sees that he's a culture hero in New York for these hilarious letters, and Twain—who was always physically lazy—thought, "Why should I work myself to death trying to come up with a funny book? Why not take these letters I wrote back from the trip, kind of throw them up in the air, have them come down in a different order, and make this my book?" He did. Called *Innocents Abroad,* this novel in Twain's day made him famous as a humorist, though it's not much read today because most of the humor has not held up all that well.

As you know, what makes him immortal today is the novel *Huckleberry Finn.* Yet when that novel was first published in 1885, it was a dud. Nobody bought *Huckleberry Finn* when it first came out. How come? Because word of mouth had let people know that its main character was not only the son of an alcoholic, but the son of such a severe alcoholic that the father had attempted to kill his own child. And people from good society thought, "Why would I waste money buying a book about the son of an alcoholic? This is so low-life. It has nothing to do with my good society." Then they found out that the second major character in *Huckleberry Finn* was a black slave named Jim. And again they thought, "Why would I waste money on a book that's about the son of an alcoholic and a black person? They have nothing to do with good society. I'm not going to read it." And the book would have died, except one woman single-handedly rescued it. It's a stirring story. You know this woman, I assume. You should. Her name? Louisa May Alcott, of Massachusetts.

Louisa May Alcott had become world famous for her book *Little Women.* She found out that Huck Finn was a "little man," figured this was her area, she'd give it a read. But she only reads half of *Huckleberry Finn,* put it down, and wrote Twain the following letter: "Dear Mr. Twain, I have tried to read your latest novel, *The Adventures of Huckleberry*

Finn, but I find the characters and incidents in this book so low, so common, so vulgar and so dirty that I say to you, Mr. Twain, if you can't write a better book for our young people than *Huckleberry Finn* I suggest you don't write anything in the future." She sent it to Mark Twain. Was he upset? You bet he was. Because Louisa May Alcott had power. If she loved a book, it sold. If she hated a book, it died.

But poor Louisa May didn't know when to quit, and of course she had already been upset by Twain's less-than-flattering portrayal of the Massachusetts Episcopalians in *Innocents Abroad*. She hated *Huckleberry Finn* so much, because it was so low and dirty, that she went to the library board of her state of Massachusetts and got a law passed that banned the sale of *Huckleberry Finn* or its rental in libraries because of all its dirty incidents. Twain found out that his book was banned in Massachusetts. Was he upset? No. He simply took out huge ads the following week in magazines and newspapers throughout the country. They all said the same thing: "My latest book, *Huckleberry Finn*, by Mark Twain, has been banned in the state of Massachusetts," and then in great big letters, *"FOR ALL OF ITS DIRTY INCI-DENTS."* Sales shot up 300 percent—and that's an accurate figure—the next month. Everybody ran out to buy *Huckleberry Finn* hoping they'd get into a good dirty incident. Don't forget, this is the Victorian period. They weren't finding anything in their lives in that way, so they figured that maybe they'd find some relief in the novel. They read *Huckleberry Finn*—no dirty incidents.

What they did find was a very touching story about this little boy, Huck Finn, who had such an incredibly good conscience, though he was low in most ways, that he was risking going to hell to save his black friend, the slave, Jim. People finished the book. They liked it. But we do have letters that they wrote Mark Twain that said, "Dear Mr. Twain, I enjoyed *Huck Finn*, but you did make one big mistake. You must not have realized that you made as the hero of this book—the most kind, giving, loving, decent person in the novel—the black slave, Jim." They said, "You can't make a black person the hero of a novel. Blacks have nothing to do with good society." Twain always gave the same answer: "The reason I made the black slave, Jim, the greatest character in *Huckleberry Finn* is because since blacks are *never* taken into good society, they are currently the only people in this country who have not been warped and totally ruined by the good society of which they are not a part." He added: "Because blacks aren't taken into good society, they are foolish enough to have to live by the dictates of Jesus Christ in the Sermon on the Mount. Because blacks aren't taken into good society, they foolishly think that the last shall one day be first, and because blacks are so ill-treated by white society today, not only must they survive any way they can, but they survive today with a dignity that most white people cannot even imagine."

Well, you know, even black people weren't saying this about blacks back then. So it was incredible that it came from a white Southerner—because, don't forget, Samuel Clemens, our Mark Twain, had blood that was half-Kentucky, half-Virginia. He was thoroughly Southern in his background. English professors will tell you that even today the greatest hero in American literature is Jim, the black slave. It should not shock us that our greatest hero in our literature is black. It should *amaze* us that he was invented by a white Southerner, in the 1880s, named Mark Twain.

This novel made Twain so famous that he was a celebrity for the rest of his life. And when he was an old man, a reporter once said to him, "Of all your accomplishments, Mr. Twain, what is the one thing you are most proud of?" Twain thought about it and said, "Of all my accomplishments the one feat I am most proud of was to have been born on November 30." A rather odd thing to say. Why would Twain single out being born on November 30 as his greatest accomplishment? Here's why. Had you been alive on the night Mark Twain was born—he was born at 11:10 P.M., November 30, 1835—had you walked out of your log cabin that night and looked up into the sky, you would have seen a streak of white light go by that we call Halley's comet.

If you know anything about that comet, you know it can only be seen from earth once every seventy-five years or so. You can look up and see the comet, then it's gone for about seventy-five years, and then it comes back. Mark Twain, when he was ten, heard his mother say that on the night he was born, Halley's comet was in the sky. This so impressed Twain that for the rest of his life he told almost everybody he met—it became a bit boring after a while—"I came into the world with Halley's comet, I'm going out of the world with Halley's comet." In other words, he was saying, "I'm going to die when the comet is back in the sky." A rather dangerous prediction, because not only did it mean he would have to die when he was just about seventy-five, but it would be during the few weeks that you can see Halley's comet from Earth. When did Mark Twain die? April 21, 1910. Did he die during the few weeks when you can see Halley's comet from Earth? He did. Did he put a gun in his mouth and shoot himself to make sure he'd die on schedule?

No. Surprisingly he actually died of natural causes, when the comet was in the sky, just as he'd predicted.

But when you think about it, this is not such a feat. There must have been thousands of people who were born in 1835 when the comet was in the sky, who lived for what was back then a rather long life of seventy-five years, and who died when the comet was back. The only reason I'm wasting your time with this story is this. Had you been alive on the night Twain was born, not only would you have seen the comet in the sky, but if you knew a lot about astronomy, you might have realized that Halley's comet was *exactly* two weeks away in its orbit from the place it would be closest to Earth. Twain dies on April 21, 1910. Shockingly, not only is the comet in the sky, as he said it would be, but on the night Twain died, Haley's comet was *exactly* two weeks away in its orbit from the place it would be closest to Earth. So not only did he accurately predict that he would die when the comet was in the sky, but actually the comet—to the degree—was in the exact same spot for the one and only time in seventy-five years. Now, I think Mark Twain would certainly have wanted you to know that, but given how long I've gone on with this essay, that's probably about the last thing he would have wanted you to know.

Thomas Hardy

(1840–1928)

Usually if you ask an English professor, "Who are the six or seven greatest Victorian novelists?" you get the same answer; it is a well-established canon. Their names: Charles Dickens, William Makepeace Thackeray, Charlotte Brontë, Emily Brontë, Anthony Trollope, George Eliot, and Thomas Hardy. Hardy is always mentioned last because he was born considerably later than the other six and he wrote at the turn of the twentieth century. Given that forty thousand novels were published during the Victorian period, it is impressive enough that he is one of the seven, but that is just the beginning.

Thomas Hardy did not want to spend his life as a novelist. He only wrote novels so he could earn enough money to do what he really wanted to do in life. Was he good at what he really wanted to do? Well, he was very good at it indeed. If you go to college and want to study Thomas Hardy, you have two choices. You can take a course in the Victorian novel, which will end with Thomas Hardy. But the next semester if you decide, "Well, I think I would like to try twentieth-century British poetry, I wonder whom we study in there," you will of course study W. H. Auden, T. S. Eliot, William Butler Yeats, Ezra Pound, A. E. Housman, and

Stephen Spender, but you would not start with any of those poets. All twentieth-century British poetry courses begin with Thomas Hardy. Many critics consider his poetry even finer than his novels. He is the only man or woman we study in college who is found in two different courses, under two different genres, in two different centuries; he is a nineteenth-century British novelist and a twentieth century British poet, and he is equally brilliant in both. Even Shakespeare cannot compete in that manner. And so, in studying Thomas Hardy as a novelist I want to emphasize from the start that you need also to read his poetry.

His life was rather extraordinary and certainly bizarre. If you know his novels, such as *Tess of the d'Urbervilles* or *Jude the Obscure*, you comprehend that this man must have been familiar with the grotesque. Drastic things happen to his characters, and you may surmise where he found his inspiration . . . from his life.

He was born in Dorchester, in southwestern England in the county of Dorset. Hardy's ancestors were all masons and bricklayers. He came from rural lower-class people, long before industrialization made them factory hands. His father's name was also Thomas Hardy, his mother's name was Jemima Hand. They married in 1839 because she was pregnant, and on June 2, 1840, she gave birth to a stillborn son. They put the supposed corpse to one side, and then fortunately, because of the "watchful optimism of the midwife," she noticed that the child was not dead but would survive to become Thomas Hardy.

But because of this near trauma the parents formed no emotional attachment to this child; they did not know if God would take it again. Not until his sister Mary was born two years later did they treat the older child as something that would live and be part of the family. So he received no nurturing in those cold first two years. If you love Hardy's works, you know that there is no more detached, omniscient, and in many ways cruel narration in the history of the novel than the third-person, omniscient narration of Thomas Hardy. That detached, capricious, godlike presence must have had its beginnings in those early years.

Thomas Hardy's father was lazy; he did not really do much, did not ever want to do much. But Hardy's mother was an incredibly ambitious woman on behalf of her son. If you have ever read D. H. Lawrence's *Sons and Lovers*, the father and mother of the hero Paul are exactly like Thomas Hardy's parents: the father alcoholic, the mother driving the son all the time. His mother worshiped Thomas Hardy, perhaps trying to atone for the neglect of the early years. Hardy, in his journal, said an interesting thing—and I think many men can identify with it. His mother wanted to protect him as much as possible from growing up because she wanted to appreciate the childhood so nearly lost. Hardy wrote, "Because of my mother I was a child until sixteen, a youth until twenty-five and a young man until nearly fifty."

Hardy is the great poet and the novelist of rural nature. The description of Egdon Heath at the beginning of *The Return of the Native* is one of the finest descriptions of landscape in literature:

> A Saturday afternoon in November was approaching the time of twilight, and the vast tract of unenclosed wild known as Egdon Heath embrowned itself moment by moment. Overhead the hollow stretch of whitish

cloud shutting out the sky was as a tent which had the whole heath for its floor.

The heaven being spread with this pallid screen and the earth with the darkest vegetation, their meeting-line at the horizon was clearly marked. In such contrast, the heath wore the appearance of an installment of night which had taken up its place before its astronom-ical hour was come: darkness had to a great extent arrived hereon, while day stood distinct in the sky.

The face of the heath by its mere complexion added half an hour to evening; it could in like manner retard the dawn, sadden noon, anticipate the frowning of storms scarcely generated, and intensify the opacity of a moonless midnight to a cause of shaking and dread.

Because Hardy was poor, he traveled on foot or, at best, in a wagon with a slow horse, everywhere. Because of this Hardy said he knew "every twig, every gate, every cottage, and every field in the county."

Above all, because he grew up in the rural class, he was surrounded by macabre tales and gossip. He was an excellent fiddler, as was his father. Together they would fiddle at local events; they heard not only all the local gossip that furnished Hardy with ideas for characters in the future, but they always fiddled to music in ballad form. The ballad form of literature became what Thomas Hardy's novels and many of his poems have as their skeleton.

It is important to understand what a ballad is. As you know, a ballad is never cosmopolitan; it is rural, about country people. It can be about a variety of subjects, but two subjects must be in all classical ballads—love and murder.

Hardy, when asked why love and murder are so ingrained in ballads, replied, "Ballads must be about blood, and since love is the rising of the blood and death is the spilling of the blood, that is the focus of ballads." Rising of the blood, passion, which leads to love, or vice versa, the spilling of the blood, murder. If you consider *Tess of the d'Urbervilles* or any of Hardy's novels, they are ballads stretched out to five hundred pages, and many of his great poems are ballads as well.

Hardy's childhood can only be termed grotesque. He was born alive but thought dead. Later he became interested in science, and when he was nine, his parents gave him a little telescope. He took it outside to look up in the sky or at a distant object to see if it could be brought closer. He saw movement at a barn at some distance that he certainly could not make out with just his normal eyesight, so he thought that would be a good thing to test the new telescope on. He put it up to his eye, focused on the barn, and just at that moment a young farmhand was hanging himself. So his first close-up view through the telescope was of this unfortunate youth swinging, having just broken his neck committing suicide. If you can name a more depressing novelist than Thomas Hardy, I would be surprised; this sort of experience tells you why.

He had very little schooling, perhaps a seventh-grade education. He was not going to be a writer, he was not going to be a poet; he wanted poetry to be what he did for love. He wanted to be an architect, and he became a good one. In his novel *Jude the Obscure*, Jude is an architect, just as Charlotte Brontë's Jane Eyre is a governess because this is what she knew. Hardy was apprenticed to an architect who specialized in rebuilding and restoring churches from the twelfth, thirteenth, and fourteenth centuries. The medieval period, both its grotesqueness and its beauty, fascinated Hardy as he was learning how to restore ancient churches.

Not a lot of money was to be made by restoring churches, but it seemed a worthwhile profession. Hardy went to London when he was twenty-one, convinced he would never return to Dorset. I would not be writing about him today had this happened, but fortunately for readers his stay in London was not productive. He was lonely. He tried to stick it out for six agonizing years, but he eventually knew he could not live in London. He also knew church architecture was not really what he wanted to do. He returns home at twenty-seven as a failure and moves in with his parents.

Moving in with an alcoholic father and a mother with a miserable husband and no place to go was difficult. Hardy's emotions, particularly concerning women, were tangled. Though very physically attracted to women, he was not, in terms of physical appearance, a Romeo. He was frustrated by urges that could never be fulfilled.

If you read his journals at this point—depressed, he tried to take a few day trips just to get away from his parents—they are interesting in the honesty of what he observed about women. One of his journal entries, when he was twenty-eight, reads, "Went to Lolworth on a steamboat. There was a woman on a paddlebox's steps near me, all laughter, white feathers, hat, brown dress, Dorset dialect, short upper lip, a woman I would have married offhand on the spot, probably with disastrous results." Throughout his entire life he was falling in love with women he glimpsed on streetcars, trains, and tops of buses—any public conveyance seemed to get Thomas Hardy excited if an attractive woman was attached to it.

Hardy loved to write poetry, but he knew he could not make a living as a poet. He decided to write a novel to earn enough money to allow him to be a poet. The first novel he wrote, which no one ever reads now, was about a poor man and a wealthy lady, a lady who would not return his love. He called it *The Poor Man and the Lady*. The novel's problem was not its depiction of the poor man; Hardy got him down exactly. But Hardy knew absolutely nothing about upper-class ladies. What he wanted to do in the novel was satirize upper-class manners and show how hostile wealthy people are to the poor. It was a valid idea, but to do it the author had better know something about the class he is satirizing. Hardy did not; he sent the manuscript to Macmillan's, and it was immediately rejected.

He wrote another novel, a better one called *Desperate Remedies*. He recognized his limitations at satirizing society, so *Desperate Remedies* was a sensationalist novel with murder, abductions, illegitimate children, sexuality bubbling beneath. It was rejected too, but with some encouragement along the lines of "Shape it up a bit better, there is excitement here but there is not art, resubmit it." He resubmitted it and it was published—anonymously. That was fine with Hardy; he understood that the publisher was attempting to avert personalized attacks should the public find the book too violent.

Unfortunately Hardy was the most thin-skinned of novelists, and believe me, most novelists, Dickens and Thackeray included, hated criticism. But they took it well compared to Thomas Hardy. He never wanted to hear anything negative about any of his poetry or novels. He almost quit as a novelist because he was so sensitive. There had been no reviews of the novel because it was not important enough—but as he was catching a train about nine months later, there in a wagon, under a sign saying "Remaindered and Cheap," were copies of *Desperate Remedies*. He was appalled. Even though his name was not on it, he was devastated that his book could hardly be given away. This incident almost cost us the great novelist Thomas Hardy, but he wanted to write poetry desperately and knew because there was no money in it that he had to keep going.

Since *Desperate Remedies* obviously was not selling well, Hardy had to return to restoring old churches in Dorset. One day he was sent to an old church, and when he knocked at the door expecting to see the curate or the vicar, the door opened and on the other side was a young woman, Emma Gifford. She was the rector's sister-in-law, and a conspiracy was afoot. The rector did not really want Hardy to restore the church, but he had heard Hardy was young, and not married. Poor Emma Gifford was not going anywhere on the marriage market, so the rector had sent for Hardy and arranged to have Emma Gifford open the door. She was twenty-nine, intelligent, but possessed of a rather scattered nervous energy.

When she opened the door, she saw Thomas Hardy, a bookish, pale, little, balding man, and she decided this man would be her husband. As you will discover, it was not a good marriage from start to finish, and yet Thomas Hardy was a sentimentalist about women. If you visit his home today in Dorset, you will see on his desk a calendar that is set on March 7. It is not his birthday. It is not his death day. March 7 was the day Emma Gifford opened that door, and for the rest of his life to honor their meeting he kept his calendar on March 7, a very touching gesture (particularly when you learn more about Emma).

Before they got married, Thomas Hardy figured out what he needed to do to sell a novel: do not write about the upper classes, do not write about abductions and illegitimate children. He did not know about that at all. What he knew backward and forward was rural life. Up to then only George Eliot had portrayed rural life. Hardy was far more rural than she was. She was at least from dairy-farm people, with a father who had worked for a squire. Thomas Hardy was from a completely different sort of menial people. And so at thirty-two, in 1872, he wrote *Under the Greenwood Tree*, his first rural novel. It was a modest but firm success. The next year he wrote *Far From the Madding Crowd*, the novel that made him a notable Victorian author. It was popular and thrust him up, not at the Dickens, Thackeray, George Eliot level, but right below it.

On the strength of these two novels Hardy had enough money to marry; he and Emma married right after the publication of *Far From the Madding Crowd*. They were not at all compatible, as is clear from their journals, even the journals kept on their honeymoon. If you read Thomas Hardy's journals, you find thoughts about whatever city they might be visiting, rather abstract, rather intellectual, very interesting. If you open up Emma's journals, they too are full. But the only things Emma put in her honeymoon journal were complete menus from every dinner at every hotel they visited. On the one hand you have abstract thoughts about Scotland and Ireland, and on the other hand you have four entrées, two desserts, and a starter.

They never had any children. We are not sure why, but we do know that Hardy was peculiar. He could not stand to be touched by anyone. If he was touched, he shrank back as if, one person who touched him said, "an electric jolt had been sent through his body." What he loathed—because he was small, five feet six—was when a larger man put an arm around his shoulder. As he put it in his journal, "the condescending air of a larger person thinking he has a larger soul, trying to console a smaller person who he thinks has a smaller soul."

In 1877 he becomes immortal in the Victorian novel by writing *The Return of the Native*. If you have not read it or if you were forced to read it at too young an age, you need to read it. And then something terribly exciting happened to Hardy. It sounds at first so dull. He loved Dorset, his home county, and he wanted to know everything about it. In 1878 he visits what we would call a library, though there were no public libraries until 1891. It was the repository of the archaeological and sociological history of the county. He came across a journal called *The Dorset County Chronicle*, which had been published weekly since 1826. It related everything about every acre, practically, of Dorset. This gave him an idea—why not set the rest of his fiction in a particular locale of Dorset that had never existed?

He decided to call his imaginary setting Wessex. There is no Wessex on the map; it existed only in Hardy's mind. The county seat would be called Casterbridge. Thus by re-creating the actual past, but putting it in a place that never existed, Hardy was creating something that many twentieth-century novelists adopted. Probably the greatest twentieth-century American novelist is William Faulkner, and if you think that his Yoknapatawpha County just came to him full bloom, it did not. He got the idea for it from two authors, Thomas Hardy and Anthony Trollope, who invented Barsetshire. Hardy's idea was brilliant and freeing—he could put everything about the past and the present, all the universal truths of human experience, into a place where no one could protest, "How dare you use this town and talk about my dead ancestors this way!"

The first Wessex novel is *The Mayor of Casterbridge*. Casterbridge, of course, is rural because Dorset is rural and Wessex is Dorset. Hardy thought, "What if I put a mythological person, a man of such power . . ." He made Michael Hinshard the mayor of the title, a combination of Oedipus Rex, King Lear, and Samuel from the Bible. Hardy put this strong archetypal figure in the middle of Dorset/Wessex, in the town of Casterbridge, and he gave him all of the qualities that mild Thomas Hardy lacked. He made Hinshard ambitious, authoritative, vigorous, violent, and sexually aggressive. And it worked. People had never read anything like it. It was classical Greek tragedy set in their backyard.

His wife, Emma, though, was jealous. Now that Hardy had become famous, Emma could not understand why she was not achieving anything herself. They did stay together. A plain woman when she married, she became plainer as she aged, while here was Thomas Hardy, full of passion that spills into his novels. Emma loved cats—cats everywhere. Hardy liked dogs, and he was not enamored of cats, particularly since Emma gave her cats names that she insisted Hardy call them. Her favorite cat was Kiddeley-wink-em-poops. Hardy refused—he would not call the cat by that name. He said, "Could I call it by a nickname? Trot." Emma also insisted that if a kitten was born, Hardy was not allowed to wear shoes in the house for the first two months, because the shoes might crush the kitten if he did not see it. So Hardy went barefoot in his own home for two months just to please Emma.

He was, perhaps understandably, unfaithful to Emma. He was very unfaithful to Emma, yet he never had an affair. How? He imagined Tess, of *Tess of the d'Urbervilles;* he created the sensual Arabella Allan in *Jude the Obscure.* He invented all sorts of beautiful and sexually charged females—and he made love to them through his novels, through his male characters. It was an extremely healthy and extremely prosperous way to express his yearnings without straying from the marriage. He could imagine anyone he wanted, and this eased his marital captivity.

From 1891 until 1895 he wrote *Tess of the d'Urbervilles, Jude the Obscure,* and *The Mayor of Casterbridge,* his three major works. And he could only get better. But in 1895 something happened that led Hardy to say he would never write another novel. There was a circulating library in England, Mudie's, named after a tiny bookstore in Bloomsbury in London that a Mr. Bede had started in 1842. Bede had the good idea of charging an annual fee to join his private circulating library; for that fee you could borrow the popular three-volume novels, however many you wanted, over and over. His idea paid well because middle-class people who could not afford the expensive novels, who could only afford Dickens in cheap paper versions, could get what they wanted and then return it.

Bede had a monopoly eventually. By the time Hardy started to write, any aspiring novelist had to sell to Bede. He would buy three hundred copies of the novel and put them in his own yellow bindings that said *Bede* on the outside, so the novel became an advertisement—it was seen as a Bede novel. So, novelists could not afford to write something that Mr. Bede did not like. Novelists in the Victorian period had to kowtow to Bede because he purchased large quantities and then spread them throughout England. He made a fortune on it and eventually the author did too, so everyone was happy. But since Bede lived during the Victorian period, a novel's suggestive subject matter might prompt letters from irate fathers or clergymen saying, "How dare you sanction a novel where these two people run off together doing goodness knows what before they are married!" Bede began to insist to his authors that if they wanted to be Bede novelists, they had to adhere to high moral standards in their writing. And most gave in, because they could not fight Bede's popularity.

But Bede met his match in Thomas Hardy. Bede immediately expressed disapproval of *Tess of the d'Urbervilles*, which is a vividly sensual novel, and he insisted that Hardy revise it. One scene in particular he objected to. Hardy had created a man named Angel Clare. He was the most handsome man in the dairy where Tess worked. Three different women, Tess and two other dairymaids, fell in love with him; all they thought of day and night was Angel Clare. There is a scene when the four of them go to church on Sunday morning, handsome Angel and the three beautiful women. They walk down toward the church, but there had been a big rainstorm, which flooded the stream. The gushing water had destroyed the bridge and the four were not going to be able to get across, though it was only a narrow stream. Angel's solution is to carry each girl in his arms safely to the other side.

It is a sensual scene, each woman being carried by her dream man. Hardy described what they were thinking when Angel carries them across and how disappointed they were when they reached the other side. Bede said, "This is filthy and must go." Hardy demurred, "It will not go, it is central to the plot." Bede said, "No, you do not have to remove it from the novel. I have read enough novels; I have come up with how you should revise it. All you need to do is, when they come to that little stream, you have Angel Clare say, 'What are we to do?' Then, he could look to his left or right and say, 'Ha, a wheelbarrow,' have him get the wheelbarrow, put each of the women in one at a time, and wheel them across." You can guess what such a change would do to the romantic nature of Hardy's scene. Hardy refused. Amazingly, the public followed Hardy; they did not want his work changed. And within three years of Hardy's defiance of Bede, Bede was gone, out of business.

Jude the Obscure is so peculiar, and so antireligious, that a bishop of Wakefield had a public burning of the book thirteen months after Hardy's confrontation with Bede. Hardy, burdened by the criticism, and by his unhappy marriage, had had enough. He hated the publicity, he did not want to be associated with it, and so he vowed he would never write a novel again. In 1895 he stopped and turned to writing poetry.

He was a brilliant poet. He became so recognized for his poems that at the turn of the century he was offered a knighthood. This is what Emma had always wanted; to be Lady Hardy would be her ultimate fulfillment. Hardy turned the honor down, and Emma died not long after. The cause was a heart attack, but really it was a broken heart, broken and frustrated. Hardy was not a public man who liked public recognition.

A female secretary, Florence Dugdale, worked for Hardy and had been friendly with Emma. Florence admired Hardy tremendously. We do not know what he would have thought about her had she had a different personality, but she was perfect for Thomas Hardy's temperament because she was extremely depressed most of the time. They married a year and a half after Emma's death.

Hardy was by now almost seventy, still writing poems. World War I broke out and became a sad source for his poetry. The modern world was coming in and Hardy tried to adjust to it. There is a long diary entry for the day he received his telephone.

In 1920 he turned eighty, a grand old man of literature. To live to be eighty years old, having been born in 1840, and to be regarded as a brilliant novelist and poet, is something praiseworthy. He was honored everywhere on his eightieth birthday, and poets, the ones who would after World War I become major names in English poetry, came to sit at Hardy's feet. He would have them over to the house and they would talk of poetic theory, of modern poetry, of what it was like in the eighties and nineties of the last century when he was writing novels.

Poor Emma would have loved this. Money was plentiful; people who read Hardy's poetry discovered that he was also a novelist and bought all the novels. The people who had read him as a novelist learned he was a brilliant poet; people who would never buy poetry bought his because they loved

Hardy as a novelist. And he was the first author to make significant money from film rights. In the 1920s the movie studios, particularly in England, were desperate for stories that were gripping and, better yet, rather depressive. Hardy was their man. They made movies of *Tess of the d'Urbervilles*, *Jude the Obscure*, and *Return of the Native*. The films did so well that the film scripts were adapted for the stage.

Tess of the d'Urbervilles in particular was every stage actress's dream. One of the great stage actresses in England was Gertrude Bugler. She was a beautiful young woman and a brilliant actress, and the Haymarket Theater, probably the most prestigious in England, wanted to put on *Tess of the d'Urbervilles* and make Gertrude its star. Hardy had to approve her as the choice for Tess. He not only approved her, he fell in love with her. The first time he saw her was when he went up to Haymarket. She was late for the appointment, and, wouldn't you know it, she was on a public conveyance rushing there. He saw her feathers in the distance, and it was love at first sight.

He was not allowed in at the rehearsals; they did not want a sensitive novelist looking over their shoulders at how his work was being adapted. But he loved Gertrude so much—he was eighty-four and she could not have been thirty—he stood outside the theater during the rehearsals just to be on the street where she was. Hardy's wife did not take this well at all. She went to the theater a couple of weeks before the play opened and confronted Gertrude, telling her that if she played Tess, the Hardys would be ruined. And Gertrude withdrew from the play. Tess was a part actresses would die for, but she was so touched that Florence would humiliate herself in front of this "other woman" who really was not an other woman except in Hardy's mind, that she agreed to relinquish the role.

Hardy brought out a volume of verses in 1925 called *Winter Words*. It is excellent poetry. The most remarkable thing about *Winter Words* is that when it was published, Hardy was eighty-five years old and these were all new poems. It is one thing to collect a poet's works at eighty-five. Most of us, if we live that long, would not have the energy to go through the old poems and figure out what to include, but Hardy was writing new poems.

On the last day of his life, in the morning, he asked the maid Eva to please get a rasher of bacon, bring it up to his bedroom, and grill it in the fireplace, a peculiar request. She complied and asked him why. And weakly from the bed he answered, "My first memory is the smell of my mother grilling bacon for me in my bedroom." He wanted to come full circle. As she was grilling, he rose up from the bed and looked behind Eva. He started to raise his arm and said, "Eva, what is that?" As she turned, he died. She was convinced it was death he was staring at.

He was buried in Westminster Abbey. To emphasize what a tribute this was to Hardy, let me say no novelist since Charles Dickens had been buried in the Abbey, and no poet since Alfred, Lord Tennyson. No one else in the history of Westminster Abbey was buried as a poet and a novelist. Actually, they only buried most of him in Westminster Abbey. People noticed that the local vicar, after the service, stood there with a biscuit tin. He was asked what was in the biscuit tin. It was Hardy's heart. He had asked that if he was buried in Westminster Abbey, his heart be removed and buried with Emma in the churchyard. Was it guilt? Was it because the second marriage to Florence was unsatisfactory? Whatever the reason, you have to admire a man who has his heart buried next to the wife who caused much pain in his life, a man who insisted that the date of March 7, the date they met, be constantly on his desk as it is today.

To put a seal on Thomas Hardy's literary stature, let me share a list of the pallbearers at his funeral:

Sir Stanley Baldwin; James Barrie, who wrote *Peter Pan;* John Galsworthy; A. E. Housman; Rudyard Kipling; and George Bernard Shaw—impressive company at the last hour for a man sprung from England's rural class.

250

Sir Arthur Conan Doyle

(1859–1930)

I would like to quote to you something Sir Arthur Conan Doyle said, because I think it is significant: "If in one hundred years I am only known as the man who invented Sherlock Holmes, then I will have considered my life a failure." Well, unfortunately for Doyle, I do not think there is anyone who when you mention his name thinks of anything *other* than Sherlock Holmes. Few of us would call it a failure to have invented such a world-famous character, but unfortunately Doyle did, so desperate was he to be known for so much more than Sherlock Holmes.

Let me tell you a few details about his life that will show you how Doyle came to invent such a memorable detective. First of all, quite a few people forget Doyle was a Scot. A good part of his life was spent in England, but he was born on May 22, 1859, in the middle of the Victorian period, in Edinburgh and was reared there. Edinburgh turned out a good city to be born in if one was going to invent a detective who would look beneath surfaces and see the unsavory side of people who seemed respectable. Edinburgh was just that type of city; on the outside it looked beautiful and quite genteel, but underneath it was a seething den of vice and poverty. If you turned down some of the side streets of

Edinburgh when Doyle was growing up, you would find filth, corruption, decay, smallpox; stranglings and knifings were rampant. A man from England visited Edinburgh the very year in which Doyle was born, and he wrote back to his wife a description of the city: "Edinburgh reminds me of a grand duchess with gonorrhea." A vivid image, and it is indeed what we think of as Edinburgh in the middle of the 1800s: beautiful on the outside, corrupt within.

Doyle's home life as a child was not good. His father, to put it quite bluntly, was a failure. Charles Doyle was the youngest son of a famous family; his father and his brothers were brilliant artists and illustrators, so good that they had worked with Charles Dickens and William Makepeace Thackeray on their novels. Unfortunately Charles was not gifted that way. He was emotionally distant, with a great sense of inferiority; he felt himself a failure and certainly became one.

Doyle's mother, whose maiden name was Mary Foley, married Charles Doyle at seventeen. She was obsessed with the notion that her family could trace its roots all the way back to the Plantagenet kings, so she always believed she came from royalty. In her mind she had clearly fallen on very hard times by marrying Charles Doyle. To compensate she distanced herself from her life. She was always reading stories written by Sir Walter Scott about the early great days of Scotland, stories about chivalry and romance. She was so in love with the Arthurian legend—King Arthur, Queen Guinevere—that she named Arthur Conan Doyle for the mythical King Arthur.

So Doyle grew up in this strange, shabby, genteel family where the father could not do anything right and the mother had reverted into the world of damsels in distress being saved by knights in shining armor. If you think about it, Doyle would invent a detective who often had damsels in distress come to his door, and in his own way Sherlock Holmes would be the modern knight in shining armor, dashing off to rescue, through his brains, these helpless maidens.

Arthur as a boy was big, burly, broad-shouldered, and because his mother had trained him from an early age to be chivalrous, on the playground at school he would beat up the bullies. On the other hand, when he came home from school in the afternoon he would weep over novels such as *Ivanhoe* or the death of Little Nell in Charles Dickens's *Old Curiosity Shop*.

Meanwhile, he sought to escape his off-kilter family. Both the mother and the father made his life miserable in different ways, and he decided he would certainly not go into architecture or anything artistic like his father—he would go into medicine. He studied medicine at the University of Edinburgh, and when he graduated at twenty, he became a ship's surgeon. He left Scotland and set up his medical practice in England. He did not know anyone in England; he did not even know where to set up his practice. He decided to move to Portsmouth, on the south coast, to begin his career.

He picked Portsmouth because it was the birthplace of his favorite author, Charles Dickens. It is a lovely reason romantically, but it was a stupid reason practically. It is risky to open up a practice in a town where you know no one, just because you like an author who was born there, and Doyle certainly suffered for his choice. He had no connections and therefore no patients. He put out his shingle, to no effect. So to pass the time while he was waiting for patients who never came, he wrote stories. Not detective stories, as you might think—he wrote horror stories. He wrote about ghosts and ghoulies and the kind of spirits found in Scottish homes, stories told to him as a child. But he still received no patients.

One day, a middle-aged man showed up at his door and Doyle was delighted. He took him into the examining room, where the man sat, saying nothing. Finally the man cleared his throat—nothing else. Then the man cleared his throat again. Using his powers of deduction, Doyle asked him, "Bronchial trouble, I assume?" And the man said, "I was hoping I would not have to say it, sir, but I have come to collect on the gas meter." But shortly after that, right outside Doyle's front door on the street, a horse fell on a wealthy pedestrian. And although the pedestrian was not Doyle's patient, the pedestrian could not actually get up and move anywhere, so Doyle treated him. As he said later, "I ate for a week off of that horse falling."

However, he could not count on horses falling on people right in front of his door for a medical practice. Just as he was about to leave the medical profession in despair, a widow who had come to Portsmouth on holiday came to his rescue. She had a son and a daughter; the son had meningitis, and because she did not know any doctors in Portsmouth, she brought him to Doyle to be treated. Although the young man did die, Doyle took great care of the young man and made his last days painless. It was a turning point for Doyle—not in his medical profession, but because the sister of the young man who died, Louise, fell in love with him and he returned her love.

Ironically, once they married, his business began to thrive. He did not realize just how good for business it was that he

had married Louise. Now that he was married, all the families who had young women in them, who had been looking
for a family doctor but would never pick Doyle when he was
a bachelor, sent the whole family to be treated.

With his business thriving and his married life happy and
settled, Doyle decided to stop writing the horror stories that
had reflected his unhappy bachelor mood. He turned to
writing detective stories and immediately invented a detective named Sherringford Hope. Louise, ever polite to her
husband, informed him that such a character was not going
anywhere in fiction with such a dreadful name. Doyle dutifully changed the last name of the detective from Hope to
Holmes because at about this time the great criminal psy-
chologist and jurist, Oliver Wendell Holmes, published the
first book on criminal psychology. And he took the name
Sherlock from his favorite musician, a famous violinist
named Alfred Sherlock.

Doyle began writing stories about Sherlock Holmes, but
he was unused to writing fiction of quality. He had really just
written horror stories before, which were hardly realistic; he
did not even know how to describe Sherlock Holmes. He
could not picture him vividly enough in his imagination, so
he simply decided to give Holmes a purple dressing gown,
luxurious slippers, and a pipe. These accoutrements have, of
course, stuck with Sherlock Holmes from the first story on—
and Doyle invented them because Doyle himself, when he
was finished with patients, always put on a purple dressing
gown and slippers and smoked a pipe. Then he had the inspiration to invent for Sherlock Holmes a sidekick, John
Watson, a doctor.

Actually Doyle had broken up his own personality into

two different characters. He gave Watson all the medical skill that Doyle possessed, and he gave Sherlock Holmes all the deductive skills that Doyle had always been proud of in himself. As you notice, he always put Watson and Sherlock Holmes together. They live side by side, almost like a married couple, and this is because they are one personality, Doyle's, split into two. He makes sure only Holmes and his detections stimulate Watson, and Holmes is only stimulated by crime—an easy way to slip into all the ensuing adventures.

In March of 1886 a snowstorm raged in Portsmouth. For three weeks no one could get out and around, so Doyle had no patients at all come to see him. While he was stuck in his office with nothing to do, he began his first Sherlock Holmes adventure. He called it *A Study in Scarlet*, and he brilliantly decided on the most offbeat plot possible. *A Study in Scarlet* is about, of all things, Mormons in the state of Utah—something no one would ever expect. When he finished the story, he rolled it up in a cardboard cylinder and sent it off to a publisher. It came back rejected. He sent it off again; it was rejected again. And what depressed Doyle so much was that when he opened the returned cylinder, he noticed that no one had even flattened out the manuscript; it had been rejected without being read.

But the next year *A Study in Scarlet* appeared in the most unlikely place. In the 1880s publishers traditionally published Christmas annuals, ornate magazines full of sugarplum fairy stories appropriate for the season. In 1887 the publisher of *Beaton's Christmas Annual* was desperate for more material, and when Doyle's Sherlock Holmes piece was sent to him, he decided to put it in the annual. It had no effect on the public at all; Sherlock Holmes was not a phenomenon overnight. One reason for the lack of enthusiasm for this very good Sherlock Holmes adventure was probably the illustrations that accompanied it. Doyle had sent in illustrations that pictured Holmes as a plump, foppish, rather stupid-looking man. It was totally wrong for the character of Sherlock Holmes. Why would Doyle choose such terrible illustrations? Sadly, the illustrator of that first story was none other than his father, Charles Doyle, who was by now in a mental institution. An alcoholic, he had broken down entirely. Doyle felt so sorry for his father that to give him something to do, he sent him that first Holmes story to illustrate. The illustrations were so terrible that most people probably looked at them and decided not even to read the story when it appeared in *Beaton's Christmas Annual*.

Doyle was convinced that he was not a great detective-fiction writer. He decided what he really wanted to be known for was writing historical novels. He wrote a novel called *Micah Clark*, which took place in the seventeenth century. The one review it received said, "This novel's principal defect is a complete and utter absence of any interest whatsoever." You would assume that when Doyle read this, it would warn him that he should probably not write historical fiction; but it did not, he kept at it.

One day a Philadelphia publisher, one of the few who had read the first Sherlock Holmes mystery story and liked it, approached Doyle in Portsmouth. He gave a dinner for Doyle and another young author, Oscar Wilde, and he proposed to each that he write something brilliant and give it to him to publish. Indeed, Oscar Wilde then wrote *The Picture of Dorian Gray* for this publisher. And Doyle, deciding to give Sherlock Holmes one more try, wrote the second Sherlock Holmes story, *The Sign of Four*, written in 1889. And what's remarkable about *The Sign of Four*, even today, is that early in the story Doyle has Sherlock Holmes injecting cocaine into his veins. Here was a detective who was not only brilliant but also vulnerable. This vulnerability made Holmes's personality absolutely riveting. But even this story did not make Sherlock Holmes famous; it too was ignored and did not give Doyle any kind of remuneration or fame.

Meanwhile, Doyle's medical practice in Portsmouth had fallen way off, and he and his wife decided new steps needed to be taken. Sherlock Holmes seemed to be going nowhere, no one cared for the historical novels, and Doyle felt he must stick with medicine. A new specialty was developing at this time, ophthalmology, the study of the eye. But to become an ophthalmologist, one had to go to Austria for six months for study. Louise and Arthur Conan Doyle decided to go to Austria so he could become this new kind of physician and perhaps earn a better income. When they returned from Austria, they decided to open his ophthalmology practice in London. Doyle rented an office directly across the street from the British Museum, thinking this would be a good location. It was indeed an amazing practice—amazingly nonexistent. According to Doyle, not one patient came to see him. Discouraged, he felt that he really would have to make a career of writing.

This was the turning point of his life, because right when he opened his ophthalmology practice, a new magazine made its debut. Called *The Strand Magazine*, it was the first mass-market publication, a glossy magazine with photographs—photography was still fairly new, even in the 1890s—on every page. Basically the magazine was a series of interviews with celebrities of the day, going into their homes, getting pictures, relating intimate scenes with fashionable folk whom people were interested in. It was the *People* magazine of the 1890s, and it was hugely successful. But the editors of *The Strand* decided that what would really capture the public's imagination was a serial, a series of short stories with a recurring character. They had read Doyle's two Sherlock Holmes stories, and they asked him to submit more Holmes exploits as a possible serial. Doyle, knowing how important this commission was to his career, wrote two Sherlock Holmes stories in less than two weeks. He sent them in and the editors loved them. They also understood that the illustrations for the Sherlock Holmes stories would be terribly important—so important that although they paid Arthur Conan Doyle thirty guineas for his stories, they paid the illustrator twenty.

The illustrator they found, Walter Paget, was the perfect choice. Rather than showing Sherlock Holmes as Doyle had thought of him—tall, ugly, and rather gawky—Paget said, "Absolutely not. We need to make him sexually attractive to women, an 1890s dandy. I am going to draw a Sherlock Holmes that all the women will yearn for and all the men will want to emulate in his flawless tailoring," and that is exactly how he drew him. The stories came out, the illustrations were brilliant, and Sherlock Holmes became wildly, wildly famous. In a quixotic turn of timing, when the Sherlock Holmes stories started to come out in *The Strand Magazine*, Jack the Ripper was at his height in London. Here was this murderous monster roaming the streets of London, killing women, and here was Sherlock Holmes in fiction ingeniously solving crimes.

The success of Sherlock Holmes was so immense that Doyle knew he could give up his medical practice. He still spent hours researching events that he wanted to turn into historical fiction, but he was also furiously writing Sherlock Holmes stories because he knew they would sell. He did two series of Sherlock Holmes stories—two series of twelve in less than two years. If you are familiar with the intricacies of the Sherlock Holmes stories, you are no doubt amazed Doyle could write twenty-four of them in such a short period.

His wife, Louise, contracted tuberculosis, what they called consumption back then. Even though Doyle was trained as a doctor, he did not catch the symptoms of his wife's illness because he was so busy writing the Sherlock Holmes stories. Because he was so pressed, and because his wife was so ill, he began to hate the character he had invented. Sherlock Holmes was taking over all of his time, and he blamed his creation for his wife's illness; he felt if he had had more time to spend with her, he could have caught her symptoms much earlier. They traveled to Switzerland for treatment. In Switzerland, they toured a place called Reichenbach Falls, a vast waterfall with its bottom a boiling pit of water and ice. It looked like a whirlpool or a maelstrom down below. This scenery so impressed Doyle that he decided he was going to kill off Sherlock Holmes and get rid of him once and for all. This story, called *The Final Problem*, would come out in *The Strand Magazine* in 1893. Sherlock Holmes and his arch-enemy, Moriarty, would fight to the death and both of them would plunge over Reichenbach Falls. The *Strand* editor begged Doyle to reconsider, because Sherlock Holmes's death would be disastrous for the magazine.

Sure enough, *The Final Problem* was published, and as the editor feared, twenty thousand people canceled their subscriptions in protest. Young men actually wore black silk bands, a sign of mourning, on their hats on the streets of London as protest against the death of Holmes. The Prince of Wales, Queen Victoria's son, an avid Sherlock Holmes fan, wrote the magazine saying how upset he was that Holmes was dead. But Doyle did not care. He was only thirty-four. He had made a great deal of money on the Holmes saga, enough so that he had the luxury of continuing to write what he really wanted to, historical novels.

His wife did survive this first bout with consumption. Doyle, however, fell in love with another woman, Jean Lecky, in her twenties. But his mother had taught him the duties of chivalry, and even though he loved this other woman, writing her daily for ten years, it never went beyond that.

By 1901, eight years after he had killed off Holmes, even Doyle began to have second thoughts about it because his other novels were failures. The public was still eager for more Holmes, and now that enough time had passed, Doyle started to reconsider. A theater producer asked Doyle to write a play about Sherlock Holmes. Doyle pointed out that he could not, Holmes was dead. The producer wisely pointed out that Holmes could have had many earlier adventures that had never been brought to light. Doyle thought this was not a bad idea, and he wanted to try his hand as a playwright, and so he wrote a play based on one of Holmes's earlier adventures, "The Adventure of the Empty

House." This play is famous today not because it was good, but because one of the young boys hired to be one of the Baker Street Irregulars was a twelve-year-old who had had no stage experience before. His name was Charlie Chaplin.

The play went so well that in 1902 Doyle decided to bring out another adventure, this one in the form of a long story featuring Sherlock Holmes. To me, and to most critics, it is the best thing he ever wrote, *The Hound of the Baskervilles*, which caused a sensation throughout England and Europe. Even Doyle now saw it had been a mistake to have killed off Holmes, and he agreed to write further adventures. The former Prince of Wales, now King Edward VII, was so pleased that, on the strength of *The Hound of the Baskervilles* and the promise of more Holmes, he knighted Doyle.

As Sir Arthur Conan Doyle, he embarked upon further Sherlock Holmes cases. If you read these later stories, you notice that the clientele, the people who hire Sherlock Holmes, are much wealthier than before. Doyle, with all the money pouring in, had become much wealthier himself, with friends and social acquaintances from a much higher class.

Sherlock Holmes had by 1903 taken on mythic proportions. Letters poured into Baker Street, since that was Holmes's address. People knew there was no real Sherlock Holmes, but they wrote letters asking him to solve problems in their lives. Doyle thought this was so delightful that he would take some of the more interesting letters and answer them as Holmes. My favorite is one a woman wrote: "Dear Mr. Holmes: Can you help me? I have lost recently a brush, some golf balls, a dictionary, a bootjack, and many tin cans, and I can not imagine who has stolen them." Doyle wrote back, as Sherlock Holmes: "Madame, why don't you check to see if your neighbor recently purchased a goat. Sincerely, Sherlock Holmes." Indeed, the neighbor *had* purchased a goat and the goat had eaten all of the items.

At this time Doyle's wife, Louise, died. He now married Jean, the woman he had been in love with for ten years. Arthur Conan Doyle was such a gentleman that he waited exactly thirteen months after Louise had died, to mourn her, before remarrying.

World War I broke out, and Doyle lost both his son and a brother during the war. England was decimated by this war—so many young men went off to France and died that after the war a new movement caught on that Arthur Conan Doyle, unfortunately, would become close to. The movement was Spiritualism, a religion espousing the existence of a world inhabited by the spirits of the dead that a medium, as a guide, can contact. We all know the stereotype of Spiritualism: people sit around a table, hold hands, and try to communicate with the dead. The table levitates and the medium will claim that he or she is speaking through the voice of the dead. This idea of Spiritualism and its claims for contacting dead relatives became popular in England for the obvious reason: so many families were devastated and in deep mourning from losing their young sons that they would try anything to reach them in the other world. Doyle, because he had lost a brother and a son, devoted himself to Spiritualism. He would travel and talk about Spiritualism; his name became connected with it, and because he was so famous, people tended to listen.

There is a wonderful story about the largest group he

ever addressed, in New York City at Carnegie Hall. The event was sold out since, though people did not so much care about Spiritualism, they certainly cared about meeting the author who had created Sherlock Holmes. In the middle of the meeting, a strange, high-pitched whistle suddenly permeated the air of Carnegie Hall, an eerie, unsettling sound. Doyle became so excited when he heard it, he called out to the audience, "Is this a spirit manifestation?" And a little man from the middle of the audience stood up, red-faced, and said, "No, Sir Arthur, it is just my hearing aid on the blink again." And of course the audience dissolved into laughter. This was printed in the papers and became the sort of thing that made Doyle rather a laughingstock to the public. They resented that he was so involved in this kind of nonsense and was not writing more Sherlock Holmes stories.

Doyle could not get himself detached from Spiritualism, nor did he want to, and thus he tarnished his reputation. For the first time the complete collected tales of Sherlock Holmes were published, and the sales were mediocre. The 1920s, however, saw a rebirth of interest in Sherlock Holmes because the famous actor John Barrymore decided to portray Sherlock Holmes in the movies. Once again the name Holmes was on everyone's lips. Today there are more films about the character Sherlock Holmes than any other character in the history of imaginative literature—158 films that feature Sherlock Holmes.

Doyle died in July 1930. Even his death, and what happened immediately afterward, was marred by his obsession with Spiritualism. His wife, Jean, maintained that Doyle's passing would mark a new stage of Spiritualism. This was the time when airlines were becoming popular and people with money could have their own private planes. Jean had the notion that if you would conduct a séance in a plane, you would already be thousands of feet higher and closer to heaven, to the other world. Right after Doyle died, Jean, accompanied by reporters, went up in a plane to see if she could contact her husband.

The event became a media circus. Jean did not contact her husband. In fact, there was more "interference" at this séance because of all the static from the radio of the plane. Jean decreed this was static from heaven. The fiasco was reported tongue in cheek by the reporters, so even Doyle's death was marred.

Doyle wrote thirty full-length books and numerous short stories, poems, plays, essays, pamphlets. To me, his greatest accomplishment was that he changed the nature of the adventure story once and for all. Before Doyle, an adventure story, the archetypal one, was always about a knight who had a quest and a zest for an adventure, a physical trial. He would ride off on a steed, lured or carried to the adventure in some interesting manner, and would fight evil with the strength of his arms and legs. Physical prowess was required to conquer chaos and restore order. Once Sherlock Holmes entered fiction, however, everything changed. Suddenly you did not have a knight in shining armor as your protector; you had a hyperintelligent dandy, Sherlock Holmes himself. And rather than being introduced to an adventure by some exciting creature—a leprechaun or a witch, as in fairy tales—now you had Holmes simply getting a letter or a telegram, or reading something in a newspaper that interested him. And rather than dashing off to fight evil on a fiery steed, Sherlock Holmes and Dr. Watson took the most prosaic means, public transportation, or sometimes they would walk. Rather than fighting with physical strength, Sherlock Holmes restored order by mentally sifting masses of information that he had accumulated about the crime until he had the solution. In a way, in Sherlock Holmes we have the first living, breathing computer. He restored order intellectually.

Of course the other reason you like to open up a Sherlock Holmes story is because then it will always be 1895, it will always be London at the end of the Victorian period, a far more romantic period than we live in today. Although Arthur Conan Doyle considered it a failure to be remembered for Sherlock Holmes, those of us who love the adventure story will be eternally grateful to him for changing it in such an ingenious way.

D. H. Lawrence

(1885–1930)

D. H. Lawrence wrote novels that movingly plead for sexual liberation and sexual fulfillment; he is probably the greatest writer we have in lyrical descriptions of the ultimate female fantasy of the perfect illicit lover. There is even an adjective that has not yet made the dictionary but has certainly made the literary vocabulary—*Lawrentian*—which means "incredibly sensual." Lawrence was born in 1885; Queen Victoria would rule for another sixteen years, yet this is the author who would obliterate the prudery of the Victorian novel.

Usually the place an author is born is rather significant to what he goes on to write. With D. H. Lawrence it is absolutely crucial. He was born in a place I don't think any of you would know—Eastwood, in England. Eastwood is eight miles from Nottingham, and where Lawrence was born would have been the center of Sherwood Forest in Robin Hood's day, if there had been a Robin Hood. Until 1850, Sherwood Forest was one of the most beautiful, pastoral areas in England. It was paradise, untouched by the hand of man except for agriculture. In 1850 this idyllic landscape vanished with the onset of coal mining. Coal mining always ruins any beautiful landscape, but no area suffered more from it than Sherwood Forest. Heat, noise, confusion, foul air—there were all the components of hell, particularly for people who were used to saying, "I come from Sherwood Forest." Boys were forced to leave school to work in the mines. Mining has nothing to do with D. H. Lawrence's life or how he earned his living—his mother made sure his hands would never be dirty from that—but he would die because he was born there, where the filthy air ruined his lungs, killing him at forty-four.

D. H. Lawrence hated how mining butchered the landscape where he was born, but the foul industry itself inspired him. He was the first novelist to bring a Freudian outlook into literature. He was convinced that, though he was never a coal miner, by growing up seeing all these men going underground clean and coming up filthy, the inner earth taught him, before Freud did, what the unconscious and the subconscious and the inner life are all about: the deeper you go in, the dirtier, more primal you become. So it is a perfect symbol for this most Freudian of novelists that he comes from a place where, deep beneath, was fossilized fire; to him the id in all of us is fossilized fire. We cannot act upon it, we cannot break the laws of society, we cannot have our lust rule us, but it is there, fossilized, yet fire.

Lawrence's father, Arthur, was a miner, but that was not how he made his money. Arthur wasn't ambitious. His own father had been a brilliant boxer, but Arthur didn't want to be a boxer because he had a handsome face and didn't want it ruined. His father had taught him something about boxing that Arthur Lawrence turned into a nice sideline: a dance school. Here was this unusual father who is a miner and teaches dancing, who was good-looking, charming, and rough. The mother—the most important influence, unfortunately, upon D. H. Lawrence—was Lydia Beardsall, who wished all to know that she came from a prosperous Puritan family—but unfortunately of the seventeenth century. By the time she was born 120 years later, her home was the Manchester slums. She hoped to become a teacher and become respectable, but she failed the teacher test and had to take a tedious job in the lace trade that was just catching on in the Midlands.

Both parents came from the working class, but Lydia would never admit it. She was small and sharp-tongued; discipline and cleanliness were everything to D. H. Lawrence's mother. She was obsessed by propriety. They had spent their last shillings getting a good pew at the best church. If they came to church and found some uninformed newcomer actually sitting in the Lawrence pew, Lydia did not stare at that person until the person left: *that* she would consider too lowly. She stared at the minister until he told the trespasser to leave.

Lydia married Arthur in 1875. She liked him because he was rough. She did want to be regarded as middle upper class, but the sexual tension between them attracted her and she could not resist it. He liked her superiority because he came from a line of miners and boxers; he thought it miraculous that someone who came from such a prosperous family would marry him. Ten years later he couldn't stand her because she was so superior, and she couldn't stand him because he was so rough. He was the drunkard, she was the teetotaler. From his mother D. H. Lawrence would get his artistic, ambitious, and disciplined nature. From his father he would inherit intuition, vitality, and the rejection of conventional values. Both parents gave him traits equally valuable, but his entire adult life is a record of rejecting everything his mother stood for and taking up with a passion everything his father stood for.

D. H. Lawrence was born September 11, 1885. He was an unwanted infant because neither parent at this point cared for the other, and they certainly didn't want this fourth child. His actual name is David Herbert; for his entire life he was known as Bert. He was sickly as a young boy. He contracted bronchitis, which became chronic due to the foul air of the mines. His mother kept him sheltered, away from anything she considered rough. Above all she spent the early years stifling his normal sexual impulses as they became apparent, because she felt her life had been ruined when her sexual impulses led her to marry unsuitably. All the boy's love and affection she wanted for herself.

He was the first person from his town to get a scholarship and go to Nottingham High School. Had his mother not negotiated that, he would have been in the mines at thirteen, even with the bronchitis; she pushed him to work hard enough to pass the exams to get the scholarship. He had to take the train at seven o'clock every morning to get to school; he was not home until seven o'clock every evening. Thanks to his mother, he was disciplined and made a success. After graduation his mother did not want him to have anything to do with mining, so she found him a job at a manufacturer of surgical appliances and artificial limbs. He sorted the mail and copied letters; it was clean, it was safe. But he contracted pneumonia and became deathly ill. His mother nursed him back to health, but he was too weak for any job except teaching.

He hated teaching, but he went to school to train as a secondary teacher. I mention this because of his contemporaries in British literature—all of them seem to have become teachers: H. G. Wells, James Joyce, Thomas Huxley, George Orwell, W. H. Auden, C. Day-Lewis, T. S. Eliot, Evelyn Waugh. Notice the abundance of initials instead of first and middle names. These were men who were quite insecure in choosing professions as passive and almost feminine as teaching and writing at the turn of the twentieth century—a century that demanded its bright young men choose law, medicine, or business. Perhaps these authors thought that using their initials gave them a more professional presence. But only D. H. Lawrence trained as a teacher. The others went into it because they were lazy or needed a little side income while they were writing, but Lawrence actually thought he was going to make teaching his career.

He was not much to look at by the age of twenty. He was thin and rather unattractive because he was pigeon-chested and pale due to recurring bronchitis. He had had no experience with women, thanks to his mother, until he met Alice Dacks, a radical feminist who was estranged from her husband. She took an interest in D. H. Lawrence, and his first sexual experience was with Mrs. Dacks when he was twenty-two. She wrote: "I gave Bert sex; I had to. He was over at our house struggling with a poem he couldn't finish, so I took him upstairs and gave him sex. He came downstairs and finished that verse in twenty-five minutes."

He then fell in love with a young woman named Jesse, who loved him back. They tried sex, unsuccessfully. She was the first to truly believe in him. She urged Lawrence to break with his mother, which he could not do, and she begged him at least to send his poetry—poetry he had been writing from the age of sixteen—to a magazine. But D. H. Lawrence feared rejection and refused. Jesse, on the sly, sent his poems to the best magazine one could possibly be published in, *The English Review*. The editors recognized D. H. Lawrence's genius and published the poems. Think of the proud moment when Jesse could say, "Bert, I have something for you." She gave him the letter from *The English Review* accepting his poems. He opened it and read it. "You are my luck," he said. "Now let me take it to show Mother." He could not escape Lydia's influence, not yet. How impressive was it to be published in *The English Review* at age twenty-two? If you look up the issue where his first poetry appears, you will also find poems by Tolstoy, Hardy, Galsworthy, and Henry James.

Lawrence's mother contracted stomach cancer and died in 1910. He was twenty-five. He finished his first novel, *The White Peacock*, in 1911. The novel introduces us to what so much of D. H. Lawrence's writing will be about. The novel had two basic types of men: cultured men who completely lack passion, and passionate men who completely lack culture. Of course Lawrence saw his father as the passionate man lacking culture, and he saw himself as the cultured man—but not one who lacks passion. D. H. Lawrence had passion, but he didn't know what to do with it until he met someone who figured it out for him, Freda von Richtofen, in 1912. (If the name von Richtofen sounds familiar, it's because her first cousin was named Manfred. Two years later in World War I he became Baron von Richtofen, the Red Baron.)

Freda, at thirty-two, was six years older than Lawrence.

He was not, physically, a gift to womankind but something sensual was burning inside him; Freda saw something in him that she liked. Unfortunately she was married to Lawrence's English professor at the University of Nottingham, a dull, dull man. Named Weekley, he called his wife his "pure white lily." Not only was he dull, he was extremely naïve; Freda had had lovers, time and time again. She was tall, blond, pretty; she wore peasant scarves and exotic embroidered blouses. She was also selfish and lazy, and highly sensual. She is the archetypal Lawrentian woman before Lawrence became the Lawrence we know.

The professor naïvely held seminars at his house, and his wife served the refreshments. She served more than refreshments to D. H. Lawrence—within two weeks she told Lawrence, "Let's become lovers." He answered, "No, let's become man and wife." After only five weeks of acquaintance they eloped, causing a terrible scandal; she had three young children she abandoned for Lawrence.

D. H. Lawrence now began his most creative period. World War I broke out, and because Freda was German, the British deported them, which Lawrence would never forget or forgive. When they were banished from Cornwall, where they had been living, Lawrence said, "We will never come back to England to live." They never would; he remained outside of England for the rest of his short life.

Despite this, within three months, because of the inspiration Freda provided him, he wrote the novel that made his name in his day and in ours as well, *Sons and Lovers*. Because it is so famous today, we don't realize what a revolutionary novel it was. Freud had just posited his theory of the Oedipus complex; the general public was just beginning to study it. Lawrence took this theoretical concept of Freud's and turned it into life and blood in *Sons and Lovers*, because it was his own story.

Freud developed the Oedipus complex to illustrate how males develop an adult identity. He stated that as infants we are all masses of impulses. We have no sense of our own separate selves when we are born; all we consist of are a medley of drives—sadistic, anarchic, aggressive, and all obeying the pleasure principle. Every impulse is to seek pleasure by any means. Of course the mother is the primal source of the greatest pleasure, and so Freud says that at a very young age the mother becomes the primary attraction of all the individual's drives, including the innate sexual drive. The father becomes a rival in this ruthless search for pleasure that we all go through, until at age three or four, the little boy stops wanting to murder his father and remove him as a rival. Instead, because the father has all the power, Freud says the child therefore fears castration by the father. The child represses the incestuous thoughts he has about his mother and identifies with the father. The father becomes the reality principle; the mother always stays the illusion.

The child, because he has identified with the father, now has urges that he knows he cannot satisfy. To cope with these urges, he invents the unconscious. He puts all of his repressed incestuous fantasies into that unconscious and develops for himself the ego—how he will behave in society, the conscious semblance of identity that is separate from the unconscious desire.

What so fascinated D. H. Lawrence was what then happens at puberty a few years later, according to Freud. In puberty, when the boy can actually perform sexually for the first time, he cannot direct these ideas toward the mother because he knows that outlet is taboo. He seeks a safer outlet in girlfriends. But if the mother has made herself attractive to the son because she gets nothing from the husband in a bad marriage, she can ruin her son forever, because he must find the opposite of the mother for sex. And for the rest of his life, Freud says, where there is love for a woman, there will be no desire, and when there is desire for a woman, there will be no love. The man will only physically desire those women who are not like his mother, women he cannot respect at all. If he does respect a woman, he can never marry her because the desire is stifled.

In D. H. Lawrence's notebooks, written as he worked on *Sons and Lovers*, he underlines and stars a paragraph from Freud's book. This is what Freud said about Leonardo da Vinci: "In the manner of all ungratified mothers, she took her little son in place of her husband and robbed him therefore of part of his virility by maturing too early his erotic life." Freud doesn't mean that the mother had sex with Leonardo. But because she took the son as her husband, put all of her hopes and fears and love upon him, she therefore ruined the son. When he can then act on his eroticism, he can only seek women he cannot respect as a sexual mate. But he cannot ever find a decent wife because he can't marry a decent woman and perform sexually. This in a nutshell—a really big nutshell—is what *Sons and Lovers* is about.

Amazingly enough, however, *Sons and Lovers* is not a landmark in the history of the novel because it was the first to draw upon Freud's theory. Even more impressive is that *Sons and Lovers* is the first novel ever written where the main character is from the working class on both sides of the character's family. Paul Morel, the young hero of *Sons and Lovers*, is the first hero in English literature, in any significant novel, from a working-class background. Think a minute—given that Charles Dickens came one hundred years before, are none of Dickens's heroes from just a working-class background? No. In one case after another, though it seems they're working class, at the end we discover that actually they are of noble birth. Thackeray, Hardy, Gissing, Trollope—none of them created a working-class hero.

Sons and Lovers was a success, but it didn't make much money because it was shocking. It is not that it treated sexuality explicitly—we know where that will come in Lawrence's life—but it did open the doors of the unconscious. Only the brightest readers understood, and because the brightest readers were usually from the upper classes, a working-class hero repelled them.

Lawrence and his wife didn't know where to turn at this time. They could not live in England, so they ventured to Italy, as most great authors who leave England do. Lawrence said about Italy the first year they lived there, "One must love Italy. It is so nonmoral, it leaves the soul so free. Over Germany and England like a gray sky lies the gloom of dark moral judgment and condemnation and reservations about human beings. Italy does not judge." Despite this liberty from judgment, Lawrence had to wander. Italy was followed by Australia, Mexico, New Mexico, and the south of France.

In New Mexico, when he was looking at the tombstones of old cowboys who had been buried on a ranch, Lawrence found the epitaph he wanted put on his headstone. What Lawrence wanted to be remembered for—because he had fought convention all of his life—was that though he might not have been right all the time, he gave 100 percent of his effort to try to expand the sensuality that could be put into a British novel. This tombstone that so impressed him simply said, "Here lies Jack Williams. He done his damnedest." His wife wouldn't allow the inscription after he died, but goodness knows he went on to do his damnedest—he published *The Rainbow* in 1915 and *Women in Love* in 1920.

What saved these novels from the terms *graphic* and *explicit*—terms that make us think of pornography—is that as explicit and graphic as they are, they are so beautifully poetic, so sensuous and sensual, the writing in no sense seems like pornography, it seems like poetry. But make no mistake—he wanted to open that frank and vivid aspect of sexual love to the novel, and he sacrificed himself to do it. *The Rainbow* and *Women in Love* caused him much trouble with the censors, but didn't stop him.

In 1926 he wrote his last novel, *Lady Chatterley's Lover;* it took him two years. *Lady Chatterley's Lover* was the frankest description of the physical side of sexual love ever to have appeared in any work of English literature. He knew when he wrote it that it could not be published in either England or America, so he hoped an Italian publisher would bring it out. This was done, and in English, but the novel reached only a few people. People in England and America, so fearing what they heard about the novel—that it was just a sexual manual and completely pornographic—rained down criticism on D. H. Lawrence without even having read the book. The rejection really did help to kill him.

He died in 1930 at the age of forty-four. It would be thirty more years until we in America could get our hands on *Lady Chatterley's Lover* without any abridgment. In 1960

Grove Press brought out what they called the "complete authorized and unexpurgated text of the definitive version," which had originally been published in Italy. The postmaster general under President Eisenhower, Summerfield, banned the book from the mails, meaning it couldn't be sent to bookstores in America. Only when the ban was overturned in a district court in New York in 1961 was the novel allowed to see the light of day in America.

What Lawrence maintained through his whole life was that all he ever wanted to do was to bring into modern times one of the most beautiful myths that had ever been written as a fairy tale. According to Lawrence, if you wanted to know the plot of each of his books, all you had to do was read "Sleeping Beauty." He reworked, again and again, the theme of "Sleeping Beauty," where a rescuer breaks through a tangle of thorns to release an unawakened woman; every one of his novels fits that plot. The unawakened woman is not sleeping literally—she is sleeping sexually. She is usually married; she has certainly had sex, but not the sex that D. H. Lawrence was talking about, not sex with any fulfillment. Her lover, who is usually illicit, someone she cannot marry for one reason or another, doesn't break through a literal tangle of thorns but breaks through conventional social morality. And by breaking through that conventionality, by running off together, they both receive sexual fulfillment. He tells that same story over and over—not in *Sons and Lovers*, but in everything significant that he wrote afterward. In *Lady Chatterley's Lover* he was able, in his final version, to say exactly what he wanted to say about sex, about the beauty of sex and its capacity to rescue women. Here are the first two paragraphs of *Lady Chatterley's Lover*,

showing how cleverly he tells you all you need to know of
the theme:

> Ours is essentially a tragic age, so we refuse to take it
> tragically. The cataclysm has happened, we are among
> the ruins, we start to build up new little habitats, to
> have new little hopes. It is rather hard work: there is
> now no smooth road into the future: but we go round,
> or scramble over the obstacles. We've got to live, no
> matter how many skies have fallen. This was more or
> less Constance Chatterley's position. The war had
> brought the roof down over her head. And she had
> realized that one must live and learn.
>
> She married Clifford Chatterley in 1917, when he
> was home for a month on leave. They had a month's
> honeymoon. Then he went back to Flanders: to be
> shipped over to England again six months later, more or
> less in bits. Constance, his wife, was then twenty-three
> years old, and he was twenty-nine. He didn't die, and
> the bits seemed to grow together again. For two years
> he remained in the doctor's hands. Then he was pro-
> nounced cured, and could return to life again, with the
> lower half of his body, from the hips down, paralyzed
> forever.

There is the setup: a husband and wife who can no longer
have sexual relations, and the gamekeeper, Mellors. You are
given the sensuous setup from a logical situation and everything flows from that. We forget that the story is not just
about some woman running away from her husband. There
is a reason the affair starts; there is a reason neither of the

lovers feels terribly guilty. The descriptions of the act of love are not only the first in the history of the novel, but as most critics say, they are probably still the finest.

The later authors who claimed they wrote because Lawrence opened up the novel to sexuality would have disgusted Lawrence. Henry Miller, Norman Mailer, and James Gould Cozzens—they are the ones who said, "Thank you, D. H. Lawrence, for letting us describe sex explicitly." Lawrence said the year before he died, "I am equally against dry-necked Puritans, the smart, jazzy young crowd that takes sex like a cocktail, and low-minded people who revel in dirt for dirt's sake. These three groups show the perversion of Puritanism, the perversion of smart licentiousness, and the perversion of a dirty mind." He was against graphic and explicit portrayal of sex for sex's sake. In each book that he wrote sex is the prince who awakens the princess who has been sleeping forever.

We are now only forty-some years past the publication of *Lady Chatterley's Lover* in America. We have in that time gone so far in explicitness that Lawrence becomes linked with authors who gratuitously delineate violence and sex. Gratuitous violence and sex—Lawrence would be appalled.

F. Scott Fitzgerald

(1896–1940)

As mentioned in my commentary on Ernest Hemingway, it is usually agreed, by lovers of literature, that there were only four true giants in the ranks of twentieth-century American novelists: Ernest Hemingway, William Faulkner, John Steinbeck, and F. Scott Fitzgerald. There is no fifth. These four are so important and so far beyond any other American fiction writers in terms of lasting power that, when we look back at the twentieth century, those will probably be the only four novelists regularly studied.

Most English professors would say that of the four William Faulkner would be considered the greatest genius. Why do they pick him? Because they know that if the average American picks up a typical Faulkner novel and reads it through, he will likely not have the vaguest idea of what is going on. How much more eminent can you be than to confuse the general American public?

Seriously, it is true that Faulkner's is the finest talent, yet of the four it is Fitzgerald who most draws our sympathy and fascination. He is the saddest, even compared with Hemingway, and the most vulnerable. The other three authors, like Fitzgerald, are known for one primary contribution to American literature. Hemingway changed how we write modern prose: the short, brief sentences, the hard-hitting verbs, these are his legacy. John Steinbeck defines our image of the Great Depression and the working poor in *The Grapes of Wrath* and *Of Mice and Men*. Faulkner takes a vast and mysterious region of America, the South, and immerses us in the antebellum and post–Civil War Southern mentality with a genius that no one else has matched.

And then we come to F. Scott Fitzgerald. No matter what work of his you read, you come away with a sense of that vivid decade we call the Roaring Twenties. And because he represents the Roaring Twenties, he seems to be the least of the four in talent, because of all our history that era seems the most frivolous, the most superficial. With Steinbeck you get the heaviness of the Depression; with Hemingway you get a whole new prose style; with Faulkner you get the men-tality of a crucial and troubled part of our country. On the surface, with Fitzgerald it seems as though all you are getting is a picture of the Jazz Age. So let us look more closely at this man and see that indeed he is far more than a chronicler of the Roaring Twenties.

He certainly has an odd name. F. Scott Fitzgerald. It is hard to think of any other famous author in America or England who is known by the first initial, full middle name and the last name. We certainly have initialed authors, e. e. cummings, T. S. Eliot—but it is difficult to come up with one who goes by an initial, middle name, and last name. He was not born F. Scott Fitzgerald; to understand why he chose F. Scott Fitzgerald, you have to understand his father. His father was from a Southern family, but not from the Deep South. He was from a prestigious Maryland family; his grandmother's first cousin was Francis Scott Key, the writer of *The Star-Spangled Banner.* And that is Fitzgerald's name: Francis Scott Key Fitzgerald. Of course he did not want to always be in the shadow of Francis Scott Key, so he went by F. Scott Fitzgerald.

His father was from a gentle Southern family of extremely good breeding but low vitality. If you remember Ashley Wilkes in *Gone With the Wind,* you will have a fair portrait of F. Scott Fitzgerald's father. He went into business, which was a big mistake. In 1890, during the same decade that F. Scott Fitzgerald was born, he opened a store called the American Rattan and Willow Works; he sold porch furniture. Fitzgerald's mother was Molly McGuin, from a rich but less well-bred family of St. Paul, Minnesota. Her parents had made their money in the grocery business. She was from a devout Catholic family that limited her social encounters with men. She did not marry Fitzgerald's father until she was thirty; at the end of the nineteenth century, not to marry until thirty would be equivalent today to not marrying until fifty. She was not stylish; on their first date Mr. Fitzgerald pointed out to her that she was wearing one black shoe and one blue shoe. He might have married her for her sense of humor, because when the mistake was pointed out, she replied, "Isn't that strange. I have a pair just like it at home."

They married and planned to have a large Catholic family. In fact, there were two children before F. Scott, both girls, but in the year Fitzgerald was born, 1896, there was an epidemic and both girls died within months of Fitzgerald's birth. With the birth of a son, and because of what they had gone through, the Fitzgeralds vowed they could not stand to lose any more children; they would have no others. It is no surprise, then, that the boy was spoiled and coddled. A large part of Fitzgerald's troubles throughout his entire life was that he was looked upon by his parents as a pampered survivor. When F. Scott was eleven, his father's business finally failed once and for all. The feckless entrepreneur telephoned Fitzgerald's mother to give her the bad news of bankruptcy. Fitzgerald remembered that when his mother hung up the telephone and told him what lay ahead, all he could say, over and over, was "Dear God, please do not let us go to the poorhouse. Please do not let us go to the poorhouse."

The Fitzgeralds had lived in the East near Maryland; now with their tails tucked between their legs they returned to St. Paul to the house of the mother's wealthy parents. They lived on the charity of the parents, who constantly reminded their daughter that she could have, should have, married someone better. Fitzgerald's mother did her son no favor by putting every hope she had upon him. She doted on him endlessly; she was going to make him her shining winner to compensate for her irresponsible husband. But as you may guess, as much as she doted on him, Fitzgerald did not really love his mother. He resented her for smothering him with maternal solicitude, and of course he resented his weak father. Years later, when Fitzgerald was terribly depressed and in therapy, he said to his therapist, "Why shouldn't I go crazy? My father is a moron, my mother is a neurotic. Between them they haven't the brains of Calvin Coolidge."

Minnesota felt like slumming to F. Scott Fitzgerald—he thought he was reared for better things. His grandparents sent him to a fancy summer camp, where boys who were far wealthier surrounded him. F. Scott's father could only scrape up enough money to give him a dollar to spend at camp. The note tucked in the envelope with the dollar read, "Scott, spend this dollar liberally, generously, carefully, judiciously, sensibly. Get from it pleasure, wisdom, health and experience. Your Father." This was a dollar. Even back then one could barely get pleasure from it, let alone wisdom, health, and experience.

The grandparents also sent the teenager to a private Catholic school in St. Paul, but then decided he was really too superior to stay there, so they transferred him to the Newman School, close to New York City, when he was sixteen. This school was where the upper-crust boys from the East Coast went, to be prepared for prominent roles in society. Suddenly Fitzgerald forgot his St. Paul, Minnesota, roots and became a starchy, self-important, serious-minded prig. He wanted to impress the other boys, but he offended everyone because he tried too hard. When it was time for college, his parents told him in no uncertain terms it was to be the University of Minnesota. F. Scott Fitzgerald knew he was Princeton material, and he knew he had the grandparents who could send him there. He wrote his grandmother telling her the distressing news that her grandchild was to be sent to the University of Minnesota and begged, "Can't you do something?" She did, in unexpected fashion: six weeks later she died suddenly, and in her will was money for Princeton.

F. Scott regarded Princeton as Camelot rising out of the flatlands of New Jersey. As a freshman on his first day, he was described as tall, yellow-blond, and willowy. His roommate wrote to his parents about F. Scott: "My roommate looks exactly like a jonquil." At the turn of the century, Princeton was not Harvard or Yale. If you were dedicated and serious and obnoxious, you went to Harvard or Yale, but if you were only obnoxious, you went to Princeton. Ennui, being bored with the general world, was the attitude of Princeton. But even with this kind of lackluster competition Fitzgerald was a terrible student; in his freshman year he failed math, Latin, and chemistry. He was very soon on probation because he drank too much in his mission to cultivate the image of a decadent dandy.

But no one really cared by 1917, because at that point America entered World War I. Everyone at Princeton left to join the army—not to actually fight but to go to Brooks Brothers, where one went to be fitted for a well-cut uniform. Fitzgerald wrote home to his father when he dropped out of Princeton to join the war, "One should go to war as a gentleman, just as one goes to college. It's best to leave the blustering and fighting and heroism to the middle classes, since they do it so much better than we do." He had hurriedly begun writing his first novel because he was certain he would be killed in the war. As he said later, he saw action in Kentucky, West Virginia, and Georgia during the war but survived. He sent his novel off to Scribner's, having persuaded a Princeton senior to write a supporting letter to his manuscript that said, "Though F. Scott Fitzgerald is still alive, the book has some literary value which of course, if and when he is killed in battle, should be greatly enhanced." The novel was rejected and he survived, and then he was sent to the last war front he would see, Montgomery, Alabama. And in Montgomery a life-changing event happened to Fitzgerald— the event that gilds his romantic image.

If you know even a minimum about F. Scott Fitzgerald's life, you know that as an army officer in Alabama he met Zelda Sayre at a country club dance. Zelda was the youngest of five children, spoiled rotten, and the pet of the family. As the daughter of an Alabama Supreme Court judge she thought her future was unlimited. Zelda was named for a Gypsy queen in a novel that her mother had been reading when she went into labor, and Zelda fit the role. Even before Fitzgerald met her at the dance—he was twenty-two, she was eighteen—she was famous for wild escapades. She hated boredom and avoided it by any means. She drank, she smoked, she had a tomboyish body, and as they said to each other in their first letters, it was not enough in life that they should be lovers, they should be accomplices. Together they would scheme to bring attention to themselves. Years later Ring Lardner, the author, met them, and in a letter he wrote to a friend who had asked what the Fitzgeralds were like, he simply said, "Mr. Fitzgerald is a novelist. Mrs. Fitzgerald is a novelty."

The war ended before Fitzgerald could be ordered overseas, but Zelda refused to marry him until he had a job. He began writing billboard ads in New York City for $90 a month, not much money even in 1920. He wrote one short story after another in the hours before and after work—all were rejected by the magazines. He was literally reduced to putting cardboard in the bottom of his shoes in the winter as he walked to work in Manhattan. Finally he could understand what it was like not to be wealthy and privileged. He knew he could not succeed in business; literature seemed the only means to a career. He returned to St. Paul, to his grandparents' home. He decided to rewrite the novel that had been rejected and send it out again. He had called it *The Romantic Egoist*, but now he decided a better title would be *This Side of Paradise*. He sent it off to Scribner's again, and this time it was read by an editor named Maxwell Perkins, the most famous editor of twentieth-century America.

Maxwell Perkins saw in this upstart young man the new era, the 1920s, which were now dawning. He accepted the novel, and Fitzgerald's life, for the only time, became a fairy tale, a happy fairy tale rather than a sad one. Once Scribner's accepted his novel Fitzgerald once again sent out the previously rejected short stories, and in the cover letter he said, "My novel by Scribner's will be published on such and such a day." All the stories were immediately accepted. In 1921 he got $400 for a story called "Head and Shoulders." Filmmakers wanted it for Hollywood; he would get $2,500 for the film rights. He used every penny of the money he was given as an advance to buy a platinum watch for Zelda. Here was a young man about to get married, thinking about having a family, and all his money was spent on a platinum watch. They married, and the society pages referred to it as a wedding between a goddess and an archangel.

This Side of Paradise sold well—forty thousand copies. (But to keep that in perspective, when Sinclair Lewis brought out *Main Street* the same year, it sold two hundred thousand copies.) But Fitzgerald had arrived at the crossroads that would ultimately destroy him. He needed to decide whether to devote his talent toward writing for art's sake, with its accompanying poverty, or toward wealth, through the slight, easy magazine articles that could be tossed off. His father told him to consider his family and what he needed to do for them. Fitzgerald had just married Zelda and cared little about his mother and father, and so he wrote back, "I've made the decision. It seems at this point my family needs a fur coat." He decided to write for the magazines rather than for eternity.

The money came in, and he and Zelda spent it freely—so quickly that they were always in debt. In 1919 he could not sell a short story for more than $200. Because of his rising fame, two years later he would get $1,500; two years after that, $2,500; three years later, in 1926, $4,000. He was writing at the height of a magazine war between the *Ladies' Home Journal* and the *Saturday Evening Post*. Both publications had grown dissatisfied with their images. The *Ladies' Home Journal* was Victorian, conventional; it sold to the mothers of young daughters, and the young daughters bought the magazine too. The *Saturday Evening Post* was a man's magazine, covering finance, printing hunting stories, action stories. Kipling and Jack London were keeping the *Saturday Evening Post* alive. The *Saturday Evening Post* decided it wanted to edge into the *Ladies' Home Journal*'s female readership, and through Fitzgerald's first novel, and his short stories like "Bernice Bobs Her Hair," they figured out how to do it. They would give Fitzgerald top billing at their magazine, higher than Jack London, higher than Rudyard Kipling, because Fitzgerald wrote about the 1920s flappers. That would attract the young girls as readers, and then their mothers would have to read the *Post* too to figure out what the young girls were doing on dates when they went out. Fathers, in turn, would be appalled at these new young daughter/flappers and they would read the *Saturday Evening Post* to figure out what their children were thinking.

Fitzgerald changed the conception of what we considered the all-American girl. Before Fitzgerald, if a girl was deemed sexually attractive from, let's say, 1896, when Fitzgerald was born, until he started writing in the twenties, that girl was called a vamp. She was elegant, she was extremely curvaceous, and she looked like a Gibson girl. Fitzgerald's heroines changed this image once and for all. His women were all flappers, and they looked nothing like a Gibson girl. They were boyish and flat-chested, with bobbed hair; they wore nothing but rayon and silk and always had a cigarette in one hand and a martini glass in the other. Where did he get the model for this new girl? He looked at his wife, Zelda, and made the image we have of the twenties, the ultimate flapper girl.

Meanwhile, F. Scott and Zelda felt they had to live the life of the characters he was writing about—sophomoric antics became their signature behavior. One evening they were at a rather dull party, and Zelda, because she could not stand the boredom, pulled a fire alarm and reported a three-alarm fire. The fire trucks pulled up, the firemen rushed in. When they asked the source of the fire, Zelda pointed to her heart and said, "Here."

F. Scott was pressed to keep writing the short stories to keep them in money. He knew he needed another novel, but rather than a novel he got a daughter, their only child, Scotty, named for her father. They still had enough money from his sales of the early works to rent, in 1923, a vast house on Long Island where every night they threw wild parties exactly like the parties in Fitzgerald's masterpiece, *The Great Gatsby*. But they were running out of money, and so they went abroad. There Fitzgerald decided he would write the novel that would make him even more famous, and rich besides. On April 10, 1925, *The Great Gatsby* was published. To his astonishment and to ours today, the praise of the critics could not have been higher and the sales could not have been lower. This masterpiece was in no way understood or appreciated in its day. With a wife like Zelda and having a child to raise, Fitzgerald could not have been more disappointed; he never got over the disappointment that this novel did not sell well. Ironically, today many Americans call *The Great Gatsby* the greatest single novel they ever read in school.

Let me remind you of what makes Fitzgerald an enduring author and not just a magazine writer who wrote a few novels. Like the great dramatist of our day, Tennessee Williams, Fitzgerald could write prose so beautifully imagistic that it reads like poetry. The most famous line in the novel is a description of Daisy Buchanan's voice: "Her voice was full of money, the inexhaustible charm that rose and fell in it, the jingle of it, the symbol song of it, high in a white palace, the king's daughter of it, the golden girl of it." It's not the voice he's describing, it is the soullessness of Daisy Buchanan. Interestingly, the two most used adjectives in *The Great Gatsby* are *careless* and *pointless*; he defines his era as the most pointless age in terms of having no goals morally worthwhile. In *Great Gatsby* is a description of Daisy and her wealthy, stupid husband, Tom: "They were careless people, Tom and Daisy. They smashed up things and then retreated back into their money or their vast carelessness or whatever it was that kept them together, and let other people clean up the mess that they had made." An accurate description, from all we read, about how the wealthy were acting in this age.

Zelda by now realized her husband was too like his ineffectual father, and she indulged in a damaging affair with a pilot. She also decided she wanted her name to be remembered in the twenty-first century, and so she set out to be a great ballerina. Then, of course, the crash of the stock market in 1929 brought the Jazz Age to a devastating halt. People were worried, and suddenly Fitzgerald found he was writing about a bygone age, though it was only yesterday. He could not adapt to the new age, the Depression, as Steinbeck could. But he knew he had one more great novel in him.

For eight years he worked on this next novel. It would be about an alcoholic doctor and his wife, Zelda fictionalized once again. He first called it *Drunkard's Holiday*, then realized that title sounded like a Victorian melodrama. He changed it to *Dr. Diver's Holiday;* his editor said it would not sell. That night Fitzgerald was reading Keats; his favorite poem by Keats was "Ode to a Nightingale," and in that poem was the line, "Tender is the night." *Tender Is the Night* was published, and Fitzgerald felt confident it would restore his reputation. Instead, it sold worse than *The Great Gatsby*, because somehow it still belonged to the Roaring Twenties. At this point people either wanted escape, such as they found at the movies, or the utter realism Steinbeck provided. Fitzgerald could offer neither, and the book was a failure. Zelda was so unhinged by this and by her own sorrows that she entered a sanitarium in Asheville, North Carolina; she would be in and out of that sanitarium for the rest of her life.

Fitzgerald turned forty in 1936, with, in his opinion, so little to show for his life. He was staying at the renowned Grove Park Inn in Asheville, where he made a terrible error of judgment. On his fortieth birthday he invited a reporter from *Esquire* magazine to interview him on what his life was like at that milestone. Well, at forty he was having a nervous breakdown, which he chronicled to the reporter, who brought it out as an article called "The Crack-Up," one of the most famous articles ever published—the pathetic remains of F. Scott Fitzgerald. From the time that article was published, the *Saturday Evening Post* and the *Ladies' Home Journal*, the two sources he could still count on to provide enough money to at least pay for his drinking, rejected every story he sent them. He had only one choice left if he wanted fast money, and that was to go to Hollywood.

Hollywood did nothing to curb his drinking, or his decline. In 1938 he was chosen by David O. Selznick to write the dialogue for Scarlett O'Hara and Rhett Butler in *Gone With the Wind*. Now, if you read a Fitzgerald novel, the dialogue is not what you love; its strength lies in poetic description. Two weeks after he was put on *Gone With the Wind*, he was fired. But at this point he did meet a successful twenty-eight-year-old movie columnist, Sheila Graham, and in Sheila Graham he found a kindred spirit. She was not really Sheila Graham at all. She had just been divorced from a titled Englishman and was actually named Lilly Shield, who had been reared in a London orphanage and had gone on the music hall stage as a little girl. She was a complete phony in terms of where she came from. She had invented her life as Gatsby did in *The Great Gatsby*. Fitzgerald, recognizing their common bond of a kindred spirit in pretension, moved in with her.

Graham forced him to give up liquor, an amazing feat, given how deeply alcoholic he was. And once he gave up liquor, he decided once again that he had yet another novel in him, which would restore his reputation and make him famous and rich. He began to write. The novel was about the thing he knew best at this point in his life, Hollywood tycoons and the degraded moral values of the movie industry. He called this final novel *The Last Tycoon*. He began writing it in 1940, and it was progressing smoothly. On December 19,1940, he wrote Zelda that there would be no Christmas gifts this year for her or for Scotty because he simply did not have any money. But, he told her, he was finishing chapter five of a novel called *The Last Tycoon*, which would restore his reputation and his income.

On December 21, 1940, Sheila brought him breakfast in bed because he was so engrossed in working on chapter six that he could not even get out of bed. He took a morning break because the mail came, containing the Princeton alumni newsletter highlighting the football team. He found the article so charming that he stood at the fireplace and read it to Sheila, eating a Hershey's bar as he read. You may wonder, why all these details here? Well, you can guess. He made it halfway through the article when he was seized with a heart attack, grabbed the chimney, and slid down—he was dead before help could arrive. Dead at forty-four.

In the 1920s, when he was primed with success, this is what he had written in his will: "Part of my estate is to provide for a fine funeral and burial in keeping with my station in life." Three years before he died, he had crossed that passage out with India ink and had written, "The cheapest funeral possible without any unnecessary expense." At his death he was worth $700; $613 went to the undertaker. Only thirty people showed up at his funeral, which was held in Maryland. He had wanted to be buried in Rockville, where his ancestor Francis Scott Key was buried, but that was St. Mary's Catholic Cemetery, and because his books were judged immoral by the Catholic Church, he was denied burial in the family plot. One of those who attended his funeral wrote to a friend about it, complaining about the poor cosmetic work on Fitzgerald's body. I think these words are a poignant view of Fitzgerald's end: "Fitzgerald's made-up face resembled a store dummy in Technicolor. Not a line showed anywhere on his countenance, not one gray hair either. This looked like a first-class production until you reached his hands. Realism began at the extremities. His hands were horribly wrinkled and thin. The only proof left after death that for all the props of youth, Fitzgerald had actually suffered and died like an old man."

If his end was sad, Zelda's was far sadder. In November of 1947, the sanitarium outside of Asheville caught fire. Zelda was locked in a room upstairs with ten other women. They could not get the door open; the fire was so severe that she was identified only by dental records. Could there be a more pathetic ending for a love story of a flapper and a golden boy?

Ernest Hemingway

(1899–1961)

It is rather easy to discuss the importance of being Ernest Hemingway; although thousands of novels poured off the presses in twentieth-century America, you can count on one hand (and still have a finger left over) the giants of the twentieth-century American novel. There are really only four: Ernest Hemingway, William Faulkner, F. Scott Fitzgerald, and John Steinbeck. Hemingway indisputably belongs in the pantheon of great novelists of the twentieth century. Yes, I know how ridiculous it is to draw up such a short list of literary giants for such a full century. And yet both the public and most twentieth-century writers themselves have mentioned these four authors far more than any others when listing those of the highest genius and influence. Certainly, no author after 1950 enjoys anywhere near the name recognition and the space in literary anthologies and school textbooks that these four do.

It is true, Hemingway has not aged as well as some of the others; we don't regard him as the artistic genius that we regard William Faulkner as today, or even F. Scott Fitzgerald. Yet he is one of the stellar four. But far more importantly than with the other three, his life must be studied because Hemingway is not only a writer, he is a Personality. His life and his works intertwine so thoroughly they cannot be considered apart from one another.

There was nothing peculiar about his birth, but there is something very peculiar about the position in society he was born into. Most writers struggle with either a middle- or a lower-class background, particularly novelists it seems; but that is not true with Hemingway. He is probably America's first great upper-middle-class, suburban author. He was born in 1899 in Oak Park, Illinois, which was considered a suburb of the huge city of Chicago. He came from a rich family; his father was a successful doctor. His father's passions—and this will not surprise you if you've read anything by Hemingway—were hunting, fishing, and taxidermy. He was a "man's man," and Hemingway would certainly take after him. On the other hand, Hemingway's mother, Grace Hall, possessed the opposite qualities. A beautiful woman who taught music and directed the church choir, she was extremely artistic and had given up an opera career to marry Dr. Hemingway and become a wife and mother. She never ever forgot to remind everyone in the family and outside the family of that sacrifice. So from his father Hemingway absorbed the love of male sports; from his mother came a love of singing, writing, art, and ballet.

The family took long vacations each summer, when Hemingway was just a child, to northern Michigan. At the turn of the century this region was utterly wild, so wild that Hemingway had as his playmates children from the Ottawa Indian tribe. Hemingway mentions that the first doll he ever had was a rubber papoose, and his second doll was a white Eskimo. He was immersed in this Indian culture every summer when he mingled with the Indian children. His mother, because she loved writing, recorded everything about Hemingway's earliest days, including his first words and his first sentence. She asked him when he was just over two years old, "Ernest, what are you afraid of?" His answer became an anthem to his writing and his life. He looked at his mother and said enthusiastically, "'Fraid a nothin'!" Actually Hemingway came to have many fears, but in the public persona he projected he was 'fraid of nothin'.

Ernest as a little boy loved making up stories, but his stories were all the same. And the stories he made up as a child virtually did not change when he became a novelist years later. His tales were always about swashbuckling heroes, and the code of behavior was always the same—a test of great physical courage. Hemingway was obsessed with physical prowess, although he did not at first look the type to be an athlete. He had been short, but when he was sixteen, he grew an inch a month for five months; from five feet seven he shot up to six feet. With this rapid burst of height, he cemented his self-image as a great male athlete. He also developed a touch of the bully. He was not one to defend the weak, but rather to show everyone how tough he was. His father saw that he loved to use his fists and taught him the art of boxing.

Though Hemingway came from a wealthy background, he did not go to college when he graduated from high school. World War I was raging in Europe, but any military ambitions he had were rendered impossible because of a congenitally weak left eye. He had an uncle in Kansas City and begged his parents to be allowed to go there after high school. Immediately he got a job on the *Kansas City Star*, a reputable Midwestern newspaper. He remained only six months, but he found something in the drawer of his desk on his first day that would forever change not only Hemingway but what we regard as American prose style in the early-twentieth-century novel. Inside the drawer was a pamphlet titled simply "Style Manual." It taught reporters, especially cub reporters like Hemingway, good sentence structure. The manual said, "You should use only short sentences, you should always have a short first paragraph, and above all, avoid adverbs and adjectives such as *grand, splendid,* and *gorgeous.*" Obviously it would be an exaggeration to say that Hemingway took that manual and derived from it his distinctive style, but it is not an exaggeration to say that those lessons of style were not only learned by Hemingway but were never forgotten in anything he ever wrote.

Hemingway felt frustrated penned at a desk when so many of his friends were overseas fighting in World War I, yet he could not get into the Army legitimately because of his bad eye. He decided to head overseas to serve as an ambulance driver for the Red Cross; he would at least be near the front, though he would not be a soldier. His actual job, which in later times he never really talked about, was hardly heroic—carrying cigarettes, chocolates, and postcards to the soldiers fighting at the front. Fate stepped in, however, and gave Hemingway a heroic role, one he could never have imagined, one that formed his early reputation.

He had been in Italy as an ambulance driver for only three weeks when he was hit by enemy fire, and though wounded, he managed to carry another injured man to safety. His heroism was reinforced by good timing: as the first American casualty in Italy, he became a magnet for publicity. Given the Silver Medal of Honor, he was sent to recover to a Red Cross station that had eighteen Red Cross nurses and only four patients because the fighting had just begun. It was an ideal situation for Hemingway, and he fell in love with a nurse there, Agnes. It was an unrequited love, unconsummated, but Hemingway would remember her in a novel, later on. Above all, he gloried in his own behavior: enduring an ordeal by fire, instinctively having the courage not only to save himself but to save another man, and—best of all—receiving recognition for his heroism. He sustained 227 scars from this accident. How do we know? Hemingway, ever the self-publicist, counted the scars so that he could regale people with the tale. He also had a ring made out of a piece of shrapnel taken from his leg, a symbol of his suffering on perpetual display. Such was the image of the man's man he hungered to promote, at nineteen.

Hemingway recuperated for six months in Italy, then was sent home. He had a cane, he had a (highly photogenic) limp, and he had a hero's welcome. He quickly became an unemployed hero with no particular skill, so he turned to writing short stories. The stories were written in the terse style recommended by the writing manual: blunt, masculine, unsentimental, and laconic. Readers did not at first care for such writing because they had never read anything quite like this before. Such unadorned brevity was unfamiliar to them, and the stories didn't sell. Hemingway was an original; he had to create the taste by which he would be judged.

Hemingway would marry four times, and none of his marriages would, as you probably know, work out success-fully at all. The first of his four wives was Hadley Richardson, who was not nearly as young as Hemingway when they met—she was twenty-eight, he was only twenty.

She was beautiful and, not coincidentally, had a trust fund. Her sophistication, physical beauty, and financial health were irresistible to the young Hemingway. The author Sherwood Anderson was a friend of the young Hemingways and told them that anybody who was anybody in culture was going to Paris. It was right after World War I, the early 1920s, and Paris was the unquestioned mecca for artists and writers. Anderson wrote letters of introduction to important cultural figures in Paris, including the most influential person in the literary circles, Gertrude Stein.

So Hemingway and his new wife moved to Paris to further his ambition to become a successful writer. Gertrude Stein looked at him and saw in this twenty-two-year-old a young man who had literary potential, even though when she first met him, he was unpublished and utterly unknown. She and a generous circle of writers sustained Hemingway, and he kept writing.

He wanted to be a great short-story writer, and to encourage himself to write the kind of prose that he thought was worthwhile, he wrote a sentence that he kept in front of him: "All you have to do is write one true sentence at a time as forceful as a right to the jaw." He wasn't at the time writing much fiction that was any good, or that people were recognizing as good, but he did write for the newspapers. He finally accumulated a number of short stories, some of them quite good, that he felt he could show to a publisher. He found a publisher outside Paris; his wife, Hadley, was to take the train and meet him, bringing the valise full of his short stories. Unfortunately, on the train that valise was stolen—all Hemingway's early work was gone and would have to be rewritten. In hindsight it was a good thing, as his rewriting probably made the pieces far more artistically sound.

About this time Gertrude Stein suggested that Hemingway and Hadley go to Pamplona for the festival of the running of the bulls. Hemingway's exposure to the intensely masculine aura of bullfighting led to one of the signature, enduring images of his writing. He finished three stories and ten poems that he thought would launch his writing career. He wanted an assertive title for these pieces, a title that would attract attention. He called the collection *Three Stories and Ten Poems*, a ridiculous yet effective understatement that proved his point—Hemingway wanted no flowery nonsense. The poems were as starkly masculine in theme as the fiction.

The collection was published and was a unique success. As someone said about Hemingway's works, he was one of those rare authors who was "praised by the highbrows and read by the lowbrows." Critics who spent their lives looking at great literature thought Hemingway had real promise, yet the man in the street—men who didn't really care about art—liked Hemingway because his themes were so identifiably masculine.

Hemingway then turned his hand to a group of short stories that were linked by theme and by a character named Nick Adams; he called this collection *In Our Time*. He couldn't find a publisher for it in America, so he sent it to Paris, to Ernest Walsh, who prided himself on publishing what we would call today cutting-edge material—the avant-garde. "All you had to do," Hemingway said, "to be sure of being published by Ernest Walsh was to send him your manuscript and include a letter where you said that you had tried to have the work published by every respectable journal in the United States but they all sent it back and hated it." Once *In Our Time* was published in Paris, it received attention in the United States, due to the support of Sherwood Anderson and F. Scott Fitzgerald. Not only did Sherwood Anderson and F. Scott Fitzgerald admire Hemingway's works, they also used their reputations to get this young unknown published in the United States.

Hemingway was always jealous of other authors, and that included his friend Fitzgerald. Hemingway wrote about Fitzgerald, "He had very fair, wavy hair, excited and friendly eyes, and a delicate long-lipped Irish mouth. That mouth on a girl would have been a mouth of beauty. His mouth worried you until you got to know him and then it worried you even more." Even in that bland description rested a note of criticism. It was difficult for Hemingway to be generous about anyone else but himself.

The success of *In Our Time* convinced him to attempt a novel, and Gertrude Stein's car mechanic, of all people in Paris, gave him the novel's focus. Gertrude Stein told Hemingway that she had been having her car fixed, and she had told the mechanic he had no competition for his job because few other young men were car mechanics. The young car mechanic pointed out the lack of young men between the ages of twenty-two and thirty as most had been killed in World War I, and he called his "the lost generation." The idea of writing a novel for that lost generation appealed strongly to Hemingway. When it came out in 1926, called *The Sun Also Rises*, it caused a sensation. Its hero, a young man named Jake Barnes, was impotent because of a war wound. He had sexual desires but was incapable of fulfilling them, a dilemma that rendered the world absurd to him—he is one of the early existential heroes in literature. Scribner's published the novel and the editor was the brilliant Maxwell Perkins, who had shaped such authors as Fitzgerald and Thomas Wolfe. It was Fitzgerald, though, who offered the most constructive advice before *The Sun Also Rises* was published. He read the manuscript and recognized it as a brilliant novel difficult to get into. He advised Hemingway to lop off the first fifteen pages. Hemingway asked Maxwell Perkins, Perkins agreed completely, and the cut was made.

Hemingway's marriage to Hadley Richardson was now failing. He had met Pauline Pfieffer, who was working in Paris at the magazine *Vogue*. She was a good friend of Hadley's—or so Hadley thought—and they had all gone on skiing vacations together. Hemingway and Pfieffer fell in love, and Hemingway wanted his freedom rather than working on his marriage with Hadley. Hadley divorced him and almost immediately he married Pauline.

Hemingway must have felt guilt regarding his relationships with women, getting rid of one and so quickly taking up with another. One critic noted that this guilt shows itself in the kinds of accidents that befell Hemingway—his mind might have been preoccupied with his love life, for he became exceptionally accident-prone. Given how important physical strength and dexterity and grace in movement were to him, it is strange to note the accidents Hemingway survived. In 1930 alone—shortly after he had broken with Hadley and married Pauline Pfieffer—he endured a series of bizarre accidents. The first was the most remarkable: in Paris when he reached up to pull the cord to the toilet to flush it, he pulled the cord to the skylight above it instead, so hard that the entire glass skylight fell down upon him, shards of glass everywhere, almost blinding him. The same year he had an anthrax infection, a cat scratch on his eyeball, a kidney infection, and he sliced his index finger so deeply he had to have thirty-eight stitches. He accidentally shot himself in both legs on two separate occasions, was involved in a terrible car accident, and while riding a horse went under a low limb and almost had his head taken off. It was best to avoid Hemingway in 1930.

With his new life with Pauline Pfieffer came a new setting for Hemingway. He discovered Key West, long before tourists made that locale popular. He loved the atmosphere of Key West and loved the fishing he could do there. It relaxed him and the atmosphere was conducive to writing, so conducive that this is where he started and finished his second novel. *The Sun Also Rises* was a success, but the novel that made Hemingway a household name was *A Farewell to Arms*. He was offered $10,000 by Scribner's, a fortune back then, for the unseen manuscript, and they certainly didn't regret that offer once they read it. *A Farewell to Arms* is the story of a nurse and a war patient—a tragic story, clearly based upon the nurse Hemingway had fallen in love with when he was in Italy recovering. A movie of *A Farewell to Arms* was made starring two of the biggest Hollywood stars, Gary Cooper and Helen Hayes, and Hemingway earned $24,000 from the movie rights, becoming one of the earliest authors to profit from the movie industry.

At this time, the end of the 1920s, something ominous happened in Hemingway's life. His father committed suicide by blowing his brains out with a rifle. The reason given was that his father had developed angina and diabetes, and he was such an outdoorsman, he couldn't bear the thought of living as an invalid. Hemingway's mother, meanwhile, was torn between pride for her son the author, because she was so arts conscious, and humiliation. She was very religious, old-fashioned, and Hemingway's novels were very realistic, particularly for that era. She called his first two novels "the filthiest books that had ever been published." At this time, as well, the stock market crashed. The resulting financial debacle did not affect Hemingway at all; because he could always earn money from manuscripts and from movies, he was in fine financial shape.

In the early 1930s Hemingway decided to write something other than a novel. *Death in the Afternoon* is more nonfiction prose, about one subject, a subject he was very familiar with because of his trips to Pamplona and other parts of Spain. *Death in the Afternoon* is probably the finest piece written about bullfighting because Hemingway saw the contest between bull and man as far more than a gory battle. To most people bullfighting seemed a barbarous sport—man versus beast, bloody and awful—but Hemingway saw it in a remarkable way, as the ultimate ballet. Because of the ornate costume that the matador wore, right down to the slippers, he looked to Hemingway like a male ballet figure, and Hemingway's point in *Death in the Afternoon* was that the matador represented the powers of civilization, discipline, grace, beauty, and power. The bull, of course, represented the opposite, utter chaos. Hemingway saw in the beautiful costuming and the graceful, delicate moves of the matador the battle that has always been on earth between the ultimate civilizing forces, represented by the bullfighter, and the ultimate animalistic chaos, represented by the bull. *Death in the Afternoon* introduced the world to bullfighting in a way never seen before, and it was beautiful and brilliant.

The 1930s were the highlight of Hemingway's life. He added to his list of sporting conquests—he discovered marlin fishing, both in Cuba and in Key West. He also traveled to Kenya, Africa, attracted by the big-game hunting. He was living every male fantasy, pursuing the things men have always dreamed about: hunting beasts in Africa, marlin fishing off the Florida coast. His book *Green Hills of Africa* did for Kenya what his book *Death in the Afternoon* had done for Spain. And then, in the late 1930s, Spain blazed to the forefront of world affairs through its convulsive civil war. Hemingway, ever anxious for the hero's role, took up the cause. Intellectuals such as Hemingway supported the communists against the fascists because they felt the poor people of Spain had far more to gain under the communists than they did under the fascist regime of Franco. A number of Hemingway's leftist friends had begun to condemn him because the heroes of his novels, though manly, were apolitical. They seemed entirely selfish (like Hemingway himself) because they were lonely, individualistic heroes with no concerns other than their own desires and wishes. Hemingway thought he could answer this criticism by writing a political novel, one that clearly took a side, and from that impulse came *For Whom the Bell Tolls*. It was a magnificent novel—condensed into a sixty-eight-hour time frame—that brought to the people of the world an understanding of the Spanish Civil War that they had never had before.

Hemingway's other interest in Spain, unfortunately for Pauline and their marriage, was a woman who, like him, was fascinated by Spain. Hemingway had been a celebrity in Key West. In a bar there called Sloppy Joe's, Hemingway loved to linger in a grubby T-shirt and shorts, and above all he loved to be recognized by the tourists who were starting to come to Key West in the hopes of seeing the great Ernest Hemingway. One day, a woman from St. Louis, in her forties, walked in with her two college-age children, a son and a daughter. Hemingway was not interested in the mother; he set his sights on the beautiful daughter, Martha Gellhorn, though he was twice her age at thirty-seven. Hemingway fell in love, or at least lust, with this young woman; she was a reporter headed for Madrid to cover the Spanish Civil War. Hemingway became involved in the cause and with the young woman as well. Pauline, however, would not give up without a fight. There was a humorous but rather sad incident, when Hemingway and Gellhorn left for Spain. Pauline went to Europe as well, confronting Hemingway with her hair bobbed in the exact style as Martha Gellhorn's, trying to make herself an older version of this woman Hemingway had fallen in love with, all to no avail.

The success of *For Whom the Bell Tolls* was phenomenal, and Hollywood, planning to use Ingrid Bergman as its star, paid Hemingway $100,000 for the movie rights. At about this time, F. Scott Fitzgerald died; Hemingway was oblivious. Even though Fitzgerald had been generous in helping Hemingway establish himself, his death really didn't register with Hemingway. All Hemingway cared about was the money he was making; as he said about *For Whom the Bell Tolls*, "It is selling like frozen daiquiris in hell."

Hemingway and Pauline divorced, and immediately he married Martha Gellhorn—but the marriage was short-lived. Martha had begun to see what Hemingway had become. He was Papa Hemingway, a mythic figure who wrote brilliant novels, a man's man, as good and courageous as he portrayed his heroes. Hemingway spent all of his time, it seemed to Martha, trying to live up to the myth. Within a few years he was ready to divorce Martha and marry his newest and final love.

In 1945, less than four years after marriage number three, Hemingway divorced Martha and married Mary Welsh, who had left her husband to marry Hemingway. Of his four wives, Welsh had the hardest role. The other three had known Hemingway when he was successful, but this last period of Hemingway's life became a nightmare, and Welsh would have to endure it. In 1950 Hemingway published *Across the River and into the Trees*, and it was a failure—critics were disappointed, and the public spurned it. This failure brought out the worst in Hemingway, who erupted in temper tantrums. When he found out William Faulkner had been awarded the Nobel Prize, Hemingway, always jealous of other authors, was furious; he wanted that prize for himself.

There was one last victory he could claim, however. He dreamed up an idea for a four-part novel, with each part based upon the sea—a work about people who either make their living from or have their struggles with the sea. In eight weeks he had written the first part, about an old man called Santiago and his battle with a marlin, and he titled it *The Old Man and the Sea*. *Life* magazine became interested in the story and decided to publish *The Old Man and the Sea* in one issue of *Life* in 1952. *Life* was so popular back then that it guaranteed Hemingway an immediate audience of 5 million readers. Hemingway allowed *Life* to publish it and it was a success. It was more than a story of one man's courage. So much meaning was underneath it that as soon as it came out, ministers and rabbis throughout the country preached sermons about the themes of *The Old Man and the Sea*. Because of this work Hemingway won the Pulitzer Prize and, shortly afterward in 1954, the Nobel Prize for literature. What he said about winning the Nobel Prize would come back to haunt him: "No son of a bitch who ever won the Nobel Prize ever wrote anything worth reading afterwards." He would live up—or down—to that statement.

Hemingway moved to Ketchum, Idaho. Idaho was the perfect setting for the ultimate Hemingway hero, Ernest Hemingway himself. He grew a big beard, let himself get downright fat, and even though he claimed he was in Idaho because he wanted the privacy, he didn't. He loved it when tourists recognized this heavyset, bearded figure as the great Ernest Hemingway, and it infuriated him one day when a whole carload of tourists spotted him and said, "Could we have your autograph, Burl Ives?" He became so impressed with his image that he was impossible to live with. His final wife, Mary, confided in a letter, shortly after she married him, that she found Hemingway "heartless, thoughtless, selfish, spoiled, unappreciative, egotistical, and a publicity seeking monster."

From 1954 until 1960, he produced nothing worth reading. His health was terrible, and he developed the same angina and diabetes his father had. In 1960 his mental health fell apart. He was hospitalized for severe depression and was given electric shock treatments twice a week. He went to Spain to recapture the glory he had partaken of, but the journey was a mistake. He was convinced the entire time he was in Spain that the FBI was tailing him, after him for income tax evasion. Some may remember the Kennedy inaugural, and how much Jacqueline and John Kennedy wanted to be recognized as cultural leaders. They invited Robert Frost to the inaugural but they had considered, before Frost, inviting Ernest Hemingway. Rather than invite him they sent him what was called a "Presentation Volume for the Inaugural." It was sent to eminent authors, who were to write in it just one sentence of congratulations or something about the new era beginning with the Kennedys. When the presidential volume was sent to Hemingway, his wife tells us he worked all day and halfway into the night, came out, burst into tears, and said to his wife, "It won't come anymore."

Hemingway was admitted to the Mayo Clinic, where he continued with shock treatments. Mary, remembering what had happened to Hemingway's father, locked all the guns in the house in a storage room in the basement. Hemingway charmed the doctors at Mayo into releasing him prematurely from the hospital. It was a thousand-mile journey from Mayo back to his home in Idaho, and the trip became a nightmare. Hemingway was convinced that every state trooper was after him and was severely paranoid. It was the end of June 1961, and the end of Hemingway. Early on Friday morning, June 30, Hemingway got up. Although Mary had locked all the guns in the storeroom, she had not removed the key from its usual place on the window ledge at the kitchen sink. Hemingway found the key, let himself into the storeroom, and took up a double-barreled shotgun. He aimed it at his forehead, right above his eyebrow, in exactly the same position that his father, years before, had placed a shotgun, and like his father, he pulled the trigger and committed suicide.

Interestingly though, this was not the end of Hemingway's writing career. Four years before Hemingway killed himself, porters at the Ritz Hotel in Paris going through an abandoned storeroom had come upon two small trunks overflowing with typed manuscripts that had been stored by Ernest Hemingway in 1928, thirty years before. The manuscripts were sent to Scribner's publishing after Hemingway died; one was a memoir of Hemingway's as a young man in Paris from 1921 to 1926. In 1964, three years after Hemingway committed suicide, this memoir was published by Scribner's as *A Moveable Feast*. It is an accurate portrayal of the man but not a portrayal Hemingway would have wanted to come out three years after his death. It mentions Gertrude Stein, F. Scott Fitzgerald, Ford Madox Ford, and others, and in every case Hemingway had drawn ruthless, vicious portraits of those people who had been nothing but kind to him.

What contributions from Hemingway are indeed lasting? First of all, there is his style. The Hemingway style caught on and American prose has never been quite the same since. His was a spare, objective, unemotional, ironic style. His dialogue was tough in the same way Dashiell Hammett's dialogue is tough, that hard-boiled-detective style. Above all, Hemingway wanted ruthless economy in his prose. He was a minimalist; he believed that less was more. He wanted no literary embellishments, few adjectives, virtually no adverbs, and no sentimentality at all. He said, "Compared to a home, a prose style should be architecture but never interior decorating."

There is also the legacy of his subject matter. He was brilliant at what he did, but the focus was narrow. He always placed his main male character in the same circumstance of physical danger, so the character could display courage. Hemingway gave a famous definition of courage as "grace under pressure," and he made sure that in all the books he wrote, his characters were measured against that unvarying standard. People who liked this kind of character said that in Hemingway you could always see perennial youth. People who didn't like Hemingway said what you really saw in Hemingway was arrested development.

My final observation on Hemingway may seem strange, but I think you'll find it true. The author I find closest to Hemingway in terms of the characters he invents is the last person in the world you might think would be mentioned in the same breath as Hemingway: Jane Austen. Jane Austen and Ernest Hemingway share a gift for taking an extremely narrow range of characters and examining them in depth. Jane Austen created the most feminine of characters, a heroine who is always a young lady, who is about to be married amid many social repercussions. Hemingway was the opposite. He wrote of men put on a battlefield or pitted against a great fish or against a bull, against something that represents chaos. But in both cases courage was tested: the physical courage of Hemingway's heroes when confronted with physical danger, and the moral courage of Austen's heroines when confronted by the ethical danger of an inappropriate suitor. Austen and Hemingway both had learned that an author's scope doesn't need to be wide if it can go very, very deep.

Robert Frost

(1874–1963)

With most authors you can view their childhood experiences and environments and receive a fairly accurate preview of what these authors will symbolize in their careers as adults. For example, if you consider Charles Dickens's childhood, you are not surprised that some of it was spent in the tumultuous city of London, in a lower-middle-class area where money was of great concern to his family. These settings and themes Dickens would carry with him, whether he wanted them or not, the rest of his life. If you look at Ernest Hemingway's childhood, you are not surprised to learn that he grew up in the Midwest, spent his summers at physically strenuous athletic camps in the wilds of Michigan, was an Eagle Scout, and loved everything to do with camping. Such very masculine themes resonate in Hemingway's later works. No early childhood, however, was less likely to produce the man we think of as Robert Frost than the childhood of Robert Frost.

If you had to guess about his childhood from the themes and images prevalent in his writing, you would, of course, assume that he had had an idyllic New England childhood spent swinging on birches, exploring the woods, looking at paths and deciding which one to take. If you had to picture

the night of his birth, judging by his poetry, you would probably assume a wintry eve, lots of snow, in a tiny town in New
Hampshire or Vermont. Actually, Robert Frost was born in
1874 on Nob Hill in San Francisco and lived there for eleven
years. He knew nothing about New England in his infancy or
early childhood. San Francisco was the wildest, most profli-
gate city of its era, and this is where young Frost spent his
most crucial years.

Frost's father was a renegade spirit. The night Robert
Frost was born, when the doctor came to the door to deliver
him, Frost's father waved a Colt revolver at the doctor and
said, "If my wife and my child are not perfect following the
birth, I'll kill you on the spot." Needless to say, it was a
meticulous delivery. When the child was born, he was
named Robert E. Lee Frost because his father, not a
Southerner at all but a New Englander, had deserted the
Yankee cause during the Civil War, joined up with the
Confederacy, and fought with Robert E. Lee's army.

Frost's father and mother were not San Francisco–born;
they were from the East. Both were teachers—in fact, his
father met his mother after the war when they were both
teaching at a school in New Hampshire. He noticed her
immediately, which was not surprising as they were the only
two teachers at the school. They married in 1873 and moved
to San Francisco because Frost's father was desperate for a
new start, and San Francisco was the place you went for a
new life. He hoped to be a journalist and might have been an
excellent one except for three problems: drinking, gambling,
and what were termed dalliances. He also had consumption.
The medicine prescribed for consumptive men: lots of
whiskey. Not a good idea with Frost's father, who had been

on that medicine long before he ever knew that he had consumption. What do we call a man like this? The only adjective that would be absolutely accurate for Frost's father is *feckless*. It is hard to think of any great author who ever had a father who was anything but feckless. *Feckless* means weak, ineffectual, unlucky—an exact description of Shakespeare's father, Poe's father, Dickens's father, Twain's father, Fitzgerald's father . . . go right down the list. Almost all great American and British male authors had feckless fathers, and Frost was no exception. Oddly, female authors seemed to have escaped the curse of the pathetic papa.

Frost's childhood was far from normal, even for San Francisco. The family never lived in a house; because Frost's mother didn't want to play housewife, they lived in one hotel after another. Because the father was so feckless, Mrs. Frost was overprotective of her son and his sister. And because she had brought from her native Scotland a dour Calvinist spirit, she nurtured her children on fear. An imaginative woman, she told the children lots of stories—scary stories with profoundly moralistic themes. Frost said years later that what he remembered so much about his mother's teaching was that all her stories were based on opposites. Her stories were always about good versus evil, chaos versus order, light versus darkness; she loved paired images. This opposition is extremely significant in Frost's work; no other poet uses paired images more brilliantly.

One of my favorite poems by Frost, "Fire and Ice," offers a vivid example of opposite images:

> Some say the world will end in fire,
> Some say in ice.

From what I've tasted of desire
I hold with those who favor fire.
But if it had to perish twice,
I think I know enough of hate
To say that for destruction ice
Is also great
And would suffice.

Frost's father did not long survive the consumption and the drinking. Frost found out about his father's death in a devastating manner. He was playing across the street from the hotel where his family was currently staying when a playmate asked, "Why are they hanging crepe over that hotel?" The crepe was for Frost's father, who had died inside. Fortunately his father had taken out a $20,000 insurance policy on his life; unfortunately it had lapsed. The survivors were left with $8, enough to pay for the coffin.

Mrs. Frost, Robert, and his sister were destitute, left with no choice but to go live with Mrs. Frost's parents in New Hampshire. So at age eleven Frost became acquainted with New England, which, at first, he loathed. The man who would introduce the glory of New England to the world despised his new environment; he resented how his mother was treated because she had married a ne'er-do-well and had come back as a beggar to her parents.

The first challenge to his dislike, the thing that first made him fall in love with New England, was the snow. He remembered that his grandfather, when it would snow, loved to take a thimble, fill it full of ice, and place it on a hot stove. And then, Frost said, "We would watch it dance on its own melting"—a wonderful image of the thimble with the ice in it, feeling the heat going all over it until the ice melted and the thimble would stop. When people asked Frost what makes a great organic poem, he answered, years later, "A poem must dance on its own melting." In other words, it must move itself organically just as that thimble did years before. And he remembered his grandfather, in those winters, taking a coin and placing it in the oven. He would take it out with pincers, and then because it was so cold and snowy one could not see out the windows, the grandfather would place the hot coin right against the window in two spots side by side. The ice would melt in two peepholes the size of young Robert's eyes, so he could look through the window.

Frost was not a good student; he was lazy. He loved only baseball, until he went to high school over the border of New Hampshire in Lawrence, Massachusetts, and met the girl he would marry, Eleanor Merriam White. And because he fell in love with her and because she was on the literary magazine and because she was going to be valedictorian, Frost's intellectual light awakened. He didn't love learning but he loved a girl who did love learning, and he decided he could not be second to her intellectually. He became joint editor with her on the magazine, and when they graduated high school, he was covaledictorian. And because she had a love for poetry, Frost decided he would develop a love for poetry; he decided he would be a ballad writer. Ballads are like songs, they have a strong rhythm. Frost told the delightful story years later that he developed an ear for the rhythm of words because as he would walk to school with his schoolbooks on his strap, he would try to compose poetry. It didn't work until he realized he could swing the books back and forth, like a metronome, and that rhythm would help him fill out a line of iambic pentameter.

Frost succeeded well in high school, primarily because of the stimulating competition with his future wife, and he decided to attend Dartmouth. But he had some of his father's failings and did not finish his freshman year. However, he published his first poem, "My Butterfly," for which he received $15—a large sum, particularly for a nineteen-year-old. Frost took this literary success as a signal that poetry should be his vocation. Unfortunately he had been reading Edgar Allan Poe, Thomas De Quincey, and Samuel Taylor Coleridge; he noticed that all three poets had been on stimulants when they wrote their best verse.

Frost went down to Boston and rented a room for a month. Before he set himself to compose any poems, he drank himself into a stupor, then sat back and waited for splendid verse to pour forth. Needless to say, this thirty-day experiment left him with a terrible hangover and not one decent poem. Frost thought this experiment was telling him he didn't have any poetry in him; what it actually told him was that one isn't likely to write a decent poem on a gallon of vodka over ten days. Frost thought his life as a poet was over. To worsen matters, Eleanor, his future wife, was furious with him for this experiment and told him she intended to end their relationship. Frost, in the manner of the Romantic poets he so emulated, decided his life was not worth living. He decided to kill himself in such a dramatically poignant fashion that Eleanor would regret for the rest of her life that she had driven him to this early death. He had heard of the Dismal Swamp on the border of Virginia and North Carolina and thought it would be the perfect setting for an effective suicide. He took a steamer to Norfolk and then . . . couldn't find the Dismal Swamp! In his search he met some duck hunters from Kitty Hawk; they invited him to go along with them, and since he couldn't locate the Dismal Swamp and he had nothing else to do in his misery, he went. Two of the hunters lived in Elizabeth City, North Carolina, and they invited him to stay there for a while. He might have lived there forever but for his reasoning that Eleanor should really be able to forgive him. He had cleared the alcohol from his system and realized that he wasn't a poet, not because of a native inability, but due to his wrongheaded approach. He had no money, however, to leave Elizabeth City. So he hitched a ride in a boxcar on a train headed north and returned to New England.

Frost and his Eleanor married—she had indeed forgiven him. They both turned to teaching because they knew they couldn't support themselves as poets. The pair, however, were not made for one another. Robert Frost, like his mother, was throughout his life nervous, tense, not given to good moods. Unfortunately Eleanor, in response to such moodiness, became utterly silent. What Frost needed was reinforcement; what Eleanor needed was a happy-go-lucky husband. They had a son, Elliot, early in the marriage. Frost then decided he could not be a poet without a college degree, and the better the degree, probably the greater the poet he could become.

He enrolled at Harvard University as a special student and was assigned an adviser to help him decide which courses to take the first semester. Frost thought he would impress this professional adviser, so the first thing Frost said was "You know, I did get fifteen dollars for the poem that I wrote." And the English professor smoking a pipe looked at him, arched his eyebrow, and said, "Oh, so we're a writer, are we?" The humbling was deserved, but here is this Harvard professor who wanted to put Frost in his place, and he did—Frost left Harvard without ever even making a decent start.

He found teaching too great a strain, and he became ill. He then thought farming was the answer to his troubles, and he and Eleanor moved to a farm in Derry, New Hampshire. Then their son, Elliot, died at the age of three; we can imagine the strain such a loss put on a marriage that was already shaky. There is an impressively somber poem by Frost called "Home Burial," about the effect of the death of a young child on a husband and wife. It is a terrifyingly realistic work and clearly based on what happened to Frost and Eleanor.

They did eventually have more children, but Frost was failing as a farmer; he had no college degree, no accomplishments in the world. He was, however, writing poem after poem, though he never submitted them for publication. When he was thirty-eight, his wife told him her vision had always been to live in one of those charming thatched homes in England, and perhaps there their luck would change.

And so Frost, thinking such a change of scene would be beneficial, moved the family to England. They arrived in London knowing no one—they had to ask a retired policeman they met on the street if he could suggest a place to rent. The policeman took pity on them, and they found a house—a thatched house. Probably the turning point of Robert Frost's life came one night after the family was all asleep in this little thatched home. Late that night he put all the poems that he had written over the past twelve years on the floor faceup. Just as a game he decided to see if he could move them around the floor and group them by theme. He discovered, indeed, a forceful pattern; some poems seemed to go together nicely, possibly as chapters of a book. Frost resolved to publish these poems as a unified work. He knew no one in the publishing industry, so, though this is hard to believe, he returned to that retired policeman who had told them where to live and asked him if he knew a publisher. And, by heaven, he did!

By good luck the policeman's former neighbor David Nutt was a publisher of poetry. Upon introduction to Frost, Nutt recognized that this American had created a vivid portrait of New England—and where would New England be more exotic than in old England? The other fascinating coincidence of this episode is that one of the people who published with David Nutt was the poet Ezra Pound. Pound heard from his publisher about this New England poet, read Frost's poems, and found them brilliant. Still more wonderment was in store for Frost: Ezra Pound's good friend was William Butler Yeats, the Irish poet. Now, of all the poets whose work Robert Frost had read, by far his idol was William Butler Yeats. Ezra Pound gave Frost's poetry to Yeats to read and critique, and Yeats liked it too. He invited Ezra Pound and the unknown Robert Frost to join him during his next visit to England. Frost had been an absolute nobody with no career that he'd ever achieved anything at—he couldn't be a teacher, he couldn't be a farmer—and here he was in England, chatting with Pound and Yeats about his own poetry.

Such good fortune so inspired Frost that in the next few months he wrote some of his greatest poems, "Mending Wall," "The Death of the Hired Hand," and "After

Applepicking." They are all brilliant in their evocation of New England, and we wonder if he could have written them had he stayed in America. He had needed to leave his country, needed to be homesick for the real New England, to fill his soul and make him write about it so movingly. He knew these poems were fine—he knew they would make a fitting second book of poetry, but he needed a good title. He remembered that farms in New England; were listed in two basic categories. Since so many were in the Boston area, a huge list of farms were under the title "Boston." Another category was called "North of Boston," all the farms in the New Hampshire and the Vermont area. He thought about that title "North of Boston" and realized that he had not been writing about all New England; he'd been writing about north of Boston, the soul of New England. Vermont, New Hampshire, Maine—the great settings of Frost's poems—this was the New England he was writing about. *North of Boston* was published to great critical acclaim.

With the outbreak of World War I, Frost and his family realized they must go home; by 1915 it was apparent they were not safe in England. Frost bought a farm in the White Mountains of New Hampshire. The *Atlantic Monthly*—one of the most respected journals of poetry—began buying Frost's poetry regularly. He found himself an established American poet, ironically because he had had to travel to England to realize the depth of his love for New England. His marriage was still not good. Eleanor had been supportive when he was a failure, but now that he had become successful, she was jealous. She had introduced him to poetry, to culture, and now he had eclipsed her.

Frost wanted money and security, and he knew these would not come from writing poetry. He resolved to join the faculty of a college as poet-in-residence. Amherst College hired him, with no good result. The faculty disliked his moodiness and resented him for earning more than they were while teaching virtually nothing. What he was doing instead was organizing readings—readings of his own poetry and that of other poets he knew, who came to read while Frost acted as master of ceremonies. His lack of popularity didn't faze him—he was making a good salary. But the faculty's animosity brought out his worst qualities, and his moody irritability lapsed into nervous depression.

In 1921 the University of Michigan offered Frost the position of poet-in-residence. Frost held off deciding until he could visit the campus, so deep in the Midwest. On a trip to Ann Arbor, it reminded him of New England, a beautiful, green, rolling land. He accepted the position of poet-in-residence, only to see it bring out again his worst qualities. The Michigan faculty did not take to him; he was being offered poetry readings at the University of Illinois and Indiana University, so he was absent from campus often. Finally a faculty member put a sign on his door when he returned from one trip to Ohio State that said, "Poet-Not-Often-in-Residence."

Frost no longer enjoyed bringing in other poets for readings because he was jealous of them. The man he hated most was Carl Sandburg. Frost despised Sandburg for always showing up at poetry readings in a flannel shirt, playing a guitar; he felt Sandburg was trying to be Walt Whitman brought back from the dead, a poet people would fall in love with as a kind of rural American who could write great poetry and sing it on the guitar. What bothered Frost most was that Sandburg's poetry, because it was song, had been translated into twenty-one different languages, and Frost's works hadn't been translated into *any* other language. Frost's comment upon Sandburg's international success was "Well, yes, his poetry has everything to gain and nothing to lose by being translated into another language." No wonder others found Frost unlikable.

The next volume of Frost's poetry, called *New Hampshire*, won the Pulitzer Prize. He had selected the poems he needed, but there was no spectacular poem in it that he felt would sell the whole volume. The poems had to be submitted the next day; he was left with twelve hours to come up with a poem. It was an unusually hot and sticky July morning—he had moved back to New Hampshire to complete the poetry—he hadn't slept well, he was desperate for some form of escape. He decided he needed to write a poem that had absolutely nothing in common with the hot, sticky now. He began to rhyme words that he loved, simple words he felt he could craft a poem around: *know, though, snow, queer, near, year, shake, mistake, flake.* And thus came about the poem that begins, "Whose woods these are I think I know. His house is in the village though"—"Stopping by Woods on a Snowy Evening," by far his greatest poem and one beloved by countless people.

Perhaps you can see how his mother's idea of opposites infused Frost's entire life. He can't write and get published in New England, so he goes to the opposite, Old England, and gets published. He's in a hot and humid room, he needs to escape, so he creates "Stopping by Woods on a Snowy Evening." Because it is so famous, I want to spend a little

space on this brilliant poem and give you my interpretation
of it.

> Whose woods these are I think I know.
> His house is in the village though;
> He will not see me stopping here
> To watch his woods fill up with snow.
>
> My little horse must think it queer
> To stop without a farmhouse near
> Between the woods and frozen lake
> The darkest evening of the year.
>
> He gives his harness bells a shake
> To ask if there is some mistake.
> The only other sound's the sweep
> Of easy wind and downy flake.
>
> The woods are lovely, dark and deep.
> But I have promises to keep,
> And miles to go before I sleep,
> And miles to go before I sleep.

It seems a simple poem, but to an English professor there
is no such thing as a simple poem. Let's go back to the first
stanza:

> Whose woods these are I think I know.
> His house is in the village though;
> He will not see me stopping here
> To watch his woods fill up with snow.

What is the main thrust of that first line that unites this stanza? Passivity and tentativeness, the very human condition of being weak and tentative. Frost didn't go all the way and say, "I know whose woods these are." He said, "I *think* I know whose woods these are." The next line is "His house is in the village though." In other words, "Yes, it is this man's, but actually it's not because his house is not here, this is just the woods." "He will not see me stopping here"—a negative. "To watch his woods fill up with snow." Frost could have said, "To watch the snow fill up the woods," but that would be an active condition; to say that woods are filled up by snow is passive. Everything in the first stanza tends toward the passive and tentative, which is the condition most humans find themselves in much of their lives.

The second stanza switches viewpoints. The first stanza has been from the point of view of a rather irresolute human being; the second stanza shifts to the point of view of the horse, which represents animal instinct and spirit:

> My little horse must think it queer
> To stop without a farmhouse near
> Between the woods and frozen lake
> The darkest evening of the year.

Horses are not tentative. They know what their schedule should be, and because the horse has stopped where it has never stopped before, it is wondering, "Why are we stopped here?" And he's going to do something about it because he's a horse, he is not a tentative person:

> He gives his harness bells a shake
> To ask if there is some mistake.

The second half of the stanza returns to the earlier passivity:

> The only other sound's the sweep
> Of easy wind and downy flake.

The man is sitting there watching the wind blow, a passive receiver of the wind and the snow. And then comes the famous last stanza:

> The woods are lovely, dark and deep.
> But I have promises to keep

The first line is eloquent of human passivity: "The woods are lovely, dark and deep." In other words, "I could just stay here, the snow would fill up, I'd die and be rid of all my obligations." The second line, "But I have promises to keep," tells us, "I don't want to leave, but like the horse I've got a schedule. I have obligations." And so we have a poem that balances, until the last two lines, on the idea "Is it best to take action, or is it best just to be passive?" If this sounds familiar, it is the exact theme of the most famous play ever written, and the most famous line ever written in the history of the English language, "To be, or not to be." That is what this poem is about, and that is why it is so famous and so beautiful. To be—in other words, to strive to make something of myself—or not to be—the seductive idea of "Life is hard, why not just give up and drift away?"

Regard the brilliant ending: "The woods are lovely, dark and deep"—that is the passive view, "I might as well stay here." "But I have promises to keep"—"But I need to keep going." We expect, then, in the last two lines, will he go, or will he stay? Frost gives us a brilliant nonanswer: "And miles to go before I sleep." Had the poem ended there, we would assume that he has decided to go on, he has, "miles to go before I sleep." But then Frost repeats it, as if hypnotized:

The woods are lovely, dark and deep.
But I have promises to keep,
And miles to go before I sleep,
And miles to go before I sleep.

You have thus absolute balance of no decision made at all. By the end of the poem, we do not know if he is the horse who is going to trudge on, or if he is suicidal and is going to stay there and let the woods close his life. We have a brilliant exposition of "To be, or not to be," in a New England poem. Frost won the Pulitzer Prize for *New Hampshire* in 1924 when he was fifty years old.

Frost was one of the first "sunbirds"—Northerners who head to Florida or Texas every winter. He went to Miami, to Naples when Naples was undeveloped, to Corpus Christi, to San Antonio. He and his wife headed south every year; in Gainesville, Florida, in 1939 his wife suddenly died, a crushing blow to Frost. They had not had the happiest of marriages, but it had been an anchor of sorts, and he felt guilty about how he had behaved. He had thought as an old couple they would have a quiet, gentle retirement. Now she was gone, leaving him filled with remorse and pain. And this began the last, grand period of Frost's life, from the time she died when he was sixty-five until he died at eighty-eight.

Frost's success as a poet was unchallenged. The older and

craggier he became, the more he seemed to embody New England, the more his poetry sold. He was one of the original founders of Bread Loaf, in Vermont, which today is one of the finest schools for writing. The Bread Loaf writers asked Frost to bring in other poets, not realizing that he despised other poets, especially those of renown. He behaved fairly well until the night he brought in Archibald MacLeish for a reading. MacLeish got up and started to read, and he was absolutely brilliant. The audience was captivated, oohing and aahing and applauding everything he read. Frost was in the back row, absolutely furious. He had brought a stack of papers with him, because he figured if MacLeish was unsuccessful, he could at least get some work done. Once he saw that the audience was enamored of MacLeish, Frost took out his cigarette lighter as MacLeish was talking and lit the top of his papers to draw attention to himself. When this little conflagration proved insufficient, Frost paced back and forth to get the smoke going and then loudly tried to put out the fire on his desk.

When people asked him, "Why do you behave so poorly?" he answered, "I have had a long lover's quarrel with the world"—an effective and romantic way to make himself sound appealing when he was actually a curmudgeonly old man. His reputation didn't stop the Pulitzer committee: Frost won four Pulitzer Prizes. He was nominated for the Nobel Prize but didn't receive it. One of the committee members, who should never have divulged the information, told him why—an insult that harked back to an earlier day—"Your poetry simply doesn't translate well into other languages."

In 1959, when he turned eighty-five, there was a huge

celebration for him. In the afternoon there was a symposium on the topic "Is Boston, Massachusetts, in decay?" Why Frost responded as he did we still have no clue. He stood up and said, "Not only is Boston not in decay, but I predict the next president of the United States will be from the Boston area." John F. Kennedy had not even declared his candidacy. Frost's prediction made the newspapers and was a forceful boost to the junior senator from Massachusetts. If you ever wondered why Kennedy invited Frost to read at his inauguration, it was because Frost figuratively launched Kennedy's presidential career. At the 1961 Kennedy inauguration, Frost was invited to read his poem "The Gift Outright." At least, that was what he was supposed to do. Frost, now eighty-seven, felt he needed to show people that he didn't just know how to read his older poetry, he would write a small new one as well, and he would read both as a surprise.

The day of Kennedy's inauguration was terribly cold, and there had been a heavy snowstorm. Right when the ceremony began, the sun came out brilliantly on all the snow. Everything around the podium at the Capitol had of course been newly painted—there was new white paint, bright sunlight, and all the fresh snow. The glare caused havoc with Frost's old eyes. He rose to speak—of course he had not memorized the new poem, he had just written it. He looked down and realized he could see nothing on the page because of the glare. And he just stood there. Vice President–Elect Lyndon Johnson got up, took his black top hat, and put it over the page, thinking shade would help. Frost pushed the hat away and said, "No, don't do that. I'll do it by myself." Lyndon Johnson shrank back to his seat with his tail tucked between his legs, which was good practice for his position under Kennedy for the next thousand days. Frost couldn't read his new poem, but fortunately he had in his memory "The Gift Outright," which he had done hundreds of times at readings. He recited "The Gift Outright," and everything went smoothly until he was supposed to sit down. Kennedy's swearing-in was coming next, and so Frost said, "And I congratulate our new president, Mr. John Finley," and then sat down. Kennedy's smile was as warm as it was amused.

Frost now considered Kennedy and himself to be good friends, so he wrote the new president a letter, saying that he would love to go to Russia and meet with Nikita Khrushchev. He felt as a poet he could urge Khrushchev to temper the Soviet rivalry with America and make it a healthier, more competitive relationship. Kennedy knew how much the world loved Frost, and he knew that Frost was now associated with the Kennedy administration; he liked the idea of a poet ambassador. En route to Moscow Frost came down with the flu. The morning he was to meet with Khrushchev he had a high fever and was confined to bed. So Khrushchev, a lover of poetry and culture, came to Frost's hotel room for a ninety-minute meeting. Those present said little was discussed other than a shared love of poetry. That night Frost left on his eighteen-hour flight home. He landed, exhausted, at Idlewild and was immediately besieged by reporters waiting for a press conference. They asked what Frost and the Russian leader had talked about. Frost couldn't tell them that they hadn't really touched upon the purpose of his mission—that would be embarrassing—so he fabricated a conversation. He announced that Nikita Khrushchev had stated that he was worried about modern liberals in the U.S. government now because he feared they wouldn't fight if they had to, a statement Khrushchev would never have made. Frost was an archconservative, so he put in Khrushchev's mouth what he was thinking himself. Then Frost ended the press conference by saying, "And I have a personal message that Khrushchev wanted me to give to President Kennedy," another fabrication. And then he waited for President Kennedy to call him in to hear whatever message he was going to make up so Frost could enjoy another day in front of the cameras and reporters.

Kennedy was furious and never called Frost to the White House. Shortly after this episode the Cuban missile crisis developed. Frost in his egotism assumed the crisis was his fault because of his fabrications and had to go public with a correction saying that he had made everything up, and he hoped he hadn't caused much of a problem.

Frost's health began to fail quickly. He was successfully operated on for bladder cancer and might have lived past eighty-eight except for a pulmonary embolism that developed from the operation. Just before he died—and he was not aware that he was at the verge of death—a statement on his condition was requested. Frost said, "Tell the newspapers that 'I find myself better than a little less than bad.'" Two weeks later he died. President Kennedy, in a magnanimous gesture given the brouhaha over Khrushchev, gave Frost a touching tribute: he shared a public afternoon talking about Frost's poetry and mourning him for the nation.

Robert Frost was in some ways humble about what he felt he could accomplish as a poet. He once said, "All I wanted to do was write a few poems it would be hard to get rid of." He certainly accomplished that. One of the most delightful remarks he ever made was "When I catch a man reading a book of mine red-handed, that man always looks up cheerfully and says, 'My wife is such a great fan of yours.'" In that anecdote is a major problem with modern poetry.

The End

Suggested Biographies
for Future Reading

I am sure that this is one of the shortest reading lists you have ever encountered. This is not because I am lazy; this is because I firmly believe that one *fine* biography is all you'll need for each author. I have winnowed and rewinnowed my lengthy biographical sources for each writer to arrive at the one most readable, most accurate, and most incisive account. Those are the criteria to determine a great and lasting biography.

You'll also notice that I only list author, title, and year of publication. All of these biographies have been quite popular since their first publication and have gone through numerous editions and, occasionally, different publishers, which I cannot imagine would be of interest to you. These are not obscure volumes that need meticulous bibliographic citation so that they can be discovered in a library or bookstore. You can easily find all of them by just title and author.

Notice that the majority of these books were written in the 1940s and 1950s. I consider this twenty-year period to be the golden age of literary biography. The dreadful jargon of academic critics that began in the late 1960s had not yet permeated these books. Thus, these writers had in mind an audience of both the college-educated reading public and the literary specialists. I am sure you will delight in the fluid, smooth, fathomable prose style in all of these biographies.

I especially recommend these books for English teachers at the high school level because all of them clearly relate the authors' most famous works to the crucial events of their lives and psychological development. The information you will find will make an excellent foundation for any introductory lecture to students.

Geoffrey Chaucer—Marchette Chute. *Geoffrey Chaucer of England*. 1946.

William Shakespeare—S. Schoenbaum.* *Shakespeare's Lives*. 1991.

Jane Austen—Park Honan. *Jane Austen: Her Life*. 1987.

Edgar Allan Poe—A. H. Quinn. *Edgar Allan Poe*. 1941.

The Brontës—Juliet R. Barker. *The Brontës*. 1944.

The Brownings—Betty Miller. *Robert Browning: A Portrait*, 1952. Taplin, Gardner. *Life of Elizabeth Barrett Browning*. 1957.

Charles Dickens—Edgar Johnson. *Charles Dickens: His Tragedy and Triumph*. 1952.

George Eliot—Jennifer Uglow. *George Eliot*. 1987.

Emily Dickinson—Richard Chase. *Emily Dickinson*. 1951.

Oscar Wilde—Richard Ellman. *Oscar Wilde*. 1987.

Mark Twain—Justin Kaplan. *Mark Twain. A Biography*, 1966.

---

*Schoenbaum uses only *S* for his first name.

SUGGESTED BIOGRAPHIES FOR FUTURE READING

Thomas Hardy—Carl J. Weber. *Hardy of Wessex*. 1940.

Sir Arthur Conan Doyle—John Dickson Carr. *The Life of Sir Arthur Conan Doyle*. 1949.

D. H. Lawrence—Harry T. Moore. *The Intelligent Heart*. 1954.

F. Scott Fitzgerald—Andrew Turnbull. *Scott Fitzgerald*. 1962.

Ernest Hemingway—Carlos Baker. *Ernest Hemingway: A Life Story.* 1969.

Robert Frost—Lawrence Thompson. *Robert Frost: The Early Years* 1966. *Robert Frost:The Years of Triumph,* 1970.